STORIES THAT FLOAT FROM AFAR

STORIES THAT FLOAT FROM AFAR

Ancestral Folklore of the San of Southern Africa

Edited with an introduction by

J.D. LEWIS-WILLIAMS

Second impression 2015 by David Philip Publishers
1st floor, 6 Spin Street, Cape Town 8001

First published 2000 by David Philip Publishers
(Pty) Ltd in Southern Africa

Published in the US by Texas A&M University Press

ISBN: 978-0-86486-462-8

Text design by Sarah-Anne Raynham
Cover photo by Craig Foster
Printed and bound by Digital Print Solutions

*David Philip is committed to a sustainable future for our business,
our readers and our planet.*

Contents

PART II: MYTH, RITUAL AND BELIEF

Acknowledgements

This book has been in preparation for over two decades. The list of people who assisted in the editing of the texts and in countless discussions about Wilhelm Bleek's and Lucy Lloyd's contribution to our knowledge of the /Xam people is too long to give in full. But I am grateful to them all.

I thank the staff of the Jagger Library, University of Cape Town, for patient assistance over the years. Especially, I mention Etaine Eberhard, Leoni Twentyman-Jones and Lesley Hart. Directors of the Jagger Library have always generously permitted publication of the texts.

We all owe a particular debt of gratitude to Janette Deacon whose work on the Bleek family and their teachers is second to none. It was she who kindly took me to /Xam-ka !au and //Kabbo's Bitterpits.

Many research officers in what is now the Rock Art Research Institute worked on transcription from micro-film, endless editing and collating of texts. Amongst those who worked for long periods are Anne Holliday, Gail Emby, Caroline Jeannerat, Jennifer Kitto and Thomas Dowson. Recently, it was Jeremy Hollmann who brought the complicated task to completion. I owe him a special debt of gratitude. We look to him for a companion volume of further unpublished texts.

The Rock Art Research Institute is funded by the University of the Witwatersrand and the National Research Foundation. Substantial grants have also been received from Anglo American, De Beers, AngloGold, Liberty Life, Hasselblad, and Murray & Roberts Construction.

Orthography and pronunciation

Many of the San words in this book contain sounds that are unfamiliar to English-speakers. In addition to the more usual phonetic representations the following symbols are used for the clicks which are a distinctive feature of the Khoisan languages.

/   *Dental click.* The tip of the tongue is placed against the back of the upper front teeth; in the release, it is pulled away with a fricative sound. English-speakers use a similar sound in gentle reproof. In Bantu languages this click is represented by *c*.

!   *Alveolar-palatal click.* The tip of the tongue is pressed firmly against the back of the alveolar ridge where it meets the palate and is very sharply snapped down on release. A loud pop results. English-speakers use this sound to imitate the sound of horses' hoofs. In Bantu languages this click is represented by *q*.

≠   *Alveolar click.* The front part of the tongue, more than the tip, is pressed against the alveolar ridge and drawn sharply downward when released.

//   *Lateral click.* The tongue is placed as for the alveolar click. It is released at the sides by being drawn in from the teeth. Drivers of horses sometimes use this sound to encourage their horses to start or to go faster. In Bantu languages this click is represented by *x*.

⊙   *Labial click.* The frontal closure is made with pursed lips; when the lips are released, the sound is like a kiss. This click is found only in southern San languages.

Another sound that appears frequently in San words is *x*. It is a guttural sound as in the Scottish *loch*. In Bantu languages the sound is represented by *r*.

For the /Xam-ka !ei and
their descendants

and

to fulfil //Kabbo's wish

* * *

The motto on the new coat of arms of the Republic of South Africa
is in the extinct /Xam San language:

!Ke e: /xarra //ke
(People who are different join together)

In this book the long-silent voices of the /Xam-ka !ei speak again.

* * *

The royalties from the sale of this book go to
the Rock Art Endowment Fund
(University of the Witwatersrand Foundation)

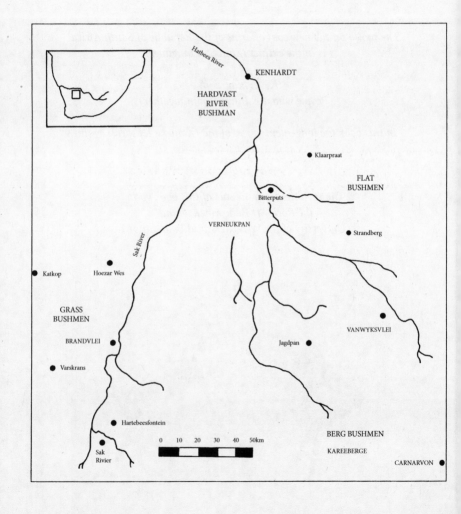

Introduction

In June 1879 a man called //Kabbo was taken to the Grand Parade, Cape Town, to witness the arrival of Sir Bartle Frere, Governor of the Cape of Good Hope and Her Imperial Majesty Queen Victoria's personal representative. Soldiers marched, cannon fired a salute, and excited citizens cheered. Dressed in European clothing yet detached from the proceedings, //Kabbo watched all the pomp and ceremony accorded to this representative of a world power that, ironically, was extending its control into the heart of his own distant land. No communication passed between //Kabbo and Sir Bartle Frere. The powerful and famous man continued on the way to his residence. Lost in the crowd, //Kabbo simply watched from afar. His own account of that poignant passing is given in this book (*Kum* 18).

//Kabbo was known to the colonists by the general appellation 'Bushman', one of the many controversial colonial words for the indigenous communities of southern Africa. Bushman groups spoke – and those remaining still speak – a large number of mutually unintelligible languages. Each group, therefore, has or had a name for itself only, and there is no word of their own to cover all the groups. We thus speak of the /Xam (//Kabbo's people), the Ju/'hoansi (also known as the !Kung), the !Kō, the Nharo, the Hei≠om, the G/wi, and so forth. Because there is no vernacular word to cover all groups, writers have to resort to words borrowed from other languages.

'Bushman', a widely used word, derives from the Dutch *Bosjesman* – person of the bush. The *Bosjesmans* were believed to hide in the bush and to spring out on unwary travellers. Understandably enough, today many people regard 'Bushman' as highly pejorative and, moreover, sexist; however, it has to be said that some Bushmen themselves do choose to use it. Some of its connotations, it should be remembered, derive from the 'Bushmen's' resistance to colonial expansion.

1

//Kabbo

The 'bush' was their land, and they were southern Africa's first free-dom fighters. Today, some of their descendants are trying to rehabilitate the word by investing it with connotations of resistance. 'San', a Nama (Khoekhoe) word, is preferred by many – but by no means all – academic writers and also by many of the people's own descendants, especially those living in South Africa. Unfortunately, it means something like 'vagabond' and is therefore also pejorative, though its negative connotations are not generally felt because few readers are conversant with the Nama language. There is no unanimity as to which word should be used and, as far as I can see, no way out of the dilemma with which history has presented us. In using the word 'San', I reject any pejorative connotations.

Way of life

To appreciate the gulf that existed between //Kabbo and the soldiers whom he watched forming up on the Grand Parade and, moreover, to understand what he and his compatriots said on many topics, it is necessary to know something about the way of life and history of his people. The San formerly occupied virtually the entire subcontinent, but today self-proclaimed San communities live chiefly

in parts of the Kalahari Desert that are now in Namibia and
Botswana. Smaller groups have recently been resettled in South
Africa. It is, however, with the /Xam San, who lived in the central
Cape Colony – //Kabbo's home – that this book is concerned. Today
there are no recognisable, self-proclaimed /Xam communities living
in the old way of life.

The sort of life that //Kabbo's people lived before the social disin-
tegration that was caused by the advancing colonial frontiers can be
pieced together, at least in broad outline, from historical records
and from more recent accounts of San life in the Kalahari Desert.
Although adapted to local conditions, all San communities practised
a foraging economy. At certain times and in certain places during the
last two thousand years, some communities departed from this
traditional way of life and acquired small herds of cattle or flocks of
sheep. In the eyes of some writers, the acquisition of cattle or sheep
caused these communities to cease being 'Bushman' in what they
considered to be the true sense of the word. Just what the 'true sense
of the word' may be is disputed, however, and there is no agreement
on the distinguishing traits of a 'true' San person or San community.
Still, there is no doubt that all San linguistic groups did at one time
practise an economy that was based on food-gathering and hunting.

Plant food or *veldkos*, as it is known in southern Africa, was gathered principally, though not exclusively, by women. According to local
conditions, *veldkos* comprised edible roots, berries, nuts, grass seeds
and so forth. In all regions of southern Africa, San women used
digging-sticks to dig up edible roots, sometimes detectable – to their
skilled eyes – by only the merest wisp of dry vegetation above
ground. In the south, /Xam women weighted their digging-sticks
with a bored stone to make digging in hard ground easier; sticks used
by men were not weighted. The women carried the *veldkos* that they
collected back to camp in skin bags or in nets made from grass fibre
or sinew. In the appropriate season, they supplemented their contribution of *veldkos* to their families' diet with insects such as locusts
and the white pupae of termites, which became known as 'Bushman
rice'. In this way they provided as much as two thirds of their community's diet.

Although they too sometimes gathered *veldkos*, the men's contribution to the San diet derived principally from trapping and hunting

with bow and arrow. Traps made from sinew were used to ensnare small animals, while pitfalls, sometimes equipped with sharpened stakes to kill any animal that fell into them, were used for larger animals.

The San are, however, better known for their bows and arrows. Throughout the subcontinent they made link-shaft arrows. These arrows comprise a shaft made from light reed, a torpedo-shaped 'link' made from bone or wood, a short reed collar and the point itself. Arrow points were made from stone or bone. In more recent times, San have been making points from metal which they obtain from neighbouring peoples; sometimes they hammer out lengths of fencing-wire for this purpose.

Link-shaft arrows are light, like the bows used to shoot them, and cannot kill on impact. The San therefore depend on poison which, in the Kalahari of today, they obtain from the pupae of a beetle; in the south, the nineteenth-century /Xam used other kinds of poison, including snake venom (*Kum* 12). The poison was placed just behind the point of the arrow so as not to blunt it (*Kum* 11). When a poisoned link-shaft arrow struck an animal, the impact caused the link to split the collar so that the shaft fell away, while the poisoned point remained embedded in the animal.

Because the bow used by the San was light and had a limited range, hunters had to stalk animals in order to come close enough to deliver a fatal shot. Sometimes hunters crouched behind bushes while other people drove herds of antelope in their direction (*Kum* 2).

This gathering and hunting way of life meant that camps had to move from place to place as the *veldkos* in an area became exhausted. They did not, however, wander randomly in a desperate search for food, as is popularly believed. They knew the land and its bounty, and were therefore able to plan seasonal moves from place to place on established, though flexible, annual migration routes. In more arid regions, such as the one where the /Xam lived, the nodes of their exploitation strategies were waterholes or patches of melons from which they could obtain water. In better-watered areas, such as the Western Cape Province or the Drakensberg, major rock shelters may have acted as settlement nodes for at least part of the year.

Where there were no suitable rock shelters, people made grass dwellings to protect themselves from the sun and the violent thunderstorms that bring rain and hail to the dry plains of the interior plateau. Usually, these dwellings were not fully constructed 'huts', which would have been too hot for comfort in the summer, but the simple shelters or windbreaks that the Dutch settlers called *scherms*.

With easily constructed dwellings and few goods to carry, people were able to move with ease from place to place. These movements were part of a larger social process. A number of camps were linked in a 'band nexus'. At certain times of the year, camps comprising a nexus or part of a nexus came together; at other times of the year they lived in much smaller groups. A camp, the smallest San social group, seems to have averaged about twenty-five men, women and children, though in some of the more arid areas a camp may, at certain times of the year, have consisted of only one nuclear family. Camps did not have fixed membership. Everyone maintained ties with people in other, sometimes quite distant, camps. These ties included kinship, fictive kinship and gift exchange. Fictive kinship allowed a person to claim a relationship with others who, while not real kinsfolk, had the same name as his or her father, mother, sister, and so forth. Gift-exchange networks cross-cut kinship. The return of gifts along lines of established exchange was sometimes long delayed, and gift partners maintained the relationship for many decades, often for an entire lifetime.

These links between camps were important, especially to groups such as the /Xam who lived in semi-arid and arid regions where rain comes in the form of highly localised thunderstorms. Under such conditions, the area seasonally exploited by a camp could, simply by chance, fail to receive rain for many consecutive years (*Kum* 3). When the plant foods withered, waterholes dried up and the antelope migrated to better watered areas, people activated one of their numerous links with those in distant camps and so moved to better endowed areas (*Kum* 2). When rain fell once more in their own land, they returned. With such movements and the constant visiting that the San enjoyed, the membership of camps was in a constant state of flux.

These very fluid social units made strong, centralised leadership or chieftainship impossible and, indeed, unnecessary. Although some people were known to 'own' waterholes, which they inherited, they did not defend territories, and leaders tended to develop influence in only those spheres in which they excelled. When decisions that affect-

ed everyone had to be taken, the entire camp sat around their fires in
the evening to talk the matter out until consensus, or near consensus,
was reached. Those who did not agree with a decision were not
bound by the will of the majority and could go their own ways.
During the last century, and probably long before that, when the San
came into contact with other people and had to negotiate with them,
leaders began to emerge, though it is doubtful if they ever became
'chiefs' in the sense that some of their agro-pastoralist neighbours had
chiefs.

Even as there were no San 'chiefs' in traditional society, there were
no pre-eminent religious leaders either. The essential elements of San
religion were widespread. Rituals that the /Xam practised 150 years
ago in the south are still performed, though in slightly different ways,
by Kalahari groups far to the north. These virtually pan-San rituals
included boys' first-kill rites, girls' puberty observances and the San's
central religious ritual, the one that brings all the people together no
matter what their age or sex, the healing, or trance, dance.

At a healing dance, the women sit in a tight circle around a central
fire. As they sing and clap the complex rhythms of 'medicine songs'
that are believed to be imbued with supernatural potency, the men
dance in a circle around them, clockwise for a while and then anti-
clockwise. In the 1950s and 1960s about half the men and a third of
the women in some of the Kalahari groups were 'medicine people' or,
to employ a word used worldwide, shamans. San shamans still enter
an altered state of consciousness, or trance, in order to cure the sick,
chase away malevolent shamans who may be marauding, so they say,
in the form of lions, travel to other parts to see how their friends and
relations are faring, and even ascend into the sky to plead with god to
spare those who are critically ill. In the south, nineteenth-century
/Xam shamans also used supernatural means to guide antelope herds
towards the hunters' ambush and to make rain fall in times of
drought. Although /Xam shamans performed these two special religious tasks that the Kalahari people of today do not, or at any rate did
not when they were studied at the beginning of the second half of the
twentieth century, there are none the less remarkable continuities of
belief across linguistic divides. Against this background of widely-
and long-held beliefs must be seen the inputs of charismatic individ-
uals. San religion accommodates a substantial idiosyncratic compo-

nent that is detectable in folklore and different versions of myths.

Moreover, the northern Kalahari people have a somewhat different conception of god from those who, like the /Xam, lived to the south. The Kalahari people believe in two gods, a greater god who lives in the east and a lesser god who lives in the west. Sometimes it is difficult for researchers to distinguish between these two gods because they share a number of names. The /Xam and other southern groups believed in one god, not two. The two gods of the northern groups and the solitary god of the /Xam are associated with the spirits of the dead, nameless shades who shoot invisible, mystical 'arrows of sickness' into people and from whom shamans attempt to protect their communities.

The various activities of shamans are at the heart of the rock art for which the San are justly famous. Painted in the rock shelters of the mountainous areas and engraved on the open rocks of the interior plains is one of the world's great aesthetic traditions. In form, line, colour and intellectual content, it is second to none. Although the Khoekhoen (formerly known as 'Hottentots', a term that is unquestionably pejorative) and Bantu-speaking farmers also made some rock art, by far the majority of these paintings and engravings were made by San.

From the Zambezi in the north to the Western Cape Province in the south, from the Cederberg in the west to the Drakensberg in the east, these images present, simultaneously, intriguing uniformities and differences. The art clearly falls into a number of geographical divisions or, as some writers put it, regional styles. These 'styles' may reflect major linguistic divisions. Anyone who knows the art well can usually correctly identify photographs of a Drakensberg painting and one from, say, the Cederberg. Yet, despite distinguishing differences, there are numerous features that are common to most regions. Certain emphases in subject matter, as well as depictions of modes of dress, weapons, distinctive ritual postures, and so forth, occur across the subcontinent. Yet few, if any, of these features can be taken as simple 'records' of day-to-day subsistence. They 'mean' far more than what they seem to depict.

The ambiguity of so many rock art images can be seen, for example, in depictions of women's digging-sticks. Many paintings depict women carrying sticks equipped with bored stones, and it has been assumed that these images show women gathering *veldkos*. There is evidence, however, that /Xam women used the same bored stones with which they weighted their digging-sticks to contact the spirit world; they used to beat bored stones on the ground as they called upon the spirits. In San thought there is little or no distinction between the sacred and the profane, and the use of bored stones for weighting digging-sticks and for communicating with the spirit world is evidence of the absence of this distinction.

This blending of the spirit world with the events of what many Westerners would see as ordinary, daily life is particularly clear in /Xam and other southern groups' concept of god. Known as the Mantis, the /Xam god was a trickster-deity. Although he created all things, he was capricious and often stupid. The /Xam people told many tales about his picaresque adventures (*Kukummi* 23, 24, 25 & 26). Sometimes he tried to trick hunters so that his favourite creature, the eland, would recover from the effects of the hunters' poison and escape. The Mantis's /Xam name was recorded by early travellers and writers as 'Kaagn', 'Cagn' and '/Kaggen' and, with characteristic colonial prejudice, was sometimes translated as 'the Devil'.

The equation of /Kaggen with the Christian religion's Devil is indicative of the colonists' attitude towards the San. It was just one of many ways in which the San were represented as unfit to occupy the land. By the middle of the nineteenth century it was clear to all, including the southern San themselves, that their way of life as gatherers of *veldkos* and as hunters had come to an end. Some groups continued to inhabit parts of the Drakensberg where they closely interacted with black farmers for some centuries. They made rock paintings up to the end of the nineteenth century and perhaps even into the first decade of the twentieth century. (The Kalahari people have no tradition of making rock art, and indeed there are few surfaces in the sandy desert on which rock art could be made.) The Drakensberg rock art of this time shows that some San shamans used their age-old spiritual weapons – those they employed in their struggles against the spirits of the dead and malevolent lion-shamans – in an attempt to protect their people from those who sought to wrest their land from them.

Farther to the west, the /Xam communities of the central Cape Colony had been destroyed by the middle of the nineteenth century.

The small, scattered remnants knew that they could not survive in the face of the land-hungry colonists and the commandos that were mounted to exterminate them. They eked out their last days as identifiable 'Bushmen' living in poverty on land occupied by farmers. One of those people was //Kabbo.

//Kabbo's home

When //Kabbo was in Cape Town in the 1870s, he spoke movingly of *kukummi* (sing. *kum*). There is no single English equivalent for his word. *Kukummi* means stories, news, talk, information, history and what English-speakers call myths and folklore (Bleek, 1956: 106). Far from home, //Kabbo was thinking nostalgically of the /Xam people whom he knew and loved, sitting at their waterholes out on the vast, dry expanses of the central Cape Colony. There they were listening to *kukummi* that, in his evocative phrase, 'float from afar' (Bleek and Lloyd, 1911: 301). Like the wind, *kukummi* moved invisibly from place to place (ibid.: 303); they were the essence of /Xam communal life, a bond between the scattered camps. For //Kabbo, that bond had been broken, and he was cut off from his own people. The white people with whom he was living in Cape Town did not, he said, possess his *kukummi*.

In the 1860s and 1870s, //Kabbo was suspended between two worlds: his own world of waterholes, springbok, rock art and *kukummi*, and the colonial world of land appropriation, servitude and 'crimes'. His ambivalence was expressed by his three names. His first /Xam name was /Uhi-ddoro, a phrase that seems to mean 'smoking tinderbox'; his second /Xam name, //Kabbo, means 'dream'; his third name, Jantje, a diminutive of the Dutch names Johannes and Johan, had been given to him by the white settlers who re-named everything as they brought people and places within the ambit of their rule.

On account of its aridity, the place where //Kabbo and his people lived – they called it /Xam-ka !au, ground, or dust, of the /Xam – was one of the last areas of southern Africa to be overtaken by colonial expansion. During the eighteenth century, *trekboers* (itinerant farmers) had begun to leave the Cape of Good Hope for the interior where they hoped to find grazing and freedom from Dutch and, later, British control. Bitter wars with Khoekhoe cattle- and sheep-herders and San communities sent ripples of violence ahead of the white settlers. Long before the whites established towns in /Xam-ka !au, dis-possessed, wandering Khoekhoen, as well as white traders and adven-turers, had been harbingers of the holocaust to come.

At first, some /Xam people exchanged ostrich feathers for traders' tobacco (*Kum* 22); later, they began to work for the *trekboers*, and the years of servitude began. At this time, the whole of Bushmanland, as the colonists somewhat ironically called the region, was open com-monage, or *trekveld*, and people from many ethnic groups exploited it at will and without regard for its inhabitants, the /Xam. Farmers did not actually settle along the Hartebeest River that flows through /Xam-ka !au from present-day Kenhardt to the Orange River until 1859.

Soon after the second British occupation of the Cape of Good Hope in 1806, the authorities in Cape Town instituted enquiries into the suffering of indigenous people. In 1862, when //Kabbo was living in the area, the Governor of the Cape Colony dispatched a magistrate, Louis Anthing, to investigate. He received horrifying reports of star-vation, frightful beatings and torture (*Kum* 21). When confronted with these atrocities, the Dutch farmers responded: 'They are our people, we can live with them as we wish.' As Anthing put it, the farmers were implementing 'a wholesale system of extermination'. Today we would use the word 'genocide'.

He found that those San who abandoned their traditional way of life and, in desperation, went into the service of the farmers were no better off:

> Harsh treatment, an insufficient allowance of food, and continu-
> ous injuries inflicted on their kinsmen are alleged as having driv-
> en them back into the bush, from whence hunger again led them
> to invade the flocks and herds of the intruders, regardless of the
> consequences, and resigning themselves, as they say, to the
> thought of being shot in preference to death from starvation.
> (Anthing, 1863: 5)

Despite these conditions, many /Xam people managed to continue living at least partially in the traditional hunting and gathering way and to pass their *kukummi* from generation to generation. Even as late as 1870, //Kabbo spoke of 'his' waterholes between which he and his family moved seasonally. At some times of the year they lived in small scattered groups within sight of each other's fires at night; at other times they came together and established camps with the grass dwellings of //Kabbo's children arranged on either side of his own (Bleek and Lloyd, 1911: 307–309). They established their camps some distance from the waterholes in order not to frighten away the animals that came to drink (Bleek, 1924: vi).

Brief sojourns

As with so many other San, //Kabbo's tragedy started with what the colonial administrators defined as a crime: he was arrested for sheep-stealing. At the time of his arrest he, his wife, his son's wife and her child, his daughter and her husband were all eating a springbok, not a sheep (Bleek and Lloyd, 1911: 295). Yet, years later, he explained that he had indeed stolen a sheep, but he had done so because he and his family were starving. The *trekboers'* presence had denuded the land and drastically reduced the herds of game that had formerly roamed the veld raising great columns of dust (*Kum* 2). That stolen sheep, he said, was 'starvation's food' (Bleek and Lloyd, 1911: 317).

But that was no excuse in the eyes of the law. Bound, he was taken first to the small town of Victoria West and then on to Beaufort West. From there he travelled to Cape Town where, together with a number of other prisoners from /Xam-ka !au, he was put to work on a breakwater that was being constructed for the Victoria Basin in Table Bay. At about 60 years of age, his life as a convict, far from his home and the *kukummi* of his people, had started. As his hard labour began, the Dutch name for the waterhole which he had inherited, via his elder brother, from his father and his grandfather took on a new and terrible meaning. One day when he was on a train travelling from Mowbray to Cape Town, a man asked him about his home. He replied, 'My place is the Bitterpits.'

Today a white farmer's windpump stands next to //Kabbo's Bitterpits. The water is still brackish and bitter. Many of the descendants of his /Xam people who continue to live in the Northern Cape Province, as that part of the old Cape Colony is now known, work on white-owned farms; because they do not live by hunting and gathering, they are no longer recognised as San. No communities speak the /Xam language. Under the apartheid system of official racial classification they were listed as 'Coloured' – people somewhere between the ruling white class and the black, Bantu-speaking farmers who, in the nineteenth century, lived largely to the east and north of /Xam-ka !au. If //Kabbo's suspension between two worlds was implied by his /Xam and Dutch names, his descendants' marginalisation was formally established by the racial designation 'Coloured'.

Fortunately for //Kabbo, some alleviation of his bitter circumstances began in 1870 when Dr Wilhelm Heinrich Emmanuel Bleek met him at the Breakwater Prison. Born in 1827, Bleek was a linguist who came from a celebrated scholarly German family. His cousin was the distinguished biologist Ernst Haeckel, for whom he was later to collect specimens in False Bay, near Cape Town. Wilhelm Bleek emigrated to southern Africa in 1855 at the behest of Bishop John William Colenso; he was to compile a Zulu grammar. While he was engaged on this task in the British colony of Natal, he heard about the San. He wrote, 'During the first few months of this year [1856] the Bushmen descended from their impregnable hiding places in the Kahlamba mountains [Drakensberg] to steal cattle again' (Spohr, 1962: 33). In addition to their apparent isolation, a characteristic of the San that greatly interested Bleek was their resistance to missionaries (Rosenthal and Goodwin, 1953: 9). Almost all the other peoples of Africa had in some measure been influenced by Christianity or Islam, but the San had remained impervious. Partly as a result of their resistance to missionaries, no one had been able to prepare any kind of grammar or dictionary of the San languages. As a linguist, Bleek was intrigued, but he was unable to do anything about his interest while he was in Natal.

In 1856 he moved to Cape Town where he became a court translator and married Jemima Lloyd, whom he had first met in Natal. Eventually he was appointed curator of the Grey Collection in the South African Public Library. Sir George Grey, Governor of the Cape Colony, had given half of his valuable collection of books and manuscripts to the library on the understanding that Wilhelm Bleek would be employed to catalogue all the items and thereby earn enough money to continue his linguistic researches.

In the year after his arrival in Cape Town, Bleek was able to follow up the interest that the reports about the Drakensberg San and their 'impregnable hiding places' had kindled in him. He was given permis-

Wilhelm Bleek

sion to interview San convicts who were imprisoned in the Cape Town Gaol and on Robben Island, the notorious island in Table Bay where, a century later, such famous political prisoners as Nelson Mandela were held. The people whom Bleek interviewed came from Colesberg in the Karoo and Burgersdorp, some 400 kilometres farther to the east. Later, in 1866, he was able to study the language of another two convicts who came from the 'Agterveld', probably the same general region where //Kabbo had lived before his arrest. None of these interviews proved very productive.

Then, in 1870, much more propitious circumstances changed the course of the Bleek family's life and, indeed, our understanding of the ancient San. Wilhelm visited the Breakwater Prison because he had heard that no fewer than 28 San were incarcerated there. Knowing that the future of the San people was in jeopardy, he wanted to study their language before it was lost for ever. He believed that this task was more important than his work on Zulu grammar and the Bantu languages in general because the Bantu languages were not threatened with extinction, and there would be many scholars who could study them in the future. He accordingly ceased that very well advanced work and concentrated on the /Xam language.

In taking this momentous decision, Bleek was flying in the face of colonial opinion. At that time most colonial people considered the San to be degenerate savages who should make way for 'higher races'. Forgetting that the land was originally theirs, writers consistently presented them as inveterate thieves, cruel, revengeful and insensitive. Above all, they were thought to lack any religion or concept of a deity. Bleek knew that this colonial view was false: the San were as sensitive, intelligent and attuned to spiritual matters as any other people.

His position was no doubt influenced by his father, Professor Friedrich Bleek, who was a well-known free-thinking, liberal theologian in the University of Bonn. Bishop Colenso, Bleek's long-time friend, held similarly liberal theological views and, in due course, these brought him into conflict with the white settlers and with the Church. Eventually, Colenso was charged with heresy. His allegedly heretical beliefs were posited on his view that God was in all people, even the unconverted 'heathen' whom he was supposed to convert. Colenso, however, refused to appear before the Bishop of Cape Town, whose authority he did not recognise, and Bleek conducted his defence in what became a *cause célèbre*. In the event, the defence was unsuccessful, and the Anglican Church eventually split into two wings, a schism that endures to the present day, though on very different theological grounds.

Throughout these unpleasant disputes, Bleek pursued his enquiries. Conditions in the Breakwater Prison, however, were not conducive to linguistic research, so he persuaded Sir Philip Wodehouse, Sir George Grey's successor as Governor of the Colony of the Cape of Good Hope, to allow some of the San to live with him at the Bleek home in Mowbray, a suburb of Cape Town. They were to be servants.

The first man moved to Mowbray on 29 August 1870. He was /A!kunta, or Klaas Stoffel, and had been declared physically unfit for hard labour in prison. He came from the Strandberg, the same part of the central Cape Colony as //Kabbo. A young man, /A!kunta was a noted mimic who loved music. With his first savings he bought a cheap violin on which, it was said, 'he played by ear with a talent which would have graced a better instrument'. His 'harmless airs and graces' afforded the Bleek family much amusement: 'A white flannel shirt, given as a precaution against the damp, was speedily converted

into a white waistcoat, in which he strutted about with the gait of a
finished dandy' (Bleek and Bleek, 1909: 38). It seems that his presence
at Charlton House, the Bleek home, and perhaps his demeanour,
were somewhat resented by the other servants; they taunted him with
being a 'wild Bushman' who had not been in the habit of wearing
shoes until he came to Cape Town. He retorted: 'I was *born* in
Veldschoen!' – the hide sandals that the /Xam people wore (Bleek and
Bleek, 1909: 38–39).

/A!kunta

//Kabbo joined /A!kunta at Mowbray on 16 February 1871, a
little-known but significant day in South African history. A much
older man, he became known as the Philosopher. Rightly, he considered himself not so much a servant as Wilhelm Bleek's teacher (Bleek
and Lloyd, 1911: 315). He 'much enjoyed the thought that the
Bushman stories would become known by means of books' (ibid.: x).
He was 'grizzled and wrinkled, lean and bent with age. Puckers of
meditation ran criss-cross by his kindly eyes … Whether trotting
meekly across the yard to do some light work, sitting to have his por-
trait taken, or enjoying a quiet smoke, old Jantje never lost his look of
mild melancholy' (ibid.: 39). According to Wilhelm Bleek, he had a

15

The Hill, Mowbray, with Wilhelm Bleek in the garden

'large swelling on [his] left shoulder, caused by the blow of a knobkerri' (Deacon, 1986: 142). //Kabbo, with his meditative, wise disposition, exerted considerable influence on the Bleek family; he seemed to be not entirely of this world: 'This gentle old soul appeared lost in a dream-life of his own' (Bleek and Bleek, 1909: 38).

The 'dream-life of his own' was no doubt created by the meditations of a long life on the significance of the *kukummi* that he wanted to become widely known. But there was another aspect of his dream-life that went beyond philosophical reflection and gives his words a special interest. It became apparent through a curious incident. While he was at Mowbray he was required to work in the garden. In October 1871, finding the ground too hard, he caused rain to fall. He accomplished this feat, he said, while he was in a 'dream'. In this state, he continued, he spoke to the rain, asking it to fall for him, just as he used to do in his own country. Still in a 'dream', he went on an out-of-body journey to the Bitterpits where he spoke with his wife and son (L. II. 5. 625–633). 'Dreaming' was one of the techniques that /Xam shamans used to accomplish their supernatural ends (Bleek translated the /Xam word *!gi:xa* as 'sorcerer' and 'medicine man'; I prefer 'shaman').

Both his /Xam names may, moreover, be linked to his status as a shaman. It seems virtually certain that the name '//Kabbo' (Dream) was given to him because he spoke often about his dream experiences (*Kukummi* 20 and 51; see *Kukummi* 8 and 9 for other ways in which the /Xam acquired nicknames). His first /Xam name, /Uhi-ddoro ('smoking tinderbox'), may be related to the word //Kandoro, which is one of the alternative names of /Kaggen, the Mantis; //Kandoro means 'tinderbox owner'. Both //Kabbo and the chief spiritual figure of the /Xam *kukummi* were thus associated, in a way that we do not fully understand, with the making of fire. This association between //Kabbo and /Kaggen seems to be confirmed by //Kabbo's special relationship with preying mantises: he was a /*Kaggen-ka !kwi*, 'a Mantis's man' (L. VIII. 23. 8033 rev.; Bleek, 1936a: 143). This state-ment was a prelude to a long tale about, not mantises, but *the* Mantis.

The type of personality that //Kabbo had – the 'dream-life of his own' – is still today associated with San shamans in the Kalahari Desert. The psychiatrist Richard Katz (1982: 236) found that these modern San shamans are 'more inner-directed' than other people and that they have 'easier access to a rich fantasy life'. Many of //Kabbo's *kukummi* are therefore precious because they come from a man who had special insights into /Xam spiritual life and belief.

At first, the authorities required Bleek to hire an ex-warder to guard wise old //Kabbo and young /A!kunta, but the precaution was soon found to be unnecessary (Bleek and Bleek, 1909: 40). Indeed, after their terms of penal servitude had expired in the middle of 1871, they stayed on for a time at Mowbray of their own free will (Bleek, 1873), though it seems that Bleek enticed //Kabbo to stay with the promise of a rifle as a gift (Bleek and Lloyd, 1911: 317).

/A!kunta and //Kabbo felt their separation from their wives keen-ly, and Bleek therefore caused enquiries to be made regarding their whereabouts, but he could ascertain nothing (Bleek, 1875: 1). In the end, their yearning to be reunited with their wives and to hear the *kukummi* in their own land proved overwhelming, and //Kabbo and /A!kunta set off for /Xam-ka !au on 15 October 1873. /A!kunta was reunited with his wife; his fate after that reunion is unknown.

But what happened to //Kabbo is known. Before he left Mowbray, //Kabbo had agreed to return to Cape Town to continue teaching Wilhelm Bleek. He even promised to bring his wife with him but, when he arrived at his home, he found her too weak to travel. She was somewhat older than he. He therefore resolved to return alone but, before he could do so, Bleek's beloved teacher died suddenly on 25 January 1876.

After the departure from Cape Town of //Kabbo and /A!kunta, Bleek began to negotiate the release of further /Xam prisoners. As a linguist, he was interested to find that the /Xam in the prison did not all speak exactly the same dialect. A hundred or so kilometres from //Kabbo's home, another /Xam group spoke a slightly different dialect. Those who, like //Kabbo and /A!kunta, lived near the Strandberg called themselves the 'Flat Bushmen' or 'Bushmen' of the plains; those who spoke the different dialect came from the Katkop, another comparatively small mountain to the west of the Strandberg. They were known as the 'Grass Bushmen'.

One of these 'Grass Bushmen' was Diä!kwain, whose Dutch name was David Husar (also recorded as Hesar and Hoezar). He lived at a place called !Kann, a waterhole where his father, Xa:ä-tin, had 'chipped gemsbok, quagga and ostriches … before the time of the boers' (L. V. 24. 5963 rev.). This link between Wilhelm Bleek's teachers and rock art is, of course, important.

Although none of them was himself or herself a rock artist, they knew that the art had been made by their own people and that it was in the recent past that they had ceased making it. Having learned that his father had made rock engravings, Lucy Lloyd, Wilhelm Bleek's co-worker, asked Diä!kwain to draw some pictures using pencil and crayon. One of his pictures shows what he called a *!khwa-ka xoro*, a 'rain-animal'. This supernatural creature was captured by /Xam rain-shamans, led across the veld, and then killed so that its blood and milk would fall as precipitation. Diä!kwain's drawing of the *!khwa-ka xoro* resembles rock engravings at a place known today as Varskans, where there are depictions of animals with the same small head, tiny legs, large body and an infill of horizontal lines. Varskans is near the Katkop, Diä!kwain's home. The first part of the name Varskans is the Afrikaans word for 'fresh'. The second part is more enigmatic, but local people believe that it derives from a San word (unknown to them) that meant 'spring' or 'waterhole'. It is possible that 'kans' comes from '!Kann', the name of the waterhole where Diä!kwain's father made rock art. It is common for Westerners to drop the clicks from San words. The rock engravings at Varskans may therefore include the ones that Xa:ä-tin made and of which Diä!kwain spoke (Deacon 1988: 131–134).

Like so many other /Xam people of his generation, Diä!kwain had had a brush with a white farmer. He described an occasion when a Boer had shot at him and his young son. He had, he said, done nothing wrong, but was simply away from home collecting poison to prepare his arrows for shooting springbok (L. V. 3. 4132 rev. – 4133 rev.).

Diä!kwain's history can only be tentatively pieced together from prison records and local traditions (Deacon, 1986: 146–148). It seems that in January 1869 Diä!kwain and his brother-in-law, ≠Kasin, had taken a sheep from one of the nearby Dutch farmers, Jacob Kruger. Kruger pursued the San. When he caught up with them, he threatened to kill not only Diä!kwain but his whole family as well – a common enough practice in those days. Diä!kwain shot and killed him. Subsequently, Diä!kwain was arrested and, as with //Kabbo, his long journey to Cape Town and penal servitude started. We do not know when he reached the Breakwater Prison, but he must have been there in June 1870 because it was on 19 June that he was sentenced to two hours' extra labour for disobedience. Diä!kwain was therefore at the prison at the same time as //Kabbo and /A!kunta. There, in their cells along with the other people from /Xam-ka !au, they doubtless related *kukummi* and shared with each other their longing to return home.

Diä!kwain did not move to Mowbray until December 1873 (the exact date does not seem to have been recorded). It may have been the more serious nature of his crime that delayed his release (Deacon, 1986: 148). Indeed, he became known as Dr Bleek's 'pet murderer', a phrase that suggests that the Bleek family's neighbours considered them more than a little eccentric. But Diä!kwain 'was a soft-hearted mortal, who would not, unprovoked, have hurt a fly'. Sometimes he escorted the Bleek family's lady visitors who were going home alone at night (Bleek and Bleek, 1909: 40). Many years later, Dorothea and Edith Bleek, Wilhelm Bleek's daughters, recalled how Diä!kwain had posed for a photograph. Dressed in his best suit and tie, he is shown 'looking down with a happy smile at his best hat, which he holds gingerly, in order to display a brass ring on one finger' (Bleek and Bleek, 1909: 40). He is holding his flute in his right hand.

Diä!kwain   *!Kweiten-ta-//ken*

Diä!kwain's father, Xa:ä-tin, was a shaman who had the ability to make rain. He had learned this skill from an old shaman called !Nuin-/kuïten. The story of !Nuin-/kuïten's death typically blends what many Westerners distinguish as real and non-real components of /Xam life. !Nuin-/kuïten had been on a shamanic out-of-body journey in the form of a lion and, in this form, had killed a Boer's ox. The Boer raised a commando, pursued him and shot him. Mortally wounded, !Nuin-/kuïten had limped home, where he told Xa:ä-tin that his end was near. He wanted Xa:ä-tin to continue singing the shamanic songs he had taught him and to make rain in the age-old way. After !Nuin-/kuïten's death, Xa:ä-tin was heartbroken. He sang:

> People were those,
> Who broke for me the string.
> Therefore,
> The place became like this to me,
> On account of it,
> Because the string was that which broke for me ...
> therefore,
> The place does not feel pleasant to me,
> On account of it.

(Bleek, 1936: 134)

Diä!kwain left Cape Town on 18 March 1874, but returned with his sister, !Kweiten-ta-//ken, also known as Rachel, on 13 June of the same year. !Kweiten-ta-//ken was accompanied by her husband, ≠Kasin, or Klaas Katkop, and her four children. ≠Kasin was 'a dark, fierce-looking man', only partly of San descent, but he spoke the 'Grass' dialect of the /Xam. His and !Kweiten-ta-//ken's children looked more like the San side of the family than their father (Bleek and Bleek, 1909: 41). They were allocated a field in which to play; their parents never had occasion to punish them and they never squabbled. !Kweiten-ta-//ken was not happy in Cape Town, however, and, together with her husband and children, left for /Xam-ka !au on 13 January 1875.

During Diä!kwain's and ≠Kasin's stay at Mowbray, Wilhelm Bleek established close contact with another researcher whose work was to became intimately associated with the Bleek family. George William Stow was born in England in 1822 and, after unsuccessful medical study, emigrated to southern Africa in 1843. After diverse employment, he became a self-taught geologist; his contributions to southern African geology are still widely respected. In 1867 he started copying rock paintings in the Orange Free State and the eastern parts of the Cape Colony. He proposed using these copies in 'a history of the manners and customs of the Bushmen, as depicted by themselves' (Stow in a letter to T.R. Jones; Young, 1908: 27–28). In 1874 Bleek expressed his 'great longing' to see Stow's copies of rock paintings of which he had heard glowing reports (Bleek, 1874: 12).

Bleek had, of course, known about rock art for a long time and must have been familiar with the copies published by Sir James Alexander in 1838. He had also seen copies made by W.R. Piers, C.H. Schunke and others, but these rather crude copies give little idea of the beauty and complexity of the art. More importantly, it was the copies that Joseph Millerd Orpen sent to *The Cape Monthly Magazine* in 1874 that persuaded Bleek that at least some of the art was a 'truly artistic conception of the ideas which most deeply moved the Bushman mind, and filled it with religious feelings' (Bleek, 1874: 13).

Then, in 1875, Stow sent 42 of his copies of rock paintings and 19 copies of rock engravings to Bleek. Bleek was delighted: 'They are of the greatest possible interest, and evince an infinitely higher taste, and a far greater artistic faculty, than our liveliest imagination could have anticipated' (Bleek, 1875: 20). He realised that the art was as complex as the *kukummi* he was recording and that, if Stow's copies were to be published, they would 'effect a radical change in the ideas generally entertained with regard to the Bushmen and their mental condition' (ibid.). Unfortunately, publication was long deferred, and the change that Bleek thought the art would effect has still not fully come about.

Even before he received Stow's copies, Bleek had set about obtaining Diä!kwain's and ≠Kasin's comments on Orpen's copies. He found that the /Xam people's explanations differed somewhat from those that Orpen had obtained from a Maluti San, Qing, who had guided him to some of the sites, but they were nevertheless essentially the same. He also found similarities between the *kukummi* that he was obtaining from the /Xam people and the tales that Orpen got from Qing (in Bleek's orthography, !King). Bleek was thus the first person to note the important continuities and differences between San beliefs in widely separated parts of southern Africa. Indeed, his remarks that were published together with Orpen's article in *The Cape Monthly Magazine* of July 1874 constitute one of the most important documents in San folklore and rock art studies.

With Diä!kwain willing to stay in Cape Town and a large number of copies of rock paintings at hand, all seemed set for years of profitable study, but Bleek, always in frail health, died on 17 August 1875 at the early age of 48. In March of that year he had said to his wife, Jemima, that he wished that his doctor would tell him the truth. He added, 'I want to know whether it will be weeks, or months' (Spohr, 1962: 40). He had to know which parts of his work he should finish off and which he should, as Jemima put it in a letter to Sir George Grey, 'lay quietly on one side' – the dilemma that faces all those who know that they have more work than time. Later, he appeared to rally and was strong enough to go for walks with Jemima, but he relapsed in June. A further recovery allowed him to return to his work at the South African Public Library and to play with the children in the evenings.

During the evening of 16 August, he worked on his Dictionary until 10 p.m. and then retired to bed. A few hours later he became partially paralysed. Three weeks after that night, Jemima described the events in a letter to Sir George Grey. 'Striking a light, I saw he was awake and looking at me, & that he tried to speak but could not.

When he saw (or felt) that the effort was in vain, a sort of wondering half-puzzled look came into his eyes, then a very sweet smile – but he never (visibly) tried to speak again.' The doctor was called, but he died at a quarter past two the next morning. 'But oh dear Sir George, perhaps you can dimly fancy what our empty home & life [are] now he is gone' (Spohr, 1962: 42).

Wilhelm Bleek was buried in the Wynberg cemetery, Cape Town, alongside two of his children. The interment was private, and only a few people were present, but the writer of his obituary in *The Cape Argus* of 19 August noted, 'Had the funeral been in the ordinary course, it would have been attended by many hundreds' (Spohr, 1962: 39). The obituary records that he was 'warmly esteemed by those who knew him most thoroughly', but he did not 'mix much with the out-erworld, and his life was essentially that of a recluse'. The extent of this retiring man's international reputation may be gauged from the fact that, in 1869, such illustrious scholars as Sir Charles Lyell, Thomas Henry Huxley and Charles Darwin sponsored a petition to the British Government to grant him a civil pension of 150 English pounds per annum so that he could continue his researches (Spohr, 1962: 32). The petition was successful, and his last years were free from financial worry.

In the doubt and confusion that followed Bleek's death, Diä!kwain did not know what to do. Although he longed to return home to obtain news of his family, he delayed his departure so that he could serve Bleek's widow, Jemima, and her sister, Lucy Lloyd. He asked Lloyd to take down a letter to his sister, !Kweiten-ta-//ken, so that he could explain the difficult situation to her. In this letter he told !Kweiten-ta-//ken that he could not leave while 'his mistress ... still weeps' (*Kum* 19).

One night, while they were waiting for a reply to this letter, a child who slept in a small room by herself was startled by an owl outside her window; it sounded like breathing. When Diä!kwain was told this, he was much pleased. He asked Lucy Lloyd if she did not 'think that Dr Bleek would come to see how his little children were getting on?' (Bleek and Lloyd, 1911: xv). The child was Bleek's youngest daughter, Dorothea, who was to play an important part in the history of San researches (Rosenthal and Goodwin, 1953: 16).

Eventually Diä!kwain left Cape Town on 7 March 1876, seven

months after Bleek's death. At first he worked for Dr H. Meyer of Calvinia, the man who had undertaken to transmit his letter to !Kweiten-ta-//ken. After a few months in Calvinia, he went to visit his family, having left some of his wages in Dr Meyer's safekeeping. He never returned, and the doctor's attempts to trace him failed. It seems likely, as local legend has it, that some of the murdered Jacob Kruger's friends shot him in revenge for the killing that had, some seven years before, led to his going to Cape Town and his meeting with the Bleek family (Deacon, 1986: 148).

The work continues

Fortunately there was someone to carry the research forward after Bleek's death. His sister-in-law, Lucy Lloyd, had worked closely with him for a number of years and had become proficient in the /Xam language. While he concentrated on linguistics, she took down the *kukummi*; all the extracts in this book were in fact recorded by her. In a codicil to his will, Bleek asked that Jemima would continue to manage the household and 'the practical matters connected with having Bushmen (men or women) on the place' and that Lucy Lloyd would continue with what he called their 'joint Bushman studies'.

Before long she set about arranging for members of //Kabbo's family to travel to Cape Town and to fill the gap left by Diä!kwain's departure. Like Bleek himself, Lloyd wished to interview older people, especially older women, because both of them realised that the women possessed information that few other people had. The *kukummi* that they were getting were all told from a male perspective.

At first //Kabbo's old widow, !Kwabba-an, or Lies, resolved to fulfil the promise her recently deceased husband had made to continue the work in Cape Town, but she died on Mr C. St. L. Devenish's farm, near Vanwyksvlei, in 1877 before she could commence the journey. On the night that she died, ghostly fires blazed on the hillside across the river, lit perhaps by /Uhi-ddoro, 'smoking tinderbox', the husband who had preceded her to the spirit world. Then, in awesome circumstances, //Kabbo himself was seen in his place among the spirits of dead 'sorcerers', waiting no doubt for his beloved Lies. The spirits of //Kabbo and his fellow 'sorcerers' were gathered around a pot, but what it contained was unmentionable (Bleek and Bleek, 1909: 41). Thus, on the night of the spectral fires, //Kabbo was eternally

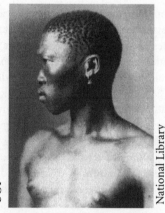

Lucy Lloyd   */Han≠kass'o*

reunited with old Lies for whom he had so longed when he was in Cape Town. In Bunyan's Christian imagery, the trumpets sounded for her on the other side.

Faced with the deaths of both //Kabbo and Lies, //Kabbo's son-in-law, /Han≠kass'o, or Klein Jantje (small or younger Jantje), decided to go to Cape Town. /Han≠kass'o had married //Kabbo's daughter Suobba-//kein, and they lived at or near the Bitterpits. His father, Ssounni, did not have a Dutch name 'because he died before the Boers were in that part of the country' (L. VIII. 1. 6052). /Han≠kass'o had been arrested at the same time as //Kabbo and, for a period, had been incarcerated in the Breakwater Prison. His second and voluntary journey to Cape Town was facilitated by Mr Devenish at the request of Lucy Lloyd (Deacon, 1986: 143). Towards the end of 1877 he set off with Suobba-//kein. In the event, they could not travel fast because 'the brutal attack of a policeman had upset his wife's health' (Bleek and Bleek, 1909: 41). //Kabbo's whole family seems to have been haunted by tragedy, and Suobba-//kein and her infant child both died on the arduous journey, despite generous assistance given to them by the Civil Commissioner at Beaufort West. /Han≠kass'o eventually reached Cape Town, alone, on 10 January 1878.

The poverty-stricken, violent circumstances of these people no doubt contributed to their willingness to go to Cape Town, but it seems that their desire to let the /Xam *kukummi* become widely known by means of books motivated them as well. They knew beyond a shadow of a doubt that they were the last repositories of these *kukummi*, and they did not want the stories to die with those into whose ears they had for so long floated in /Xam-ka !au but whose way of life was being rapidly destroyed.

Like his father-in-law, /Han≠kass'o proved to be a good narrator and teacher. It was he who recounted the mystical events of the night during which Lies died. Recalling what he had seen, he turned 'pale with awe' and spoke in a 'shaking whisper' (Bleek and Bleek, 1909: 41). When he tried to speak about the contents of the pot around which the wraiths of //Kabbo and the dead 'sorcerers' were gathered, his voice shuddered and broke off.

/Han≠kass'o was gentle and kindly. The colonial children gave him much pleasure, and he played with them and made them birth-day presents, such as a set of diminutive bows and arrows or a *!goin!goin*, a bullroarer that /Xam people used as an instrument to make the bees swarm (Bleek and Bleek, 1909: 41; Bleek and Lloyd, 1911: 352). The children loved to hear him tell his stories. They could not understand the /Xam language, so a member of the Bleek family gave them an outline before the performance began. Then, enthralled, they watched his 'eloquent gestures', feeling rather than knowing what was happening.

It was one of the colonial children's pranks that led /Han≠kass'o to draw a perceptive analogy between their mischief and his beliefs about /Kaggen, the Mantis. On 12 December 1875, when he was checking the translation of his account of the way in which the Mantis protected his favourite animal, the eland, he recalled what had happened a month or so earlier when the children had attempted to frighten him by donning a disguise.

> The Mantis imitates what people do also, when they want us who do not know Guy Fox [*sic*] to be afraid. They change their faces, for they want us who do not know to think it is not a person. The Mantis also … cheats them that we may not know that it is he.
>
> (L. VIII. 17. 5434)

By transforming himself into other creatures, /Kaggen was able to distract hunters from observing the necessary avoidance customs. He thus ensured the eland's escape.

Like Diä!kwain, /Han≠kass'o knew something about rock art. When he was giving Lloyd the tale 'The girl of the early race of people who married a baboon' (L. VII. 18. 7608–7609), he mentioned two of the ingredients of the paint that the artists used. One of the girls in the tale says that she will draw a gemsbok and a baboon because she has some //hara (black specularite). The other girl responds that she will draw a springbok because she has some tò (red haematite). Unfortunately, /Han≠kass'o did not mention the medium with which these two pigments were mixed.

/Han≠kass'o was very lonely, having no one with whom he could converse in his own language. Lucy Lloyd's efforts to secure companions for him proved fruitless. Then she learned from J.M. Orpen, who a few years earlier had obtained valuable information about rock paintings, that a small San family living near Kimberley was willing to go to Cape Town. The help of a number of highly placed people was enlisted, but the family was in poor health, and a child died on the journey, years of poverty and malnutrition having taken their toll. When the family finally arrived in Cape Town, Lloyd found that they were not San after all, but Khoekhoen. It seems that the misunderstanding arose in part from people's unfamiliarity with the Khoisan click languages, but the head of the family, Piet Lynx, who belonged to the Koranna section of the Khoekhoen, explained that people like him and his family were styled 'Bushmen-Hottentots' in the part of the country from which he came (Lloyd, 1889: 4). The distinctions between ethnic groups were far from clear-cut. Nevertheless, Lloyd took the opportunity to record some additions to the very limited amount of Khoekhoe folklore then known. On 13 January 1880 the family left Cape Town to return to Kimberley. They arrived safely and were found employment.

Another disappointment was in store for /Han≠kass'o. Wilhelm Bleek had wished to learn the San languages spoken by the people living in the Kalahari Desert, but it was not until 1 September 1879 that Lucy Lloyd finally managed to arrange for two young boys, !Nanni and Tamme, to journey to Cape Town. They were later joined for a time by another two boys, /Uma and Da. All four boys belonged to the group known as the !Kung or Ju/'hoansi. At first /Han≠kass'o was dismayed to find that their language was unintelligible to him; nor could they understand him. Yet, after a while, /Han≠kass'o remarked that he could discern some resemblances between the language spoken by the so-called 'Grass Bushmen' of the Cape Colony and that of the !Kung (Lloyd, 1889: 4). Exactly what those resemblances were was unfortunately not recorded. While they were at Mowbray, these boys provided a valuable amount of !Kung folklore (Bleek, 1935b). !Nanni and Tamme returned to the Kalahari on 28 March 1882; /Uma and Da were found employment in December 1881 and March 1884 respectively.

/Han≠kass'o himself returned to /Xam-ka !au in December 1879. He particularly wished to see his son who was 'indentured to a farmer, who would not let him go' (Bleek and Bleek, 1909: 42). His fate, like those of most of the Bleek family's teachers, is unknown.

A few years later, in 1884, the Cape Government arranged for a group of starved, impoverished /Xam to go to a place of safety at Salt River, near Cape Town. But the place where they were settled was damp and, after their semi-desert life, they found it very trying. One day, a large number of these people visited the Bleek family at Mowbray. A small boy dressed up in beads and a skin apron to show how they dressed at home in /Xam-ka !au. When one of the *kukummi* that the other /Xam people had given Wilhelm Bleek and Lucy Lloyd was read to them, they were able to pick it up and 'continue in almost the same words' (Bleek and Bleek, 1909: 44).

One of these people, an old woman, stayed with the Bleeks for a short time. But, although her granddaughter was with her and she had other relations nearby, she was too homesick. 'She longed to return to her own country, so that she might be buried with her forefathers' (Bleek and Lloyd, 1911: xi). Her name was recorded as Mikki Streep, and it was she who demonstrated how /Xam women weighted their digging sticks with bored stones. A photograph was taken on this occasion.

Soon after Mikki Streep had rejoined the others at Salt River, the whole group stole away one night without leaving a trace. Edith and Dorothea Bleek surmised that they made their way back to their homes in /Xam-ka !au, but no one knows what happened to them. They and all the other people with whom the Bleeks worked came from obscurity, lived briefly in the Western *milieu* of Cape Town, and

Mikki Streep with digging stick

then returned to obscurity and the appalling, deteriorating conditions of their land. So little is known about them. Their voices, fortunately, though imperfectly, preserved in the Bleek and Lloyd Collection, were heard for a short time only; the rest is silence. The nocturnal departure of the people from Salt River was a poignant African *fin de siècle*.

Recording the *kukummi*

/A!kunta, //Kabbo, Diä!kwain, ≠Kasin, !Kweiten-ta-//ken and /Han≠kass'o were the Bleek family's principal teachers at Mowbray. There, in their colonial garden, Bleek and Lloyd learned the *kukummi* that meant so much to the /Xam. To facilitate their work, Bleek developed a phonetic script that could encompass the click consonants, glottal stops, tones (though only partially), and other sounds of the /Xam language that are, for speakers of European languages, so difficult to pronounce.

Using this script, Bleek and Lloyd recorded the *kukummi* in quarto notebooks. The right-hand pages were divided into two columns: word by word, sentence by sentence, the /Xam text was entered in one column, the other being reserved for the translation. Dates in the notebooks show that the translations were done more often than not within a few days and then checked with the narrators. While the checking was being done, the narrators sometimes offered further observations or clarifications; these were noted on the opposite, left-hand pages. This was the next best thing to a tape recorder.

Bleek and Lloyd's learning of the phonetically complex /Xam language was at first helped by their teachers' knowledge of Dutch, albeit limited. Recalling her childhood, Wilhelm Bleek's daughter Dorothea remembered that the /Xam people's broken Dutch was often unable to cope with person, number, mood and tense. To check his translations, therefore, Wilhelm sometimes resorted to acting the words or asking his teachers to act them. Sometimes he and Lucy Lloyd called in Dorothea herself – she was only two years old when her father died – to assist in getting 'plural, dual, exclusive and inclusive' correct (Bleek and Bleek, 1909: 40). /Xam words were also elicited by pointing to pictures in little Dorothea's and her elder sister Edith's books. For their part, the /Xam were also good learners, and they rapidly picked up English.

As we have seen, Bleek and Lloyd also resorted to another, today particularly tantalising, way of eliciting information from their teachers: they asked them to comment on Orpen's and Stow's copies of rock paintings. In 1875 Bleek wrote, 'An inspection of these pictures, and their explanation by Bushmen has only commenced; but it promises some valuable results, and throws light upon many things hitherto unintelligible' (Bleek, 1875: 20).

Wilhelm Bleek's untimely death soon after Stow's copies arrived at Mowbray meant that he himself was not able to find out more about those 'many things hitherto unintelligible', but Lucy Lloyd pursued the matter. She stated, 'It is impossible adequately to acknowledge the enormous help in the Bushman researches which has been afforded by copies of Bushman drawings and paintings' (Lloyd, 1889: 28). 'Some very curious ideas' that would otherwise not have come to light were indeed revealed when Bleek and Lloyd's /Xam teachers discussed the copies. Some of their explanations are preserved in the notebooks (e.g. *Kum* 50). Unfortunately, others are known only from extracts that Dorothea Bleek published in 1930, together with a selection of Stow's copies, in the magnificent book *Rock Paintings in South Africa*; the notebook in which the /Xam people's comments were recorded has been lost. Lucy Lloyd bought the entire collection of copies from Stow's widow after he died in 1882.

Sadly, neither Wilhelm Bleek nor Lucy Lloyd ever saw original rock paintings, nor were they able to visit the homes of their teachers. They never saw the dust rise in a springbok hunt, a 'sorcerer' bleed from the nose, a 'new maiden' secluded in her hut, or the glow of a distant camp's fires far off across the veld. Nor did they taste the water at the Bitterpits. All the places, rituals and many of the artefacts about which their teachers spoke were unknown to them. Getting the /Xam names for animals and insects not found in the Cape Peninsula was a particularly difficult task, so they took their teachers to the South African Museum in Cape Town and asked them to give the /Xam words for a large number of the specimens. Inevitably, a few of the plants and insects of which the people spoke could not be identified.

The work was laborious, and the Bleek family and their teachers must have been extraordinarily devoted. Lloyd noted that //Kabbo 'watched patiently until a sentence had been written down, before proceeding with what he was telling' (Bleek and Lloyd, 1911: x). A few days after Diä!kwain's arrival at Mowbray, Lloyd wrote on one of the left-hand pages: 'It was difficult for him to dictate at 1st, which is probably why I could not get this properly and as he 1st told it to me. I have now heard again that this is the right story' (L. V. 1. 3612 rev.). Even with practice, this sort of narration must have been very disconcerting for the /Xam people, and it appears that a few of them simply could not cope with it.

Today we cannot tell to what extent the process of dictation led to digressions, omissions and embellishments. At home in /Xam-ka !au the tales were dramatised and acted out in very different conditions from the sober circumstances demanded by the process of dictation. But there were informal times when the narrators could give free reign to their considerable histrionic skills. As a child, Dorothea's favourite piece was the death of a monster that had frightened and was going to eat the /Xam children. When /Han≠kass'o told this tale, he performed the awful noise that the monster made and his final death-splutter over a hot stone. /Han≠kass'o 'clapped his hand to his mouth and rocked himself in agony' (Bleek and Bleek, 1909: 42).

The narratives were also often interspersed with songs which, according to Dorothea and her sister, Edith, 'had a most dramatic effect' when they were performed with appropriate tones and gestures (Bleek and Bleek, 1909: 37). The narrators also imitated animals well, croaking and hopping like a frog or miming the antics of a monkey. A 'mournful chorus of enchantment' accompanied the transformation of a person into a frog that hopped away in the rain. This sort of dramatisation has, of course, been lost, though something of it does occasionally come through to a sensitive reader of the notebooks.

Another difficulty that modern students encounter is that Bleek and Lloyd did not record their own questions. Often one does not know what prompted the telling of a *kum* or what elicited one of the left-hand page notes. Certainly, different performances of some of the tales, such as those about /Kaggen and the eland, were obtained in response to requests for them. Yet, despite all these limitations, it is clear from the manuscripts that the /Xam narrators displayed varied personal skills and styles of storytelling (Hewitt, 1986a; Guenther, 1989).

The Bleek and Lloyd Collection, as it is now known, comprises approximately 12 000 numbered pages of texts, word lists and notes, and this total excludes the supplementary left-hand pages. Managing this large collection was a major task to which Lucy Lloyd dedicated herself after Wilhelm Bleek's death in 1875. She prefaced the number of each notebook with 'B' if Bleek had recorded the texts and 'L' if it contained her own work. The roman numerals that follow 'B' refer to separate notebooks. In the case of Lloyd's notebooks, the roman numerals designate the narrator. The principal narrators were allocated the following numbers:

I	/A!kunta (Klaas Stoffel)
II	//Kabbo (Oud Jantje Toorn)
IV	≠Kasin (Klaas Katkop)
V	Diä!kwain (David Husar)
VI	!Kweiten-ta-//ken (Rachel)
VIII	/Han≠kass'o (Klein Jantje)

The arabic numbers that follow these roman numerals give first the number of the notebook and then the page number. Lloyd added the page numbers after the completion of the entire collection; they run consecutively through the Bleek notebooks and then, starting again at one, through all the Lloyd books. She numbered the right-hand pages only; she referred to the left-hand pages as 'reverso'. A reference such as 'L. V. 17. 5317 rev.' thus indicates material obtained by Lloyd from Diä!kwain and noted on the back of page 5317 in notebook 17.

Publication of the texts proved problematic. Victorian prejudice against women 'scientists' made it difficult for Lucy Lloyd to find a publisher. It was not until 1889 that she managed to persuade a London publisher to issue the catalogue of her part of the collection. It was entitled *A Short Account of Further Bushman Material Collected.* The presence of 'further' in her title is explained by the fact that two reports that Bleek himself had prepared had been published by the Cape Government in the 1870s.

Much later, plagued by ill-health and disheartened by the indifference of publishers, Lloyd none the less managed to see to the publication of a monumental volume, somewhat austerely entitled *Specimens of Bushman Folklore* (1911; reprinted 1968). At the beginning of her Preface to this volume, she mentioned the 'great difficulties' that she had encountered and pointed out that the passages she had selected for publication formed but a small part of the collection: 'Whether future days will see the remainder of the manuscripts, as well as the fine collection of copies of Bushman pictures made by the late Mr. G.W. Stow, also published is a question that only time can answer' (Bleek and Lloyd, 1911: vii). *Specimens of Bushman Folklore* contains /Xam texts together with translations, as well as valuable work on /Xam grammar.

When Lloyd realised that her ill-health was jeopardising the work with which Wilhelm had entrusted her, she handed the collection over to his daughter, Dorothea, who, as a child, had known the people from /Xam-ka !au. Lucy Lloyd died in 1914, at the age of 79, a year after receiving an honorary D.Litt. from the University of the Cape of Good Hope (now the University of Cape Town). Her younger sister Jemima, Wilhelm Bleek's widow, had died five years earlier on 26 October 1909.

Dorothea proved to be a faithful member of the Bleek family and continued the work with great devotion. In 1910 she went to the Prieska and Kenhardt districts where she met 'the children and nephews' of the people who had been at Mowbray. She tried to col-

UCT

Dorothea Bleek at a scientific conference in Berlin

lect folktales from them, but in vain. She found that, if she read to
them some of the material that her father and aunt had collected in
the 1870s, one or other of them sometimes recollected an old custom:
'But the folklore was gone, it had been completely forgotten' (Stow
and Bleek, 1930: xviii).

Later, Dorothea saw to the publication of numerous *kukummi*
about /Kaggen, the trickster-deity, but without the /Xam texts. She
whimsically entitled the collection *The Mantis and his Friends* (1924).
Whimsy is, indeed, all that some readers see in the /Xam *kukummi*,
yet it is the last quality we should associate with them. Quaintness sits
well with the distasteful stereotype of the San as small, childlike
people, but not with the reality that lies beneath the narrative surface.
In the late 1920s Dorothea Bleek published a 'grammatical sketch' of
the /Xam language in the *Zeitschrift für Eingeborenen-Sprachen*. Also
in the 1930s, she published a series of nine extensive extracts from the
collection in the journal *Bantu Studies* (now *African Studies*). These
extracts include /Xam texts and translations.

Dorothea extended her work far to the north, visiting Angola, East
Africa and Lake Chrissie in what is now Mpumalanga. She also studied the Nharo San of Ghanzi, Botswana, and published a short book

entitled *The Naron: A Bushman Tribe of the Central Kalahari.* Never
lacking industry, she found time to prepare *Comparative Vocabularies
of Bushman Languages* (1929a) that brought together eleven
Northern, Central and Southern San languages, as well as Nama, a
Khoekhoe language.

Like her aunt before her, Dorothea Bleek became widely respected
as the greatest living authority on the San but, when Eric Rosenthal
asked her if she had ever thought of joining the staff of a university,
she replied, 'My dear, I haven't even got a degree' (Rosenthal and
Goodwin, 1953: 21). She had in fact been offered an honorary degree
by the University of Cape Town, to which institution she bequeathed
the collection, but she declined on the grounds that there could be
only one 'Dr Bleek' – her revered father. She died on 17 June 1948, as
she was completing the monumental *Bushman Dictionary* on which
her father had started work over eighty years earlier. The *Dictionary*
was published in 1956, exactly one hundred years after Bleek had first
noted his interest in the San of the 'Kahlamba Mountains'. A truly
remarkable family endeavour thus ended.

Editing the *kukummi*

Despite Lucy Lloyd's and Dorothea Bleek's efforts, much of the
collection remains unpublished. When, in 1974, I left the published
texts and began to turn the pages of the notebooks in the Jagger
Library, University of Cape Town, I found that the collection was far
larger than I had imagined. No *kukummi* had been published for
nearly forty years. No one had worked at all extensively with the
notebooks since Dorothea Bleek's death. At first, I spent nearly three
months reading the 12 000 pages. In the mornings I worked through
the notebooks; in the afternoons I indexed my notes. Many times
after that initial read-through, I returned to what seemed to be an
inexhaustible source of insights into a long-vanished way of life.

These, I had to keep reminding myself, were the actual notebooks
that had lain on the table between //Kabbo and Lucy Lloyd as they
together struggled to get down the /Xam words and then to translate
them into English. These books had been part of her and Wilhelm's
daily life. They had carried them to and fro between the house and
the garden where they sat conversing with //Kabbo and the others.
//Kabbo too had no doubt held some of these books as he watched

Bleek and Lloyd writing down his *kukummi*. He knew that it was these notebooks, the ones that I now held, that would one day fulfil his desire to have the /Xam *kukummi* widely known. He and the others spoke from those pages directly to me. My decision was quickly made. This book is an attempt to do what //Kabbo wanted and to bring the *kukummi* to a wider readership and, especially, to make known hitherto unpublished material.

When I began work with the Bleek and Lloyd Collection, it seemed to me that the material was grossly undervalued and far too little known. Curiously, given the importance that Wilhelm Bleek, Lucy Lloyd and Dorothea Bleek all accorded the rock art copies that they obtained from J.M. Orpen, G.W. Stow and others, rock art researchers had done little more than acknowledge the existence of the collection; they never analysed the /Xam people's explanations of the copies. Moreover, very few people other than Lucy Lloyd and Dorothea Bleek had tried to place the texts before the public. One of the few was Käthe Woldmann. In 1938 she published extracts from *Specimens of Bushman Folklore* that she had translated into German. Much later, Arthur Markowitz (1956, 1971) brought some of the published narratives to a wider English-speaking audience by arranging them as poetry.

The same approach was more recently adopted by Stephen Watson (1991) in *Return of the Moon: Versions from the /Xam*. Some of his work was also reproduced in Pippa Skotnes's art book *Sound from the Thinking Strings* (1991). Although he calls his versifications new translations, they are not strictly speaking so, for he simply rearranged Bleek's and Lloyd's translations; it is hard for a reader to know how much of the resulting 'poems' are Watson and how much are Bleek and Lloyd – let alone /Xam. Certainly, his verses and stanzas are imposed on the /Xam texts and, as he says in his introduction, he has gone so far as to rearrange sequences to satisfy modern expectations of literary structure.

Another approach was adopted by Roger Hewitt who, in the 1970s in London, was studying microfilms of the Bleek and Lloyd Collection in preparation for his Ph.D. thesis (1976). He eventually published his work under the title *Structure, Meaning and Ritual in the Narratives of the Southern San* (1986a, 1986b). In his thesis, though not in the published version, he gave two of the tales in /Xam language versions that he had prepared by standardising the spelling in accordance with the *Bushman Dictionary*. Bleek and Lloyd wrote down words as they heard them, and there is therefore some variation in spelling in the manuscripts and, it should be added, in the *Dictionary* as well.

Most recently, Mathias Guenther has compared the oral traditions of the Botswana Nharo San with those of the /Xam. His book *Bushman Folklore* (1989) gives a number of narratives that had not been previously published. Avoiding any rearranging or paraphrasing, such as that employed by Watson, Guenther keeps his version as clearly as possible in Bleek's and Lloyd's translations.

In recent years there has been a significant increase in interest in the Bleek and Lloyd Collection. Short summaries of many of the *kukummi* appear in Sigrid Schmidt's monumental and scholarly *Catalogue of the Khoisan Folktales of Southern Africa* (1989). In 1991 an international conference on the collection was held in Cape Town, the proceedings of which were published as *Voices from the Past: /Xam Bushmen and the Bleek and Lloyd Collection* (Deacon and Dowson, eds., 1996). This volume contains chapters dealing with many aspects of research on the collection. Despite the interest to which the holding of this conference points, there has been no major attempt to publish the texts since the *Bantu Studies* extracts appeared in the 1930s.

In 1997 Karel Schoeman published an excellent biography of Lucy Lloyd and her correspondence with Stow. This invaluable publication provides far more details of the Bleek family and their research than can be accommodated in this brief introduction. In compiling the present volume, I decided to include only texts that had not been previously published by Bleek and Lloyd or by Guenther; Watson's work aims at something quite different and, in the comparatively few cases in which he has reworked unpublished material, the result is very different from the original texts. All but two of the *kukummi* given here (*Kum* 21 in Skotnes 1999: 40–41; *Kum* 37 in Lewis-Williams 1981) are therefore being made available in full for the first time.

Apart from the selection of texts, the most fundamental decision that I had to take was whether to publish the original /Xam language versions, as Lucy Lloyd did in *Specimens of Bushman Folklore* and as Dorothea Bleek did in *Bantu Studies* (though not in *The Mantis and his Friends*), or to give translations only. Scholarly imperative seemed to demand the inclusion of the /Xam texts, but the specialised type-setting that their transcription would necessitate and the fact that their presence would double the length of the book counted against their publication. The labour involved and the size of the resulting book would increase the price considerably and so defeat one of the principal aims of the project – to make the *kukummi* as widely known as possible. In any event, the texts are today accessible on microfilm, a technology that was, of course, not available to Lucy Lloyd and Dorothea Bleek when they published parts of the collection; the very few scholars who wish to study the /Xam language by means of the original phonetic texts can obtain them in this format. For these reasons I reluctantly decided to omit the /Xam texts of the *kukummi*.

In editing Lloyd's translations I have tried to make as few changes as possible. Except in one instance (*Kum* 1), I have resisted the very real temptation to arrange the often poignant narratives as verse (but see Lewis-Williams and Dowson, 1989: 98, 110, 125). Perhaps versification comes close to prettification, and the starkness of the narrators' dictated text, in its very proseness, better conveys the tragedy that permeates the whole collection.

I found that the amount of editing required varied considerably from narrative to narrative. Both Bleek's and Lloyd's translations were always as literal as possible, though it is clear that they found it easier to translate some texts than others. In writing the translations in the notebooks, they tried to keep the English version aligned with the /Xam text. They therefore never developed the longer, grammatically coherent sentences that are characteristic of English. Instead, long stretches of translation are sometimes punctuated by only a series of commas, some of which are clearly in a 'wrong' position and may have been inserted to indicate a mid-phrase pause in the narrator's delivery. As a result of this loose punctuation it is sometimes not clear if, say, an adverbial phrase or clause should be placed at the end of one sentence or at the beginning of the next.

Another result of Bleek's and Lloyd's very tight transliterations of the /Xam texts is irregular word order. For instance: 'These things they are those which, we who (are) ill, we are finished, our thoughts ascending, leave us, while our bodies, our bodies are those which are in (or lie in?) the earth' (L. IV. 1. 3445; Lloyd's parentheses). Guenther (1989: 25), who also faced this problem, gives a similarly convoluted example: 'hold thou strongly fast for me the hartebeest skin'. Most readers will, I feel sure, require a more idiomatic English word order. They will also appreciate the elimination of the archaic 'thee' and 'thou' usages that in some passages, such as the one Guenther gives, impart a biblical air that is foreign to the original /Xam texts.

Once an editor has sorted out the word order and punctuation, the next problem is paragraphing. For the most part, neither Bleek's and Lloyd's translations nor the texts themselves give any indication of where paragraphs begin or end. In any event, paragraphing is not, of course, characteristic of oral literature. Readers should therefore remember that the paragraphing is mine, and that it is imposed on the original continuous text to make it more readable.

The seamlessness of the /Xam texts accords with the way in which narrators sometimes slipped from one tense to another and from one person to another. An account being given in the past tense often contains a sentence or two (sometimes more) in the present tense. In some cases the narrator was probably dramatising parts of the tale; in other instances I am not sure if the aberrant tense is a result of an error in recording what was said or a faulty translation. In instances where the aberrant tense is limited to one or two verbs, I have altered it to conform with the narrative as a whole; I have left the tense as it is in longer variations.

A different kind of editorial problem is created by the ways in which Bleek and Lloyd annotated their work. Unless otherwise stated, all the notes at the ends of the passages given in this volume were made by Lloyd. Usually these notes derive from the left-hand, reverso pages of the notebooks and are linked to the adjacent, right-hand page /Xam texts by asterisks of different kinds. I have substituted consecutive numbers for these asterisks. Some notes concern the meanings of /Xam words that came up in conversation during the narration of a passage but are not directly relevant to the narrative; I have omitted these. While some of the notes are clearly Lloyd's, others are brief remarks and explanations obtained from the narrators. Still other notes are longer passages that the narrators added when the texts were being read back to them for checking; sometimes, but not always, these explications are accompanied by /Xam versions. The

notes that I have added are marked 'Editor'. Throughout I have
refrained from adding interpretative notes (for interpretations of
/Xam texts, see Lewis-Williams, 1981, 1983, 1996; Lewis-Williams and
Biesele, 1978; Hewitt 1986a, 1986b; Biesele 1993; Vinnicombe 1976).

From time to time one finds that Bleek and Lloyd left /Xam words
untranslated; they were evidently defeated by them. Sometimes they
discovered the meanings of these words subsequently, and they can be
found in the *Dictionary*. When this is the case, I have supplied the
English word. When the correct translation cannot be ascertained in
this way, I have indicated this in square brackets; round brackets in
the translations indicate the original translator's parentheses.

Although I have arranged the *kukummi* under two major headings, 'Daily Life' and 'Myth, Ritual and Belief', I am sensitive to the
fact that the word *kukummi* covers all the texts I have selected. For
the /Xam, what we may see as a spiritual realm was as real as the
affairs of daily life: life was a seamless, mythic unity that was played
out in more than one realm of human experience. Even as the
kukummi linked the scattered camps in /Xam-ka !au, so too did they
blur distinctions between daily life and spiritual experiences. To
counterbalance the dichotomy implied by the two major headings, I
have allocated all the texts consecutive numbers.

Each *kum* was given by an individual person. Bleek and Lloyd did
not conflate their teachers and the people of whom they spoke into
an anonymous collectivity. The 'ethnographic present', the convenient
fiction that collapses time and person, has no place in the Bleek and
Lloyd Collection. A /Xam equivalent for 'the Nuer herder' or 'the
Trobriand Islander' and the like, the anonymous sources of so much
ethnographic information, is never allowed to take shape. Instead,
real people who lived at particular times and in particular places and
who have personal – if little known – histories speak their views of
life and belief. We do not read what 'the /Xam' believed, but rather
what //Kabbo, Diä!kwain, /Han≠kass'o and the others believed or,
perhaps more accurately, what they had been told by, again, particular, named people of the generation that preceded them, people who
lived in /Xam-ka !au before the land was settled by colonists.

This individuation of knowledge and its location in real history
should reverberate through all that we henceforth think about 'the
San' and, perhaps especially, in our responses to southern African

rock art. Even as each *kum* was given and moulded by a specific narrator, each rock art image was made by a specific artist, or artists, in specific historical circumstances. We can no longer think of the 'San' as a 'race', or as a simple, diminutive, childlike 'people', or as now long departed and largely forgotten 'hunters'. They were individual men and women, tellers of *kukummi* and makers of extraordinary rock art images. Both the *kukummi* and the art speak eloquently of their suffering and destruction and, in doing so, are a powerful riposte to the demeaning stereotypes which have diminished their stature as human beings.

Notwithstanding the problems of translation and the dilemmas of editing, I hope that the *kukummi* that this book contains will contribute to the fulfilment of //Kabbo's wish that the /Xam stories become widely known. In those days of 120 and more years ago, the *kukummi* floated from afar across the plains of ravaged /Xam-ka !au. Today they still float from afar, from those distant, tragic times to our new millennium. As they join the past and the present, they carry intimations of unity and our common humanity. The Republic of South Africa's new motto is in the /Xam language, and San rock art images are at the centre of the new national crest. The /Xam *kukummi* can live again in a South Africa free from racial discrimination. They can, in some way, continue to play a healing, unifying role. That would certainly have been //Kabbo's wish. It will be //Kabbo, not Sir Bartle Frere, who will be remembered.

Kukummi

PART I

Daily life in /Xam-ka !au

Life and death in /Xam-ka !au

The Bleek and Lloyd Collection contains more accounts of distress than joy; the final years of the /Xam were indeed tragic. The first text (*Kum* 1) captures this all-pervading sense of death. It provides a fitting introduction to the texts that follow.

The second, into which the first directly leads, is one of the longest. It is noteworthy for a number of reasons. First, the omission of people's names gives the impression that //Kabbo was creating the sequence, almost in a reverie. Some of the details, however, do suggest real people and events. Perhaps it is a summation of a number of //Kabbo's memories. In any event, it provides a vivid, first-hand account of what it was like to live in /Xam-ka !au. Second, many details of the hunting and gathering life emerge, and we are able to experience the varied human relationships and values of the time almost as if we were there. Events are dramatised, and //Kabbo no doubt vigorously acted them out.

Kum 2 deals with issues raised by the San custom of bride-service. A young man was required to live with his bride's family until a couple of children had been born. It seems that the young man in this narrative failed to fulfil his bride-service obligations.

Kum 2 is also remarkable because of the extended period over which it was narrated. //Kabbo managed to preserve the direction of his narrative despite, as the intratextual dates show, long breaks in recording.

The third *kum* is a very brief account of life on the semi-arid plains where temperatures soar to more than 40°C and the night temperatures fall below freezing point.

Together, these three texts reflect the close personal relationships, tensions and concerns of //Kabbo's people.

A litany of death

//Kabbo

L. II. 12. 1173–1179
12–13 APRIL 1872

When a Bushman dies,
he goes to this place.

An old man wastes away and dies;
he goes to this place.

An old woman becomes lean;
her flesh vanishes away;
she dies;
she goes to this place.

A little child who is very small dies;
it too goes to this place.

If a man shoots another with an arrow
and the other dies,
he goes to this place.

If a man cuts another man with a short knife
and the man dies,
he goes to this place.

When a man shoots another with poison,
the man dies from the poison
and goes to this place.

A man stabs another with a dagger;
the other one dies
and goes to this place.

If a man shoots a woman with an arrow
and the woman dies,
she goes to this place.

If a man shoots another man with an arrow
and the man dies,
he goes to this place.[1]

When a Bushman shoots another with arrows,
the other Bushman dies
and goes to this place.

A Bushman knocks down another man
with a knobbed stick;
the man dies and goes.

Bushman stabs another with an assegai,
making him fall to the ground;
the stick's knife.[2]

A man cuts another with a knife;
the man dies,
he goes.

The very old man whose head becomes white,
dies of hunger;
he goes.

The man who shoots well lives.
The man who shoots amiss dies of hunger.

The very old woman whose flesh is dry,
dies of hunger.

The young man dies of hunger,
if he shoots amiss.

If he shoots his fellows with an arrow,

then the other man shoots another with an arrow;
the other man dies.

Sometimes folk who are many
go together to fight other people
who are also many.
They fight one another.
A man dies from fighting
because they are angry with him.
They go to shoot their own people.
They must avoid the arrow,
when they shoot their own people.

[13 April] The man who dies
because of his anger
is killed by another man.
They shoot their own people.
They shoot the other man
with the arrow.
He is wounded;
they leave their own people.[3]

NOTES

1. *[26 May 1879]* A mine/opening must be what he speaks of. The people call it 'grave'.
2. Editor: Lloyd's translation suggests an iron-bladed assegai.
3. Editor: This account of death and conflict leads directly into *Kum* 2.

Death on the hunting ground

//Kabbo

L. II. 12–14. 1179–1396
13 April – 19 September 1872

A man kills another man while they are shooting springbok. The man is wounded. The other men leave the springbok and run to him as he sits in pain. Weeping, they stand over him.

They say to the other man, 'What is this thing here which shoots our brother?'

The man says to them, 'I did not mean to shoot our brother, for I was shooting springbok. Our brother was wounded when he was behind the springbok's back. [*15 April*] I did not mean to shoot our brother; I was shooting at the springbok. The arrow went into the springboks' dust. Our brother was near and did not see. He did not see the arrow coming, so that he could avoid it, because he was looking at the springbok. So he did not see the arrow so that he could avoid it. I weep for our brother because he is our friend. He is not a stranger who is different; he is our friend. So I worry about our brother. My heart cries for our brother. My heart is not happy about our brother.'

The other man says to him, 'It seems to me that you did not think of our brother's children; you shot him among the springbok, when he could not see because of the dust. You did not wait to shoot the springbok, as the springbok passed by his side, so that you could shoot the springbok in this place. As you came, you did not see our brother coming to the place. I saw him coming towards you, as you too were coming. I saw you come near to our brother. I saw our brother and I saw you, as you were meeting each other. Stooping, you approached each other, while the springbok looked between you. [*16 April*] You did not seem to see our brother.'

The man said to him, 'I did not see our brother. I did not see our brother coming; for the dust had shut in. I could not see well because of the springboks' dust; for the springbok were many. That is why I did not see.'

The wounded man said, 'Our brother is angry with you, but I am the one who did not see well because of the dust. The dust was dense because the springbok were many. I am wounded because I was watching the springbok. I did not look carefully on this side, for, if I had, I should have avoided the arrow. I should have avoided it and so prevented our brother's fear. You scold our brother as if the arrow did not come in the dust. But that is how it was: I did not see the arrow. I could have avoided it and prevented our brother's fear. So our brother must not fear. I should have kept still, then I could have avoided the arrow. I should have avoided it nicely.

'Lift me up and carry me away to the house; I do not feel as if I can walk, for I am in great pain. So you must carry me; I must go to lie by myself in pain at the house. You must leave the springbok; you must leave the springbok; you will shoot another day. My blood is out; I was wounded early. That is why I cannot see well, although it is very early. The shade is great, the shade of the tree. The springboks' dust closed my eyes. I am wounded because the dust shut my eyes. We did not see each other.'

The other man said, 'Three of our men must come to carry you; they will lift you and take you to the house. They will put you in the house. Another man will also go to carry you. I shall also carry you. We did not kill any springbok. We ran to see because we wanted to see if you were wounded. You sat down. Our brother sat near you; you did not look out for the arrow. We know we are right. [*17 April*] Our brother was near you; you did not watch out for the arrow. We know we were right. We came running so that we could see. We ran along, talking. We were right in what we said to each other.

'We said, "That man sitting far over there looks as if he is wounded. Over there another man is running to him, as he sits. The man helping him sits down. Yonder, he looks at the other man. He holds and turns the other man over so that he can look at the wound. They are both sitting. They beckon to us to go and see. You must see them, that we may go to see."'

The other man said to him, 'Come, we shall go to see. For it seems that the wound is great indeed. Our brother beckons that we may go to see.'

The other man said to him, 'We agree.' The man is right, he agrees with him. The man agrees with him, 'We must run; we must run there together so that we may go quickly to look; [*18 April*] for the man far over there beckons. He knows there is much blood. He beckons.'

The other man says to him, 'Our brother beckons. We must run together so that we may go quickly to see; the place demands haste. Our brother beckons to us urgently, that we should run very quickly. We must run very quickly; because our brother seems to be shot through. The man over there beckons to us very urgently, so that together we can go quickly to see. We must be correct when we talk to the people back at the camp, when the women question us. We ran so that we could see how badly wounded our brother was. We think the wound is ugly. Our brother seems to be calling. The women will not speak nicely; they will ask why we were not near our brother, so that we could look at him as he was writhing about because of his painful wound. The wound seems to be large, for the arrowpoint is still on the shaft. So the wound is deep.'

The other man says to him, 'The wound is like that. We must run very fast, so that we may go quickly to see. We shall speak nicely to the women, as we speak making their hearts stand still.'

[*19 April*] They run strongly; they run fast. They run to the other people. They look at the wounded man. The other man holds and sits next to the wounded man who sits, writhing. He sits moaning, the other man holding him tightly. They are sitting.

One of those who have just arrived puts down his bow and holds the wounded man. He holds the wounded man tightly. He says to the other man, 'The wound is serious.'

The other man says to him, 'Yes, the wound which is here is serious.'

Then the wounded man shows him and says, 'The wound goes in here; that is where the wound is. That is where the arrow point stood, where I drew it out. That is where the pain is. It hurts in here. The wound's mouth hurts; the wound's mouth hurts. The pain will almost kill me, as I go to the house, as you carry me away to the house. It seems as if the blood will not staunch; it is still flowing.'

The other man said to him, 'The blood is still flowing; you must bind up the wound so that we can carry our brother. If the wind blows into the wound, the wound will become cold. The wound will swell.'

The wounded man said, 'The wound is aching. We do not know when I shall reach the house. Then I shall smell the smoke of the fire. I feel it myself.'

The wounded man tells the others that they must speak gently, not angrily, to the man who shot him: 'You must not scold your friend; you must remember that it was the arrow's fault.[1] So we must not speak angrily to our friend; the arrow hit me of its own accord.[2] Our brother did not see me. If I had seen our brother, I would say that I had seen him and that he also saw me. I would have told you that our brother shot me himself. Our brother speaks the truth: he did not shoot me. We say truly, we did not see each other. [*20 April*] The arrow flew over the dust. I did not see him either; if I had looked, I might have seen him coming, while he was still approaching. Then, stooping, I should have gone round and sat down. For we approached each other in a direct line. The springbok ran through between us. The dust was dense because there were many springbok. We not see that we were shooting at each other because we were shooting in the dust. The springbok were in the dust; the dust was dense. The dust which blows[3] rises up and blows over the springbok. The springbok ran into the middle of the dust; the dust of the springboks' feet was dense.[4] The springbok ran under the dust, because they were many. Sitting, we shot at the springbok. Therefore I was wounded, as I sat. I sat drawing the bow.[5] I was completely still while I waited, because I did not shoot.'

Then people carry him. They carry him away to the house. They set him down in the house. His wife cries. The other women cry.

They ask the men, 'You others, your friend seems to have been fighting; you have shot your friend.'

The men say to the women, 'We did not do it on purpose, for it was a false-shooting. A false shot's arrow it was. You did not tell the children to play away from the house.[6] That is why this man accidentally shot the other man. My wife is stupid. [*22 April*] She does not listen to what I say to her; she still behaves stupidly towards me. She does not behave as if her father and mother had told her. She is still stupid.'

The other man said of his wife, 'My wife is doing foolish things. But I want her to see that it was a false shot's wound. That is how it happened. It is ugly. The wound makes people afraid. She cries because of her fear. I might also have been wounded, because she did not say to my boys, "Go out of the house." For dust covers my bed when I return. My house is as if she had gone away; the house is not nice.'

An old woman says, 'A false shot's wound is just like this. They are not good [4 April] because the children played in the house. Therefore the boys must play away from the house. My son has been wounded by a false-shooting arrow, because his children do not understand. My son's wife does not understand what I said to her; she ought to drive her children away from the house, from the bed from which my son went hunting.[7] He hunts the springbok; he wants to run well. He falls down and pierces himself with his arrows.[8] A wound caused by falling down is like this, because the man falls down and pierces himself with his arrows. Arrow wounds that are caused by falling down are like this. They are like the man who shoots another man. They resemble wounds caused by shooting. They are deep[9] because the arrow itself pierces a man. The knife which a man carries injures a man when he falls down. The man is also pierced by Driedoorn wood, when he has tied on this arrow. The wound of the Driedoorn wood. A stab wound is like this. It is like this. The wounds resemble the shooting's wound's mouth: they are not good. That is why the boys go away from the house[10] [April 25] so that the bed will not be covered with dust. Another man left the house; he ran and broke his ankle, because he runs strongly. He is carried from the hunting ground because his ankle is broken. He does not shoot. The women will be hungry. His children will hunger because he is writhing in the house.[11] He cannot walk; the women will have to eat old, bitter food which is nasty. The man lay writhing near sweet meat but could not shoot. They saw it with their eyes. The people could not kill a springbok because they were looking after the wounds. They really came close to the springbok, [26 April] but they did not carry any springbok home. They were carrying a man which the children cannot eat. Soon the people will leave him when he dies of the arrow's wound's mouth; an arrow wound is something of which a man dies, for the wound kills a man.'

The wounded man says to the old woman, 'I know that I shall die, for the wound is large and the pain of the wound is great. The pain of the wound is killing me: I shall die of it. I do not feel that I shall sleep

well. I want my wife to fetch much firewood and to make a fire for
me. I shall sit writhing by the fire, for I shall not sleep tonight. She
herself sees the blood flowing because the wound is deep in my flesh.
So the blood itself flows. I know I shall not sleep tonight. I do not
know about another night, whether I shall still be here, because I
think I shall not see another day break. I keep asking myself, whether
I shall see another day break. I think I shall die in the night. The
people will cry here at night because my heart will have fallen.[12] Early
tomorrow the people will cry here. My heart does not feel as if I
could smell the scent of dried springbok meat which smells; my heart
feels as if I should die of the scent of meat. That is what I think, for
my name is great. I am not a child that I should be stupid, when my
pain is like this, my body's pain. I will tell you. You will know when
the sun sets, you will know in the night. [*27 April*] I who am grown
up, I speak and let you know it. You will know it. The day will not
break quickly, for I feel all my flesh. I burn with pain, because the
wound swells, it swells greatly. Therefore I am bloated. The swelling
throbs. That is why my heart is falling.'

The wounded man's wife says to him, 'I myself, I see the swelling
with my eye. You are right.'

The man says to her, 'I am speaking to you so that you will do
well to the boys and to the girls who must fetch water for you. The
boys must seek vulture scent, for, when people shoot springbok, the
vultures follow. Therefore the boys must seek them for you. They
must also look for tortoises for you; they must bring you tortoises.
They must act sensibly, for they understand shooting; they are grown
up. They must act sensibly, because I die, leaving them. I who was
bringing them meat die; I shall not return to live again, for I die and
go.[13] I am wounded by the arrow. The wound's mouth does not heal.
A man really dies of it. The springbok really die of it. You must make
the fire well so that it will not go out because of the children,[14] so that
the cold will not kill the children, the little ones; so that the cold will
not kill you, a grown up. For I know, when I die, I shall think of
you.[15] Your brothers must look after you; you must eat good things.
They must give you fat, so that you can rub your body. It must be
handsome. This night I die. I speak to you. I shall not speak again, for
now is speaking time.[16] You must listen to see if I speak again. You
must watch by me. You must make a fire; you must sit, you must

look. You must watch me. You must speak to the people who sleep. They must wake up; they too must watch me.

'I tell you this so that you will fetch wood, that you will fetch much wood. You must make a fire, for the hour of death has come. [*29 April*] I shall not see you again; for the time to talk is over. I am still, I shall not speak in the darkness. That is why I speak now to let you know; so that you may know. I speak, holding up your heart, so that you will really know what I have said. I am speaking to you about the children, so that you will not forget. You must not leave any of the children; you must keep all the children.[17] You yourself must look after the children; you must act well to them. You must not give the children to strangers; you must keep all the children by your body. You yourself must watch the children with your eye. Your father is the one to whom you must take the children; then you will eat good things. Your brother will be there with the children. For I am dying, leaving you; I shall never again come back alive, I who gave you food. Your father is the one with whom you must eat good food. The children will be handsome. You must lift me up so that you can lay me down at the place where I shall lie. Then you will remember what I told you long ago. You must take care of me, because I am not lying in the house; I am lying outside.'

His wife says to him: 'Your nephew (or cousin) shall make a bed and lay you in that place.'

He says to his wife, 'You must make a bed and lay me in the old kaross which the blood covered. That is what I must lie on.'

Then the other man makes a bed of the old kaross.

His wife says to the other man, 'You must call your friends so that you can help each other to lift the sick man so that you can lay him down on the old kaross; he wants to lie there.[18] He has just spoken to me. I shall not listen to him again; for he told me that his death-time draws near; [*1 May*] for his night is here. We ourselves can see the wound, it is a great wound; it is deep.'

Another woman says to the sick man's wife, 'We do so. We all see the wound is deep.'

Another woman says, 'It is a large wound.'

Another man says, 'It is not a little wound; it is deep because it was a strong man who shot him. His bow was strong. His arrow was strong; his arrow-point was large. He shot the other man. You yourselves can see that there is much blood. You also see the swelling; he swelled up and his flesh was all puffed up. We have come to listen in the night.'

The sick man's wife says to them, 'You have come to listen. You must wrap the sick man in the old kaross because when day breaks you will look for a place where the earth is soft so that you can bury the man in the earth; you will work well to bury the man, so that the hyena will not be able to scratch him out. My heart thinks my husband is not a little handsome; he who is white,[19] who dies while still a young man; of whom my heart thinks not a little. My heart is not a little afraid. You must close the man in with large stones so that the hyena will not be able to roll the stones and drag him out; for my heart stands over the man. He is eyebrowed; his face is handsome; it is white. He dies before he has grown a beard, for he is still a young man; he dies from me while his children are still small. He ran well, hunting springbok. Therefore my heart trembles; for my heart is still startled. He told me that his death was near. My heart was startled. I did not marry, making my heart stand on account of him; for I still love him. We married while we were young. So I cry much because of him. He has not yet grown a beard. He has left me. I do not want to eat on account of thinking of him. I want to cry myself to death, as I starve myself.'

Her mother-in-law says to her, 'You must eat, so that you will not hunger, so that your flesh will be still handsome. The children who are small must not hunger, the little girls whose grandmother I am. I not a little [*untranslated word*] them. Your crying cannot bring back your husband, for he has indeed died, leaving us. We will not eat good things, for we shall have to eat old things which are not good. [*2 May*] You must take children away to your father; you must go with the children to your father.'

Her son's wife agrees with her. 'I fear for the man who is here. He seems to lie still. He will not return, for he lies still. He must go into a grave. When the people lift him up, they must go and carry him and put him in, so that they can cover him up and put earth on him. Then I shall go; for I shall have seen them put him in, and he will be lying still in the grave into which the people have put him. After that I shall go. I must go with the children.'

Her mother-in-law agrees with her. 'You must do so. You must truly go and look at your husband, so that you can see him. Then you will cry. You will sit by the grave; you will really sit crying. You will think with your thoughts. You will cry with your thoughts, so that you will not cry with your arms. You must hold the stick strongly. You must dig out food for the children, the earth's food; they too will dig out "Bushman rice";[20] so that the "Gambro" may not kill the children.[21] The children must eat meat; they must eat only a little "Gambro." You must not travel far from the water. You must not leave the waters on your journey; you must stay quietly at the water, so that the sun will not make the children die of thirst. The children must rest and drink water so that they will not become thin[22] from the heat. Their flesh must rest and be handsome so that they will grow up and stay handsome.'

[*3 May*] Her son's wife says to her, 'That is right; I shall go to my father, my father who lives by the water, so that I shall be able to drink, so that the children will be able to drink. I shall cry by the water, while I stay with my father, who lives by the water, for it is our water. It is our place; it is the water by which we grew up, and we drank it. It was there that my husband married me, making me his wife. I then came to his place because he had married me. I made my place here. This is his place, for it was his father's place. That is why it was his place when he married me. I had to make it my place; I lived here. Now he is dead. He dies, leaving me. That is why I shall return to our place, so that I can go and live with my father at our place, so that my children will grow up round my father. They must live with my brother, so that he can bring the children up for me, for they are many. They shoot well, they kill. Living with them is good. They are good. They are not angry. They are my children; they love them. I take my children to them; they live with our father. They do not travel away from our father, leaving him, because he does not shoot; he is an old man. He is very old; his head is white. He has no teeth; his head is white. The woman also is an old woman. When I married this man, he should have lived with them, for they are all old.[23] He who lies dead, he lies still, for he cannot speak. He has indeed left me; he cannot talk, he whom I married. He used to shoot food for my people. Now the people must lift him up; the people must go and put him into the grave. [*4 May*] Therefore I shall indeed stay with the people. I must see them put him in. Then I shall carry things; the children shall fetch me water; I must carry water. The child who is small must drink while we journey, for I shall sleep half-way. I shall go early tomorrow. I shall go to the house. I must go to speak to my father, so that he will know. If I must marry again, [*untranslated line*]. I shall cry there because the man who married me will not be with me because he has died, leaving me. He no longer moves. The day breaks, but he lies still. That is why I weep at daybreak. I must carry the child, so that I can accompany the people who lift him up, the people who must take him away to the grave. I must go early.'

She says to the children, 'Oh children! You must all fetch egg-shells of water. You must carry water because I shall be carrying the baby. We shall sleep halfway.[24] We shall go early tomorrow and look for them.[25] For they travel to another place; but he, my old father, cannot travel. You will have to seek his food by the water;[26] for he does not leave the water now.'

The widow goes,[27] and the children with her. She weeps as she goes. Weeping, her mother-in-law sits in the house; she is with her sons, they and her husband (the father-in-law of the widow). Crying, they sit in the house, for they cry about their son.

Their son's wife goes to sleep midway. She goes early the next day. She must go to the water. She must find the water. She sees her younger brother's footprints by the water. She sees her mother's foot-print by the water. She sees her brother's wives spoor by the water.[28]

She says to the children, 'Your grandparents' and the wives' foot-prints are here.' She sees her brother's footprint by the water; she shows the children her brother's spoor. 'Grandfather's people's foot-prints are here; they have been carrying dead springbok to the water so that the people can drink on their way back with the game. The house is near. We shall follow the people's footprints because the footprints are new. We must look for the house. We must follow the people's footprints. For the people's footprints were made today; the people fetched water shortly before we came, for the water is fresh on the ground.'

She drinks; the children also drink. She carries the things. She goes. She walks following the people's path. The children walk after her. They walk away from the little Brinkkop. They see the house. They go to the house.

Her younger sisters see them. They say to their mother, 'Your daughter is coming here; she is bringing the children. She is alone; her husband is not with her. All the children are with her; she is alone. She is the only grown-up, she who is bringing her children. She is coming alone.'

Her brother's wife stands up and looks. She says to her husband, 'Your little sister is coming alone.'

Her husband says to her, 'The man seems to have left her because they fought each other;[29] they seem to have fought.'

My wife[30] says to him, 'Do not say that. When my little sister reaches the house, we shall go to see why she is bringing all the children. The little girls are with their brothers. The brothers are carrying their mother's things. [*7 May*] They are all coming. They are walking near to the house. You yourself look; for you contradicted me. You did not wait. You sounded as if we should hear. We knew that was the way you went on. We do not know what has happened. My younger sister seems to be crying. For she does not look at the house. She is looking at the ground.'

Her husband stands up and looks.

His wife says to him, 'Does it not seem as if my brother-in-law is dead, for the woman comes weeping? Tears are in her eyes. She is crying afar, while I am talking.'

Her mother asks her, 'What is the matter that your husband is not with you, as if he had left you?'

Her son's wife says, 'I think your son should see; he would not believe me when I spoke the truth.'

Her husband says, 'What is that? Now I believe you were telling the truth. You saw well.'

His mother asks her daughter, 'What is the matter? Why are you alone, as if your husband had left you?'

Her son asks his younger sister, 'Was it illness?'

His younger sister, the widow, says to her mother, 'Your daughter's husband was not ill. He was shooting springbok; then he was wounded. He was wounded because of the springbok, while they were shooting springbok. [*8 May*] Another man was shooting together with him, while he was on the other side of the springbok. He was wounded as he was drawing his bow at the springbok. So he lowered the arrow and the bow. He did not shoot the arrow from his hands. He held the arrow, and he sat still. He laid down the bow; he sat. He drew out the arrow from his flesh; he put it down. He sat in pain. He spoke to me when he saw me. He spoke to his mother. I listened.'

The dead man's wife spoke to her brother. Her brother said to her, 'Your husband did not wait to shoot until the springbok had passed him. He should have shot springbok when they were in a different place, when the springbok had run on.'

His younger sister said to him, 'The people speak truly; they not did see each other coming. So they shot at the springbok, because they did not see each other; all of them did not see each other.'

His younger sister said to him, 'If my husband had seen the other man, I think he would have avoided the arrow when he saw it coming. Therefore he would have avoided the arrow when he saw it. He would avoid the arrow.'

Her brother said to her, 'The men there, they do not shoot well.'

The other man said to her, 'Our relations shoot each other together with the springbok. Therefore he shot the other man, for they do not shoot well; they shoot amiss. [*10 May*] The other people shoot badly. They are not like us; they could not see well behind the springbok, so that they could see their companion, so that they could see the other man coming. They should not shoot their companions together with the springbok. He killed her husband, the husband who was good to us. I do not think that her husband should have gone to his brothers, for his brothers always shoot badly. He would not stay quietly with us, even though we would have taken care of him, so that he would have been safe. He would still be with you, you who does not now have a husband. Your flesh will grow ugly. You will be ugly, because you will not eat good meat. You will become dusty because you will not rub your flesh, so that your flesh might have fat on it, so that you might rub the children, so that the children will be handsome, so that you all should be red, that you might rub your faces. For father cannot see. Mother also cannot see.'

His younger sister says to him: 'I should have liked to have stayed here, and not have travelled away.[31] My husband moved away because he thought of his brothers. He told me that he wanted to journey to his brothers so that he could live with them; and they would hunt springbok together. Therefore I had to go with him. I went too because I always travel with him. For I know I should not remain behind, although I did not agree when he thought that he had remained long enough with my father.

[*11 May*] 'I have now come to eat those old things; for now we will always eat them, the ugly things, because my husband is dead, with whom we all had good things. Because my husband is dead we shall always eat old things, which are bad. We do not complain, because we know that it was our husband with whom we ate good things, because he brought them to us. That is what I feel and think. Therefore I agree that I cannot eat the same sort of things which I used to eat, food which was good. My children eat them; my children grow ugly. For their father used to bring them good things. They ate fat when their father was alive. Their father is now no longer alive; for he has died, leaving us. We have come here. We could no longer see their father. Their father's brothers have taken his arrows and his bow, because they know that he has really died, leaving his things. He does not see them; he cannot take them, because he is dead and gone. The arrow which killed him was not a little thing, but a big thing. When a man shoots a gemsbok, the gemsbok dies of it. A man can shoot an eland with an arrow; the eland dies, even though it be a bull eland. When his younger brother wounded my husband, I knew that he would not live, to come again. Now he is quite dead; he is in the ground. I cannot see him. That is why I have come to our mother, for we always do so when our husband is dead. We always go to our mother. A woman is accustomed, when her husband dies, to go to her mother because her husband told her to do that.'

Her brother agreed. 'Your husband said rightly, that you should come, that you should come to our mother, for our mother's place is here, and it is our place, where we grew up, where our father used to shoot well and bring us springbok. [*14 May*] I grew up here. We took our wives, and now we live with them here. We married and stayed here, because we knew that it was our father's place; it was our father's father's place; it was our grandfather's place; it was our grandmother's place. When his old people had left it, our father properly took possession of it. Our father in his turn is growing old here. We stay here, we walk, but we come back to it for our father is dying of old age. [*15 May*] He cannot walk on account of age. He cannot travel far from his place.'

The widow replied, 'I thought that he might have travelled away; but he is at his place. I can see him now. I thought that I should have to search for him. I thought so, because I thought that I had stayed long with my brothers-in-law and my mother-in-law. My little boys grew big, while I was with my mother-in-law. That is why I thought that he may have travelled away from this place; but he is now growing old, staying at the waterhole, because he feels his knees. Therefore he cannot travel, because the place is too big for him to travel away from it. He sits waiting for the rain, as he sits in the house, so that the springbok will themselves travel to him; that the children will shoot springbok for him; that he may sit eating the springbok at his own place. That is what I was thinking as I came along, that I would first come to look at the water. I quickly sat down, thinking that you would soon miss the man who used to be with me. You would think that he was still with me, but I am alone. Only the children are with me. The children do not play far off; they play at the house, because I mourn their father. Their father who was with me is dead and has gone away from me.

'My house stands cold. The inside of the house is cold to me; the house cannot be warm; for the house is cool. The mats are not nice; [*17 May*] the wind blows inside the house because the house stands open. The wind blows, coming into the house. I have no man to fetch me wood; so my fire has gone out; for it was he who carried wood for me; he made fire for me. Getting up, he made the fire burn for me, while I was still lying down. Then I got up and I warmed myself at the fire, when the fire was burning well. The children got up and warmed themselves, when the fire was burning nicely.

'He has now received an accidental wound, because his brothers shoot badly. They do not shoot nicely. They are not like you who shoot nicely. You do not shoot your companions instead of the springbok, for you know about your companions, that another man sits behind the springbok's back. The dust is great; the springbok are many. Nevertheless, you look well, you watch between the springboks' bodies. Therefore you shoot well; you remember that you are many. You are all good. The others are people who kill their companion, and then they cry because of their companion. They seemed to be terrified by their companion's blood, when they saw it, as the blood flowed. They were screaming as the blood was flowing away. We who are women, we were screaming at home; for we were terrified when we saw younger sister's husband being carried, as he was carried back

65

from the hunting-ground. Therefore our hearts were startled, all our hearts. We screamed. We stood screaming, as we saw my husband's blood, saw that he was black with blood. The blood which still flowed, that blood was red; it was wet; it still ran out of the wound. The blood which was dry, was black. Blood which is wet, is red. Therefore we fear it, when it is still red. It runs out of a wound's mouth. It flows out. Your younger brother, my husband, died because the blood kept pouring out of the wound's mouth.

'Therefore, I came to tell you so that you would know about your companions. When you are running together round springbok, you must watch your companions carefully. You should run quickly, turning away from the other man, so that you can run to another place, so that you can shoot in a different direction. [*18 May*] That is indeed what you do. You do not shoot like the men there; those are the ones who killed my husband, my heart's husband.

'I loved him greatly, for he loved me. That is why I weep greatly because of him, he who loved me. He did not beat me. My children grew up, and he never once beat me. He died from me, while he was sweet to me, while he never yet struck me. My children grew up. That is why I cry greatly when I think that a very different sort of man will marry me, an angry man. He will not be good to me; the man who was here, he was good to me. A different man will beat my children because my children are not his; they are my husband's children. They are not *his* own children. [*Confused translation*] He will be angry. Therefore I shall not marry, because I think that my heart does not desire that I should marry a man who will be different, who will be angry. I shall have to marry an ugly man, a man who is not nice. [*20 May*] I shall not eat good things with him. I shall have to marry a greedy person who loves fat. I shall not eat fat with him, so that I can grow nicely fat and fatten my body; so that my children may eat fat and not have to crunch bones. A different sort of man will not give food to my children. He will eat the things himself. Because he is a greedy person, we shall eat bad things, things that are not good. He is a bad man. He eats far away; he eats up things on the hunting-ground. He brings ugly pieces of meat to the house. We eat them, things that are hard, things that are not tender; our teeth ache.[32] These pieces of meat are not good. [*21 May*] Our children are ugly because they have to eat bones. Therefore they starve.[33] That's why I brought

my children to you, you who are my relatives. You are my brothers.
You will give my children good things. My heart will be happy.
Therefore you know the children's share. You know that my children
eat, that they eat strongly. They are children who eat, who do not eat
gently. You see them. They know you. You also know about their
food, that they eat. They eat strongly. You know about their food, you
who gives them good things, because you know that they are your
nephews. They understand you. I brought them so that they can live
with you, so that they can drive the springbok towards you. You will
lie to leeward so that the springbok will walk to leeward, [*1 June*] and
you will kill them and bring food for the children, the springbok
breasts. They will eat the springbok hearts, so that they will quickly
grow up for me, so that they will seek food for me. For I no longer
have their father. Their father is not with us. We are alone. We do not
have the man who lived with us. He used to bring us food. We ate it.
That is why we are handsome. We would have been ugly, but were not
like that. We were handsome. We did not eat bad things. We were
handsome. Now he has gone from us. We do not see him, for he has
altogether vanished. We no longer saw him; we were looking at other
people who not did share the food well with us. We would become
ugly; we would not look as we used to look when we were eating
good things.

[*22 August*] 'My husband did not break open and finish the
springboks' bones far out there on the hunting-ground. He brought
them to the house. His children anointed their faces. They also
anointed their bodies. Their bodies were fair. They went to the water.
They washed themselves with water. Their bodies were white.

'I think I see their father in them, for their faces look like their
father. Their eyebrows resemble their father. Their eyes resemble their
father. That is why it seemed as if their father was there, when I sat
looking at the little boys, as they came home. I sat looking as they
came back, as they returned to me. It was as if I saw their father, as
they came. For their bodies look like their father. They are not black.
They also look like you; they are your nephews. You must give them
arrows. You must make them small arrowheads so that they can shoot
while they are still young; for they were young when they first shot
out blood. Their father died, while he was eating their prey.'

Her brother agreed: 'I was the one who thought that you would bring the little boys to your brothers so that they can feed themselves by hunting, so that they can grow up quickly. You must take good care of them. They must kill to feed you. They are grown up. The eldest son is a young man. His younger brother is a boy who is still growing. He must be with his brother whom I take, for he is a boy. The elder of the two boys shoots much game. They must go together. They must run together to the springbok. They must bring me the springbok from afar so that I can be near the springbok when I shoot, as the springbok run near to one. For I have not been able to shoot from nearby.[34] They will do well, because you have brought them all.

'You will live with me. I did not leave our mother. I stay with her. My older brothers travelled away to their fathers-in-law. I remained with our mother, because I think that my wife is not wild. It is her people who talk much, but my wife is quiet here. She does not talk. Her people are those who talk here. She is silent. I am one who talks. She eats strongly; but she also eats gently. She leaves the food while she is still hungry. She is still hungry; she puts away the food. She works here because she wants to work nicely with my things, so that my things may be nice. [*3 September*] When I come home from hunting, I come to see that my things are nice; she shows them to me. I agree with her. I tell her to rub[35] the thing I shall come to look at. She agrees; she will do that. I shall go to look for her food. She goes to wet the thing's skin while I search. She will rub it early tomorrow. I think that you will rub together with her; you will rub for my nephew who is here, to make him a kaross. You must make his karosses; you will sew a kaross for him, so that he can lie wrapped in it, because he is now wearing an old kaross. His mother makes my kaross. He seems to be cold when he drives the springbok in the wind, when the wind is cold.'

His younger sister agrees, 'I will do so.'

Her brother says to her, 'You can see that my springbok bags are dry. Your brother's wife rubs springbok skins so that she can make me a new kaross, because I am cold when I drive the game very early in the morning, when I think that my small nephews are hungry, so that they may eat soon. For they ask their mother for food; their hunger aches. My hands are cold because I did not cover them up in the kaross. I was wearing a small kaross; it is a little kaross. My thighs were cold, they and my hands. I shoot springbok when my hands are cold because I think that my children must eat, so that they can eat, so that they will be silent, for they were crying here in the evening. So that their mother will be quietly rubbing. Crying, they left the bad food, because they thought that the old food was nasty; it was not sweet.

'Their mother will rub the kaross nicely for me; she will sew the kaross for me so that I can wrap up my legs which were cold. We do not shoot our friends when we drive the game. You are the one whose husband gave you portions of fat. You do not look as you used to look. You were handsome; you were not still. You were handsome. That is why I think that you will make things for my nephew, who is now with me; you will make them nicely.

'Driving the game, he will go through the cold. He will come and give you a springbok head so that you can roast it. You will roast it for the children. The children will eat it, so that they will not readily think of their father, so that they will forget their father, so that they will not think of him. [*4 September*] They will eat good things that are like the things they used to eat when their father was alive. Therefore they will not think of their father quickly. Their thought will forget their father; they will eat good things which their cousin will give them. They will eat them at the hunting-ground; their cousin will give them their shares. Their cousin does so nicely. Their cousin is like me, I who used to give portions of good things to their mother. I told him that we gave our mother good things so that she could eat them; we bring our wife good things so that she can eat them because we remember that it is she who rubs clothing for us so that our karosses will be good.

'She also rubs arrow bags for us so that we can put the hunt's arrows in them. We shoot springbok, while the quiver lies at the house; our wife puts it down there. We put arrows in the quiver so that the water will not wet the feathers, so that the arrow's feathers will stay dry. That is why the arrows fly nicely when we shoot an arrow. The arrow will stand well in the springbok, in the springbok's ribs. The springbok run out, coming in front. Therefore the springbok falls down.

'We eat quickly, while it is still early. We eat early, so that we may return carrying meat, while the sun is still cool. Afterwards, in the evening, we shall run round the springbok so that we can shoot the evening's springbok when the long shadows are out. We shall come in the dark carrying meat. We shall put the springbok down. We shall first sleep; we shall eat other meat. In the early morning we shall cut up the evening springbok. Afterwards we shall hunt, when the sun is a little warm, but first we cut up meat. The women cut the meat into slices. They will hang the meat up to dry after it has been cut into slices.

'We shall eat dried meat, for it is nice; dried-meat soup is nice. We shall eat fat which has been dried. Dry fat is nice because of its nice-ness to bite, as we bite it and break it. We shall swallow it together with dried meat; therefore the dried meat goes down our throat easi-ly. We shall swallow quickly, putting in dried meat, which we eat together with dried fat. Wet fat is that into which we dip; that is new fat; the springbok is freshly dead. [*5 September*] A new springbok's fat is still white. The sun has not yet dried it; the people have not yet hung it up so that it can dry on the bushes on which the women have hung it.

'The ostrich is what the people slice and put into the pot. Its flesh has blood in it when it has just been brought home; then the people eat its fat which has been put in the soup. The people dip, wetting the meat in the liquid fat which they have skimmed off from the soup. They skimmed off the liquid fat with a spoon.[36] They skim off and place the fat into an ostrich's breastbone so that they can wet the meat in it, so that they can eat the meat when liquid fat is in it. They wet it in liquid fat. They cut up and eat ostrich skin while the fat is still on it. They cut together so that they can eat the fat together with the skin. The ostrich thigh's meat is sliced; the women slice it. They hang it up in the shade so that the sun will not burn up the meat, because the sun is warm. They must cook the meat in an earthen pot while it is cool.

'The waterholes at which we live are large; the children used to go backwards and forwards to the pits with food. We do not move away. For we know that old water pits have old water. Therefore they taste a little bitter; for they are not new water. This is our father's water where he grew up, while he lived by it. When he married, he brought our mother to this water. That is why we grew up living by it; it is our father's water. Our father knows that it was our father's father's water. Our grandfather lived at it. When he died, he left our father his water.

Our father grew up living at the water. Our father owned it; he walked about at it.

'He must hunt. He hunts round behind the Kleine Brinkkop. He steals up to the springbok. He must [*untranslated word*] the springbok. He lies behind Brinkkop when he shoots. He carries meat to the house, to the water that is near it. I live with our father because I know that I must take the water. For our father has long grown old; when he dies, he will leave me the water. I am the one who must take it when he dies of old age, and also our mother. We are the ones who shall walk about on our father's ground. Our father was the one who, walking about, owned it. He knew that our grandfather walked about this ground; our grandfather knew that it was our grandfather-father's place; our grandfather walked about it. Our grandfather knew that our grandfather's father also walked about this ground. Therefore our grandfather's father left it to our grandfather when he died. When he married, our grandfather brought our grandmother to it. It was our grandmother's water. She lived at our grandfather's father's old houses. Therefore, our grandfather left our father his old houses when he died so that our father could live at them.

'Our father also took our grandfather's honey's hole. He cut out the honey. He brought the honey home. He closed the honey with a large stone, while the honey was inside the honey's hole. He shut in the honey, so that the honey badger would not eat the honey, so that the honey would become fat, so that he could cut the honey and put it into the bag and carry the honey-bag on his back. [*6 September*] He will put the bag on his back and carry it to his house. He will go into the shade and put the honey-bag in the shade of his house. They will eat the honey liquid's fat. That is why I think you should rub a honey-bag for me, so that I can keep it. For the honey is still lean; I will fold the honey bag and put it in an old bag when I hunt honey in the morning; the sun will be still cool, and the honey bees will be sleeping. I shall go to smoke out the bees.'

His younger sister agrees. 'I think your nephews must make me a house here in this place; they will pull up (an unidentified kind of bush).[37] They will make a good house for me so that I can be sheltered. Their father used to make a house for me. I was sheltered. For his older little brother[38] is strong. The older child is strong. His little brother, who is younger, will work with him at the house. They will make a place for us where we can shelter so that we will not be burned by the sun.'

Her brother agrees with her. 'Your son will do so; for we will not travel from this house; we will live at it. The old man sits over there; he does not travel. The honey is in the hole. Your son will look for honey for you while you sit here sheltered in the shade. I shall sit waiting in the shade here for the springbok, so that the springbok will pass by me, so that I can steal up to them. I must wait for my brother, so that they will travel to me. For I must remain with our father; he does not travel. I take care of him. He does not travel because of his knees. His daughters must fetch water for him to drink. [*7 September*] He will sit drinking. He will not travel in the sun when the sun is hot. The sun must not kill him, if he wants to journey to different water-holes. The sun will not kill him if he lies down halfway, when he goes through the noonday. He must rather remain at his own water; he must sit quietly, sheltered here in the shade which feels cool, his shade.

'The springbok will return to me; [39] I must drive away the vultures so that he may eat the skin.[40] When rain falls, the springbok will return; the springbok come, smelling the scent of the rain. I shall also steal up to the game when the springbok drink water; I stalk springbok at the water. I must shoot a springbok for him as it is drinking when the sun is hot, the male springbok which is fat. The male springbok drinks. Therefore I think your eldest son should be with his cousin. Watching, they will steal up to a springbok at the water. Watching, they will steal up to a springbok at the water for us, so that we shall be able to eat by the water. It is an old waterhole near which our father sits hungry. Hunger is not soft, for hunger is hard; we do not hunger gently. [*9 September*] This hunger is strong, for there are large waterholes. My brothers moved away from me, but I remain hungry at the water.

'The springbok itself will come to me. Hunting, I go to the spring-bok, while the springbok stay in the rain's bushes.[41] I must sleep in among the springbok. In the darkness I must go in among the spring-bok. I must lie among the springbok in the night. I must steal upon them when the day breaks a little. I must watch the springbok which walk around, those male springbok, which chase their fellows, so that they can grunt at their fellows. I must shoot quickly, while the sun is still in. The springbok will soon fall down dead. Afterwards my younger sisters must drive back the springbok so that I can steal up to the springbok that have been turned back, while the early morning's springbok are still lying down. I come to shoot at the springbok that have been driven back; another springbok also falls. Two springbok lie dead. It is our springbok for which I went out of the little house. I went to follow it.

'My younger sisters come to me while I am breaking its thighs. Afterwards I go to carry the other springbok. My younger sisters take the other springbok. They bring it to our father, our father who does not walk, while I carry the other springbok. I bring it to my wife so that my wife will not have to ask for our father's springbok.

'That is why I think that you should be with me. You will drive the springbok towards me when my younger sisters are at the house. They refuse; they do not want to be with me. I go alone. Your nephew, who is a young man, will drive the springbok for me; he will not stalk the game so that he can also kill a springbok. I am the one who drives the game here, when I am alone. The springbok walk away from me, while I lie at a different place, and the springbok go to another place. That is why I cannot shoot quickly when I go out from the little house. I have to drive the game. It is hot while I am still driving game here. I return hungry. Hungry, I come to lie down, because my younger sisters refused; their legs are swollen. That is why they refuse me. They did hunt with me, but they came home in pain, bringing their legs to the house. That is why they now refuse.'

His younger sister, the widow, says to him, 'I think that your nephew (her own son), who is a boy, should drive the game for you if his aunts refuse, because he is grown up. His brother, who is a young man, must drive the game with his cousin over there. He drove game alone for his father. His father was killed, bringing springbok to the house. [*10 September*] He will lie down with you. You will all stealthily approach the springbok. They will be with you. They will shoot and drive the game towards you. Startled, the springbok will run towards you. You too will shoot, when the springbok run, completely startled. You must stand up. You must look for the arrows. The springbok will soon lie dead; all of you will have shot them.

'These springbok, the ones which were killed first are the ones which you cut up first. You must first roast[42] the springbok breasts.

You must eat. You must carry the meat; you must put the springbok in a hole. You must go to the water; you must go to drink at !Hun's water.[43] You drink plentifully, making the heart cool.

'Then you drive the game again, the other springbok which are standing in the sun. You steal up to them, while they are standing with their faces to the sun. Your nephew must drive them. He must drive them up the hill,[44] while you lie. You shoot them again. Therefore you three will throw down the springbok. You carry the meat away to the hill. You go to cut up the meat on the hill. Again you sit and eat, cooking. You all carry meat.

'You go to fetch the other springbok, which was put into the hole. Rolling away the stones, you take it out. You take it out of the hole, the porcupine's house.[45] You know that the vultures will eat the springbok from a tree,[46] if you put a springbok there. That is why you put the springbok in the porcupine's house. You come carrying this springbok and put it with the other springbok.

'You think that you will work at the house with the arrows; you will work with the arrowheads, sharpening them. You beat the arrowheads. Having sharpened them, you will set them onto the [*untranslated word*] you bend [*untranslated word*]. Afterwards you will hunt, when the women are with you. [*13 September*] They first cut up the springbok which are here. Then they will drive the springbok towards you so that you will be able to steal up to them, while the other child remains with you; for he shoots only a little; he is a young boy. He kills the springbok. He carries the springbok. His father rejoices as he comes carrying meat.[47] His father knows that he will eat that day. He will eat immediately.

'I who am a woman, I dance for joy because he kills a springbok. We did not know that he understood how to shoot a springbok when he was alone, when his brother was not with him. Therefore he comes carrying meat, while his brother remains alone at the place from which he comes. His father did not kill a springbok, but we eat because of those who are children; we eat first from them. The grown men will shoot on another day; they must kill their own springboks. Afterwards the grown men will eat springboks which they themselves have shot.

[*17 September*] 'The two children are with the older people; they drive out the springbok for the men. The older people are the ones who shoot, while the children follow the springbok behind; they stop shooting, for they do not shoot. They know that they must go behind the springbok. Their father and his brothers run across the front of the herd.[48] Therefore the old men run in front and shoot the spring-bok herd which is large, those which send up the dust. They spring in the dust, the dust of their feet. The people run into the dust. Standing, they shoot in the dust. They know that the children go on the sides to keep the springbok together. Therefore many springbok die. The old people know that the springbok are numerous. They shoot the springbok meat as the springbok pass by them. They shoot the springbok meat from near by. Together they hold and carry the springboks.

'They sit, cutting up the meat in the shade of the bushes. They roast, after they have made a large fire. Carrying meat, they leave this place; they each carry two springboks. Therefore they come to work at the house; they will hunt afterwards, when there are many arrows, so that they can shoot many springbok. They know that their shoot-ing used up all the arrows. By shooting, they broke other arrows. When the springbok fell dead, they fell on other arrows and broke them. The springbok fell on and broke the arrows. Arrows break to pieces against the springbok-legs.[49] [*19 September*] They put on their arrow heads.'

Notes

1. The 'miskit' is the arrow's own doing, as far as I can make out what J.T. means.
2. The tone ascends in a singing manner here; while in the word for avoiding the arrow the tone is least.
3. A musical 'o' here.
4. J.T. says, the springbok run towards the wind and the dust blows over and behind them.
5. Not shooting, but holding fast the bow and string, pulling the latter out.
6. J.T. explains that if the children play away from the house, and not on the man's bed, the man shoots well, but, if he thinks that they are running backwards and forwards playing on his bed, he is angry and shoots badly. He further tells me that the /Xam-ka !ei think that, if the children play in the house and on their father's bed when the men go out hunting springbok, a man will shoot another man; also

that, if they play in the house, a man will fall down and be hurt with his own arrows that he carries in his band. If the children play outside, a man will not shoot another man; he shoots the springbok well; and a man will not fall down and be wounded with his own arrows. Editor: The 'band' of skin was worn around the head, waist or biceps. Arrows were lodged in it so that they could easily be taken.

7. J.T. explains that the man sits on his bed and puts on his arrow bag, takes the bow, and goes out of the house to hunt.

8. The arrows are stuck in the band.

9. 'sit fast?'

10. Therefore the boys ought to leave the hut.

11. Turn about with pain, moaning.

12. J.T. explains that when a man dies his 'heart' falls from the throat (the hollow of the throat) to the middle of the body, where it remains.

13. Very musical intonation here.

14. Go out from the children, I believe.

15. J.T. explains that the man says he will think of his wife still, when he is dead, as to if she gets food, is warm; and that he, when dead, thinks also of the children, whether they are warm enough, get food, etc.

16. He says that he talks to her this once, and not again.

17. Let them alone/leave them in quiet, i.e. let them all remain with you and give none of them to anyone.

18. It means outside here.

19. White man with a white forehead.

20. Editor: 'Bushman rice' was termite larvae.

21. 'Gambro': if the children eat much of this they die. J.T. tells me. Editor: *gambro* was an unidentified type of root.

22. Very musical intonation of the 1st syllable here – 'mar', J.T. says. Editor: *maar* (*maer* in Afrikaans) is Dutch for 'thin'.

23. J.T. explains that the woman thinks if her husband had lived with *her* old parents, and gone out shooting with her brother, that they would have better taken care of him, and the accident not have happened.

24. J.T. explains that the /Xam-ka !ei carry on their backs, in a springbok sack, not, as the (black people) and Korannas, on the head.

25. 'Old papa' the grandfather, grandmother and uncles of the children, J.T. explains (on the mother's side, in this instance, of course).

26. //kwe (*nett so as* [just as] //kuan, J.T explains).

27. J.T. explains that she goes to see the man buried, then returns to the house, and sets off on her journey.

28. Four brothers' wives.

29. The woman thinks that the wife has fought with her husband and has been turned away for it.

30. Editor: The phrase 'My wife' may be a clue to the informant's knowledge of these events, but it is nevertheless strange that he nowhere gives the names of the people.

31. She, the widow, had long wanted to remain at her father's, but her husband

thought that they should go to another place.

32. This also means that the flesh is hard, the /Xam-ka !ei tell me; but they use the same word to express a thing which is heavy (literally 'not light').

33. An odd musical sound here, much emphasised.

34. He means that, until now, he could not, being alone. (Editor: He had no one to drive the springbok in his direction.)

35. Editor: 'rub' means to prepare skins.

36. Springbok horn spoon.

37. Some kind of bushes.

38. She speaks of the brother of her other son, J.T. says.

39. The springbok come from the west where the sun has set and go towards the rising sun, J.T. says.

40. J.T. says that the young man drives away vultures from the springbok skin, and takes it, and burns off the hair, and the old man eats it, when he has no other food.

41. That have come up, as well as the good grass, from the rain.

42. I think this is 'broil'.

43. A hole called /*kaggen tsaxu*, which he is said to have made. /Xam-ka !ei call it !*hun*. It is through a stone, and they close it up with another stone. Editor: /Kaggen is the Mantis; *tsaxu* means 'eye', and !*hun* means 'to hunt'.

44. 'Kleine Witt Kop'.

45. A house of white stones, J.T. says; not an earthen one.

46. 'De thornbushes'.

47. Editor: A boy's first-kill was marked by rituals that effected his transition to manhood. See Lewis-Williams and Biesele, 1978; Lewis-Williams, 1981: 55–68.

48. 'The 1st springbok' as far as I can understand.

49. These are broken by the springbok's legs, as the troop goes leaping along, and the /Xam-ka !ei shoot into the midst of them.

Starvation from drought

/Han≠kass'o

L. VIII. 17. 7522–7526
19–20 SEPTEMBER 1878

≠Kammi was thin from starvation, starving and lean. Drought, drought prevailed. My grandfather was also thin from starvation. My grandfather almost died, did not a little die. Drought was what he was starving from.

The ostriches were not numerous. The quaggas and the gemsbok and the hartebeest, these things did not approach him, so that he could shoot them. For we revive, we who are children, when we shoot the gemsbok and the ostrich. We also run down the steenbok in the sun, rouse it in the sun. It gets up; it is afraid that the sun will kill it, and therefore it is wounded. It is overcome when the sun is killing it, when it suffers from the heat, when it falls down from the sun, when it is stealing away. Then we hit it, killing it with a stone, while the sun is also killing us.

We reach home, where there is water. Then someone else, whom the sun has really destroyed, faints, because the sun has really killed him. Then he goes and collapses at home. Then people poured water, cooling him. Then he recovers his breath, after he has fainted.

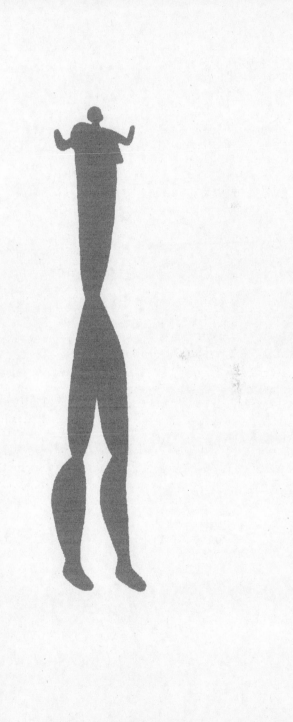

The /Xam-ka !ei
and animals

Today, a popular and romantic notion has it that the San live 'in close
harmony' with nature. They are presented as the original ecologists.
Whilst it is, of course, true that their knowledge of their natural sur-
roundings was second to none, it is wrong to think of them as experi-
encing some sort of mystical kinship with the animals. The following
texts show that life held its natural dangers. It is only a perspective
from Western industrialised cities that sees /Xam-ka !au as the
Garden of Eden before the Fall.

How ≠Kasin's eldest brother was carried off by a lion

≠Kasin

L. IV. 1. 3453–3458
6 NOVEMBER 1873

My mother sat eating while my father was lying down. My brother was sitting. All three of us were sitting down.[1]

My mother was holding the little child when the lion sprang in among us. It caught hold of my elder brother and carried him off. My mother ran after the lion, but my father caught her and brought her back. The lion bit my father's arm. My mother beat the lion's nose until it loosened its hold of my father. Then it ran away. He walked back and went to lie down. He was not strong enough to be able to walk, so he lay down. He could feel his arm swelling.

We remained at home. An old man came, another old man, while we sat hungry because my father had been injured. The other old man went to tell the people. The people journeyed to us so that they could come to see my father; so that they could give us food, we who were children, we who hungered, while they were taking care of my father.

They burned *so- /õa*.[2] They rubbed his arm. They powdered the burned *so- /õa* and mixed it with fat. They rubbed their hands with it. Then they heated their hands at the fire and rubbed his arm with them. They burned around the wound and also smeared round it fat that had been mixed with burnt powdered *so- /õa*.

My father slowly recovered. Now he walks around and gives us food, because he feels better. He walks about.

NOTES

1. This happened when they were boys, and our Klaas (the younger) was about 3½ feet high.
2. Editor: An unidentified medicinal plant. See Bleek, 1936.

A day of adventure and tragedy

≠Kasin

L. IV. 2. 3534–3585
NOVEMBER 1873 – 19 FEBRUARY 1874

I went out of the house. I walked up a little hill. I saw the mother hyena walking below along on the hill, coming towards me. She walked past and went down. She went in. I could see her no longer. She seemed to be in the hole. I now looked. I sat watching for her, but I could not see her. I sat looking for her, but I could not see her.

I spotted a crow. It was alone. It flew. It flew. It sat down.

Then I took up my bow; I took up arrows. I walked down and found the path made by the hyena. I walked along in the hyena's path. I found much hyena spoor. Then I looked in front of me, lifting up my face. I saw the earth from the hole. I took off my veldschoens.[1] I put them down. Then I turned up my trouser legs.

I walked towards the hole and peeped in. I saw nothing. I climbed up the earth from the hole and saw a little hyena's head. I walked up the earth from the hole. I saw that it sucked. I walked up and saw the mother hyena's ear. The little thing also saw me. It looked angrily at me. Then I stood still. The little thing looked angrily at me. [*20 November*] I laughed.

Then I shot the mother hyena. She came out. I stood, giving her the path, so that she could come out. She chased me, and I ran away. I ran away. I stood and looked at the hyena mother. I saw that she came to me so I ran away. She chased me. I realised that I could not get away. I ran to a bush and sprang over it. I went to stand behind the bush, while she stood on the near side, standing by the bush. She looked around, seeking me. She came to me, passing by the side of the bush. I ran, passing round behind the bush. She also ran, passing round behind. I ran again, passing behind the bush. She also ran round behind, she who was the mother hyena, while I stood behind. She stopped. She stood still. She fell down and died.

I walked round to where she lay. I pulled out the quill of the arrow. I looked at her as she lay there. I went away, leaving her.

I walked to the hole so that I could look for the hyena's children and kill them. I could not find them. I turned back. I went to pick up my veldschoens. I sat down so that I could put on my veldschoens. I went away. I went to the things, my things, which I put down, so that I could pick them up. I went to take them up.

I called the dog. I went back to the hole so that I could take the dog to the hole. The dog went into the hole and caught another little thing. He dragged it out, while I stood above on the ground from the hole. He came and laid it down, leaving the little thing at the mouth of the hole. I walked down to the mouth of the hole. I picked it up. I brought it out. I put it down on top of the earth which the hyena had scratched out from the hole. I looked at the cub while the dog bit the other little thing. The dog came out. He was alone, having left the other cub in the hole; he had left the other little thing.

I now stood up and saw springboks. I saw the springboks coming down. I tied up the dog. I fastened the dog to a bush with a *riem* [leather thong] that had been round its body. I went towards the springboks. I crept up to the springboks. The springboks ran, came running to me because they had seen a lion. Therefore I shot springboks. I shot a male springbok as they came running. I took out an arrow. I shot springboks.[2] I shot a mother springbok as they came running. I took out another arrow. I shot a male springbok as they came running. Again I took out another arrow. I shot again, [*15 December*] shot a male springbok. I shot another springbok, because all the springboks ran past me. I looked at the springboks I had shot. The springboks lay on the ground.

I went to one springbok. I went to pick it up. I carried it to the *kopje* [hill]. I went to put it down. I took bushes so that I could cover it with them. I saw a vulture, which came down because he thought that he would go to sit on the springbok. He went to sit down on the springbok. I continued running, going there. I went to pick up the springbok.

I took another springbok to the place where the other springbok lay. I went to put it down. I covered the springboks with bushes. I went to look for the other springboks. Then I saw another springbok. I also picked up that springbok. I followed the other springbok spoor so that I could look for the other springboks.

I saw a mother springbok lying on the ground; she lay. I walked up. I put down the springbok and took up the mother springbok. I went to put it into a bush. I put it down and covered it. I walked back and went to pick up the springbok which I had been carrying, the one which I had put down. I carried it to the place where the other springboks lay.

I went to cut up the springbok. I took out one springbok's liver. I laid it to roast in the fire. I cut up the springbok while the liver lay roasting. I put down the springbok and took out the liver. I took it to where the knife was. I took up the knife. I cut off the liver's other side. I sat eating.

I saw a jackal. He cantered out of the river as I sat eating. I sat looking at the jackal; and I picked up the other piece of liver, and again I sat eating it. And I saw another jackal which cantered out of the place from which the other jackal had cantered. I had now finished eating. Then I took up the springbok and laid it nicely under the bush because I wanted to go to look at the place from which the jackals had cantered. I covered up the springbok with bushes. I throbbed.[3] I covered up the springbok with bushes and took up my hat from where I had laid it on the ground. I put it on the bush under which the springbok was.[4] I picked up the bow.

Then I went toward the place from which the jackals had come. I went into the bushes. I saw the other jackals' spoor.[5] These jackals cantered into the bushes. Then I went on. I saw the place where the jackals had lain and I examined it.

Then I went on and saw a lion's spoor. I followed the lion's spoor. I went into the bushes. I saw the place where the springbok had been startled. Then I stood still and looked at the bushes, and I saw the shadow of the lion's head as he lay there. I looked again. I looked underneath the tree and saw his head. I went back across the river so that I could go along the bank to look for a place which was bare to see if I could spot the thing's head. And I saw that he lay under the tree. I shouted, but the thing was silent and not frightened. It continued to lie there. It was as if it had not heard me.

I went back to the springbok. I went to take up another springbok. Carrying it, I returned home. I went to tell the people about what I had seen today. The people then asked me what it was. I told them that the thing was not afraid of me.

And they asked, 'Why didn't you go near the thing so that you could see?'

I told the people that I was afraid, and they were silent about it. They asked me about the springboks, if I had shot one springbok. And I said that there were other springboks lying on the hunting-ground. The people asked me if it was far. I told them that it was not far.

The people then gathered together so that they could go and see what it was. Then we went. We went across the river. We climbed a little hill, climbing, going to the place at which the springboks lay. And I now showed the people the place at which I had seen the thing.

The people carried the three springboks, and we went to the place at which the thing had lain. The people went to put down the springbok, and we went near to the place where the thing had lain. I then showed the people the tree under which the thing had lain.

And another man said, 'There is a black thing over there underneath the tree.'

[*17 January*] And the other man said, 'Let us go near so that we can see what it is.'

And I said, 'It is a lion. Let us turn back, for there are not enough people to help us.'[6]

And we crossed the river and sat down. They sent me to run to the people so that they might come. I then went to the house and told them about it. [*20 January*] And the people assembled together on account of it. As they left, they slung on their quivers. Other people grasped assegais. We now went.

We went to the people, the others who had sent for help. The people were now red, as they went along. And we saw the people who stood on the top of the hill. They stood beckoning to us to go quickly. For the lion had stood up; he was going along in the river (in the dry bed, not in the water). And we ran to them. [*16 February*] They were the ones who had told us that the lion had gone down into the river bed. We ran above looking to see where the lion had gone. He went. They climbed the hill and saw the lion as it went along the river bed. And they followed the lion. They headed the lion, but it lay down on account of it. They stood as the lion lay there. And the old people[7] who had been behind came up to them.

Those who had headed the lion said to the old people, 'Here lies the lion. You should all go near so that you can look for an opening through which you can shoot.' They then did so. And another man saw the lion lying under the bush.

An old man said, 'This man must shoot the lion because his poison is strong.'

Then the old man shot. And the lion, attacking, came out of the bush under which he had lain. The people ran back because of it. They stood still when the lion also stood still. The lion lay down again at the bush under which he had lain. The men went again to the lion so that they could shoot.

Then they shot. The lion attacked, and an old man fell down as he ran. The lion then caught hold of the old man and bit the old man's knee.[8] The other men shot at the lion, but the lion would not loose his hold of the old man.

They ran up to the lion; they stabbed the lion as it was biting the old man. But the lion bit, breaking the old man's knee bone to pieces. [*19 February*] They stabbed, killing the lion, but the old man died from loss of blood.

They carried the old man home so that his children could see, they and his wife, that she might see him because he was dead.[9] They would never see him again. That they could see him for the last time. They buried the old man near his house. They moved to another place so that they could take the children there, so that the children would not think of him. If the children lived at this place, they would want to cry.

NOTES

1. Editor: Shoe made from rough animal hide. See page 14.
2. I don't understand the tenses here.
3. His flesh throbbed because he was afraid, believing that there was a lion where the jackals came from.
4. K.K. [≠Kasin] explains: 'I had put a flag (his hat which he had worn on his head) on the bush; I put it on the bush because I was going; for I feared that the crows would eat the springbok; when I went, they would eat the springbok behind my

back. Therefore, I put the flag upon the bush. For I feared that they would eat the springbok.'

5.   Jackals which he had *not* seen.
6.   Only a few men had gone.
7.   i.e. white-haired men, in this instance.
8.   The old man was too weak to run, K.K. [≠ Kasin] explains.
9.   They did not bury him on the hunting-ground, so that his family might see him once more.

Leopard-hunting: the fatal adventure of !Kwai-kwa and his companion

Dia!kwäin
From his mother, ≠Kammi-an

L. V. 18. 5419–5444
25 NOVEMBER 1875

My mother used to tell me that Gemsbok-leg[1] went hunting with another person. There were just the two of them. Then he saw a leopard. They thought that they would kill it. At first it seemed as if the leopard would run away, and they chased it. The leopard saw that they were going to hunt it. Therefore it did not run slowly. It really deceived them into thinking it had run away. As it ran along, this is what it did: it leapt and hid itself.

And Gemsbok-leg told the other man that the leopard was lying down. They said to each other they would go up to the leopard where it had lain down, so that they could shoot it. And they said to each other that they would separate, so that one man could be on the other side of the leopard and that the other man should also do this, so that they could watch.

But the leopard did this: while they were looking for it at the place where it had vanished, it rose up at another place. They were looking for it at the spot where it had disappeared. While they were looking at the place where the leopard had vanished, this is what it did: it sprang up from a place where they did not think it would be.

He was just about to shout, 'It is here!', but the leopard did not let him first tell the other man about it. This is what it did: when he tried to tell the other man that the leopard was there, it tore his throat open. [*26 November*] Before he could tell the other man about it, it grasped his throat. The other man went to help him so that he could lift him up. Before he could shoot the leopard, it sprang out and tore the skin from his face. And he asked the other man what the leopard had done; the leopard had jumped out. One man had intended to tell the other that the leopard was close to them, but before he could tell the other man about it, he reeled about and then fell down. He could not tell the other man that the leopard had come to him. They lay fainting, not seeing the leopard.

That is why our mothers tell us that we must do as follows if we see a leopard. If we chase the leopard and see that it disappears, we must not look for the leopard where it has disappeared. The leopard disappears when it wants us to look for it. Then it steals up, coming towards us, because it wants to catch us while we are looking at the place where it disappeared. That is why our mothers tell us that we must do as follows when we see that a leopard disappears: we must not look for the leopard at that place. We must first seek the leopard in front of us. For it is a thing that steals up to meet us, it holds us down before we can go to the place where it disappeared. It is a thing which does not run, but it steals up to us.

Our mothers told us about it: when dogs are attacking a leopard, we must not think that they will be able to hold it. When the dogs approach a leopard, it lies down, so that it merely looks as if the dogs are holding it down. [*27 November*] It wants us to think that the dogs are going to kill it, for it wants us to do this when we see that the dogs are about to bite it to death: it wants us to run up to it, because we think the dogs are biting it to death. Our mothers told us that we should not think that the dogs are holding the leopard down, for it is the leopard that has lain down to deceive us. It lies spitting at the dogs. Our mothers told us that the leopard watches for us, while the dogs bark round it. Then it does this when it sees us: while the dogs are barking round it, it becomes like a scrap of skin[2] which jumps out from among the dogs. It holds us down while the dogs are looking for it where they were biting it.

NOTES

1.   A young gemsbok pierced his leg; therefore they called him 'Gemsbok-leg'. Editor: see also *Kum* 8 and *Kum* 9.
2.   A very little bit of skin it is, we throw it out to the dogs. The dogs are busy with each other at the place where they saw the leopard, for they think that the 'Little skin' leopard is still among them. While they are seeking the leopard, it is biting us to death, when they were angry with the leopard.

Adventure with a family of baboons

Diä!kwain
From his mother, ≠Kammi-an

L. V. 23. 5890–5901
JANUARY 1876

The baboons used to do as follows. /Khui-/a saw them sit down to wash at the water; they sat washing their faces. /Khui-/a stole up towards the baboons as they were washing themselves. He shot a female baboon while she was holding a little baboon baby. And the baboons ran away from the water. But as the female baboon was running along, she dropped the baby baboon from her armpit where she had been carrying it. She did this: running along, she threw the baby baboon into the cleft of a rock, as she was running along.

And a male baboon stopped running. He went to see what the female was doing. It seemed as if /Khui-/a had killed the female; for it seemed as if death had settled on the female's face, as with the look with which he looked at it. /Khui-/a stood looking at what he had done. And the male baboon saw that the female was lying down. He climbed up to the rock behind which the female was lying. He sat down because he wanted to see what /Khui-/a would do.

And /Khui-/a spoke and said, 'I want to go and look, for it seems as if the mother has hidden the baby baboon in the cleft of the rock.'

And /Khui-/a went up to the place where the mother baboon had hidden the baby baboon. The male baboon sat weeping; he wiped the tears from his eyes.

And he [/Khui-/a] peeped into the cleft of the rock. He saw the baby baboon in the cleft of rock. And he put in his arm because he wanted to drag out the baby baboon. He stuck his head over the rock. And the little baboon screamed, and the male baboon rose up. He approached /Khui-/a. He spoke to /Khui-/a. He said, 'O /Khui-/a, leave me the child, for you have killed its mother. You seem to think that you will kill it together with its mother.'

/Khui-/a heard that it sounded as if the baboon would fight him.

He left the little baboon alone. He went off to his things, while the male baboon went up to the little baboon, took up the little baboon and put it under his arm. He went up to the baboon mother. He examined her, while /Khui-/a, quite frightened, went away. And the male baboon put the child down where the mother lay dead. /Khui-/a went away to pick up his quiver. He returned home.

The giving of names

We have no idea of the range of personal names that the /Xam-ka !ei used. Modern San groups that live in the Kalahari Desert have a comparatively restricted number of names. Further personal discrimination is provided by nicknames. As the following two brief texts show, the /Xam-ka !ei earned nicknames in various ways. The second text introduces the pervasive notion of supernatural power and its manipulation by shamans.

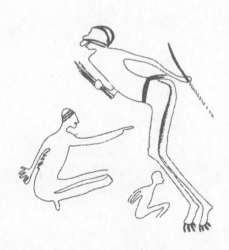

How Mansse obtained the name !Kau /noan

Diä!kwain

L. V. 20. 5605–5607
16 DECEMBER 1875

Mansse married my sister /A-kkumm. When Mansse was running after the sheep, he caught his foot on a stone and fell down. The stone cut his knee. Other people gave him his name because they knew that a stone had cut his knee. They gave him a nickname because a stone had cut his knee. That is why they gave him the name 'Stone Knee'. His name is not 'Stone Knee', for his parents called him 'Mansse'.

Why Diä!kwain's brother Tho-bbo was so named

Diä!kwain
From his mother, ≠Kammi-an

L. V. 10. 4751–4754
27 May 1875

Mamma gave Tho-bbo his name because the people continued to shout '*Bbo!*'[1] at us because of what happened at that place.[2] Therefore Mamma said this. She gave Tho-bbo his name because of what the other people had done: they truly continued to threaten us. This was why Mamma spoke like that. She gave Tho-bbo his name because of what the people had done: they worked with supernatural power; they killed my grandmother, /Abbe-ttu, with supernatural power.

And they also killed my grandfather, //Khwai-/ha, with supernatural power.[3] They said that they too had behaved as we had. This was why they did what they did: they acted because of it. They had also intended to kill us with supernatural power.

NOTES

1. Editor: *Bbo* is a /Xam interjection, apparently offensive (see page 17 in the *Dictionary*). The use of the exclamation *Bbu*, probably a variant spelling of *Bbo*, is given by //Kabbo as an example of how children might anger the moon: '*Bbu!* The great moon, which has come out! It is a great red thing; it is not small' (L. II. 35: 3157 rev.).
2. The people unjustly said that D.H.'s (i.e. Diä!kwain's) people had done the bad things which had been happening. They also killed D.H.'s maternal grandmother with sorcery. Editor: For more on 'sorcery', or supernatural power, see Lewis-Williams, 1981.
3. This happened previously, before the time when the grandmother of D.H. and also his aunt died. The two abovementioned persons had no Boer names; they did not live with Boers, who at that time were not where these people lived.

Artefacts and poisons

The /Xam-ka !ei were still making stone artefacts in the 1870s, although the tradition was fast dying out. The care with which these artefacts and arrows were made is evident in the following accounts. Stone artefacts were made by both men and women (*Kum* 29). Great interest has centred on the lethal poison which the San placed on their arrows. It is evident from *Kum* 12 that they selected special poisons for hunting different animals.

Arrow-making

/Han≠kass'o
From personal observation

L. VIII. 26. 8293–8302; 8315–8334
MARCH 1879

[*2 March*] We go to fetch reeds, to cut the reeds. We bring the reeds and bind them up with cord. We put them in the net and take them to the hut. We go and divide up the reeds at the hut.

They bind the reeds which they have straightened. They go and put the body of the reeds into the porcupine's hole.[1] They shut them in with bushes and put stones upon the bushes; they also lay earth over them because they intend that beasts of prey, which go about at night, shall not scratch it open. They bind and put the other part of the reeds away at home; these are the reeds with which they work [*6 March*] to straighten.

[*12 March*] When the arrow is like this, we are accustomed to scrape[2] them and remove the reed's excrescences. We take the !*kui* out of the fire.[3] We straighten the reed. We do it in this manner. Holding the reed, we lay it in [the stone]. We straighten the reed. We take the reed out. We do this with the reed (looking along it, to see if it is straight). If we see that it is crooked, we straighten it with our hands. We do thus with it: holding it, we lay it in the !*kui*.[4] We take the !*kui* and put it into the fire. We take the !*kui* out. We straighten the part of the reed which was bent. We straighten it again.

We cut the ends of the reed, and we also cut the upper end of the reed.[5] We split it. Then we choose a feather from among other feathers. We cut the top of the feather; we take up the reed and put down the feather, while we try the feather. We warm the reed at the fire, and we take up /Kuai juice. We rub the /Kuai juice on it in this manner. And we again warm the /Kuai juice (which is on the reed). We warm the /Kuai juice. We take up the feather. We do this to the feather: holding it, we press it and lay it along the reed. Then we take up a knife and heat it by putting it in the fire. We press the feather down into its place on the arrow; we press the feather down very nicely, and we roll the arrow into the sinew, so as to put in the sinew. We first put the quill of the feather at the upper end of the arrow. Afterwards we put on the quill of the feather. We hold the arrow and turn it. We put this on at the arrow's mouth. Then we lay down the arrow so that the /*Kuai* juice may dry.

[*16 March*] We take up the shaft and shape the shaft by removing the peel by scraping it with a knife. Shaping, we remove the peel. We warm it at the fire over the hot embers. We make it straight. Holding it, we make it straight by smoking it.[6]

Then we take up the arrow-head. We warm the tip of the shaft at the fire; we split it and we put in the arrow-head. Then we take out the arrow-head and put it on the hot embers. We take out the arrow head.[7] We put down the arrow-head.

We take up the /*Kuai* juice and we warm it. We put the /*Kuai* juice on to the tip of the shaft by means of the stick on which it is. Then we take up the arrow-head. We warm the /*Kuai* juice we put in the arrow-head. We warm the /*Kuai* juice, when the arrow-head is on the shaft. We thus press down the /*Kuai* juice. We take out a sinew, we wind on the sinew. We put the arrow-head to dry.[8]

Then we take up another reed, and straighten it. When we have finished making it straight, we put it down. We take up the reed which we first made straight. We take up the arrow-head. We put the shaft into the reed, and we sharpen the arrow-head. We sharpen the arrow-head by biting it. We polish it with a whetstone.[9] We intend it to become white. Then we put it down; we take up another reed. We cut it; we cut it; we mark it. We bind its mouth. And we put it down; we take out a feather. We hammer the inside of the quill of the feather. And we cut the tip of the feather. We put down the feather. We take up the reed. We take up the /*Kuai* juice. We warm the reed. We rub the /*Kuai* juice on to the reed. We take up a feather; we warm the /*Kuai* juice. We place the feather upon the /*Kuai* juice; holding it, we press the feather down upon the reed. We press down the sides of the feather with a knife that has been warmed.[10]

[*18 March*] We bind the reed, and we put the reed to dry. Then we take the furrowed stone. We put the furrowed stone to cool. And we stop working. We sit down in order that the reed may dry, the reed's sinew. [*19 March*] Then we take up the arrow-head with the shaft in it. We put it into the reed. And we put it down. Then we leave off working. We sit, while we feel that we have finished making them.[11] We sit thinking of other work which we shall do.

Therefore we exclaim, 'I shall first be quiet. Afterwards, I shall poison the arrows in the morning, when it is cold, for it is warm. For the poison's heat would cover my face. Therefore I am first quiet. I will poison tomorrow morning so that I will not perspire while working. For I perspire. I do not a little perspire.' Therefore we remain quiet.[12]

[*22 March*] Early, we shred it (a dried vegetable juice is that which we shred) upon a flat stone (upon which arrow-heads are sharpened). And we spit our saliva into it, and we crush it,[13] making it soft. And we take a snake's head. We take off its poison-fang's membrane.[14] We put the snake's poison fang's poison into the [*untranslated word*], and we crush it. And we take a puffadder's poison fang. We slice it (in this case the skin bag is not removed but sliced with the contents).[15] We take the poison fang out of a different snake. We put them together. A snake which is powerful (strong), it is the one that we use because we saw it at a place which is strong. It is the one of which we put in one poison fang, [*23 March*] while we leave its other poison fang alone. When we have cut it, we put in its gall. We put away the other part of the gall, while we put the other part of the gall into the [*untranslated word*]. And the poison becomes green, and we poison, [*24 March*] poison with it. We put the poison on this part. We put the poison on the sinew. This is what we do with the poison. We poison, bringing the poison down onto the shaft. We poison, laying down the poison (to the poison's lower limit about 2 inches or 1/8 down the shaft). And we work, work the poison very nicely, and we put it to dry. We put the end of the arrow shaft into a bush, put it on the back of a bush, so that a little child may not catch sight of it and take it. We take the whetstone and put it away inside the house (on the earth, under the stick), so that a little child may not see it and pick it up and break it. We stop working; we sit down.

NOTES

1. *!xo-ka //nein*: a porcupine's house.
2. With a knife.

3. It is a stone, a (split) digging-stick's stone, of which the people make a *!kui*.
4. A furrowed stone.
5. First we cut (straight) its upper end; and we straighten it (i.e., the reed). When we have finished straightening it, we cut its mouth.
6. Warm it at a fire which flames, in order that it may become black. Holding it, we lay it in the fire-tongue which is like this.
7. Jerk it out, with a stick.
8. Stick the shaft into the earth, while we intend the */Kuai* juice to dry, so that we can sharpen the arrow-head.
9. A flat whetstone, a stone which is a soft stone.
10. If an arrow-head is not there, we pull out the shaft; we heat the end of the shaft in the fire; we press down the sides of the feather (with it).
11. While they are two.
12. [Apparently unrelated note] A man who is alive, he is the one whom we ask [*/kwen*: call to, give orders to] for rain, that he may make the rain fall for us. A man who is dead, we pray to [*/gauken*] him.
13. With a 'Drie Doorn' stick.
14. The skin which is upon its poison fang's saliva. We say its poison fang's poison to it (i.e., to the dried saliva = the venom).
15. *//ka*; the name of the plant from which the *=ku* poison is obtained.

The arrow barb

/Han≠kass'o
From his maternal grandfather, Tssatssi,
and from personal experience

L. VIII. 31. 8770–8773
25 August 1879

A long wing feather. We cut off its root and split it. We work a little piece which is small, and we bind sinew over it, as we lay it on the arrow-shaft.[1] And we bind sinew upon it. And we bite the end of the sinew with our teeth.[2] We bind the sinew on nicely, and we put down the arrow-shaft because we want the sinew to dry.[3] We put it down because we want the sinew to become dry so that we can poison the arrow. We poison down, down, down. We poison downwards, over the barblet's stem, that part of the barblet's stem over which the sinew lies. The tip of the barblet is bare.[4] The barblet is that which catches the [*untranslated word*], it is under the barblet; and then the tip of the barblet is in the flesh. And then the poison[5] dissolves into the flesh,[6] on account of it.[7]

NOTES

1. Springbok's arrows do not have barblets; they are clean, handsome, because they do not have barblets. Gemsbok's arrows have barblets, and ostrich's arrows.
2. The stem of the sinew, which had been upon the bone.
3. *!guarra-⊙pua*, the name for an arrow which has no poison.
4. 'My heart stands in the hill.' Said by !Kuarra//Kau, a man who is said to have died from the effects of a poisoned arrow when he did not want to have his foot cut, in order to make it bleed.
5. The poison which is upon the barblet.
6. A whitish membranaceous-looking substance, found near the vein of the inner side of the upper arms, and also in the thighs.
7. Because the barblet catches into the flesh. Therefore the poison dissolves into the flesh.

Poisons

≠Kasin
L.C. Lloyd's paraphrase of his account

L. IV. 1. 3472–3480
7–11 November 1873

!gweh

Called by the Boers '*Malkop-gift*'. A plant with a short top and a long root in the earth; it is plentiful at Klaas Katkop's place. The large root is dug up. They get a white milky-looking juice from it which they put into a heated hollow stone, where it boils and becomes yellow. It is a strong poison. They roll it upon the end of a stick when it has cooled. They do not like to use it for hunting game for food, because it quickly runs thro'/enters the flesh of the animal killed. If they smell it when putting it on an arrow they become as if intoxicated. They are afraid to eat the flesh of an animal that has been killed with it. Cattle sometimes eat the part of the plant that is above ground, but die from its effects. Other Bushmen shoot with it, but Klaas says that 'we' do not. For he and his father (having been so advised) once went to get this poison, and shot a springbok or two with it. They took the meat home, and the mother cooked some. Klaas spat it out, but the mother nearly died from the effects of a piece which she had swallowed. They brought her round by means of water and a herb of which they afterwards made a drink, and gave to her; but she had become insensible and stiff in the arms and nearly dead – and they never shot food with the *!gweh* again.

Boom Gift[1]

There are other poisons which only burn the flesh round them like fire. You cut out the wound, which has become white, and a piece round it and burn what you have cut out in the fire, for fear that the dogs should eat it. You are well able to eat the rest of the animal killed. One of these is the blackish (or dark brown) poison which I have in the cupboard. Which Klaas calls '*Boom Gift*' or *!gao-ki*. It is brought by Bushmen who live farther away than these do; the latter buy it from them; for sheepskins, karosses, handkerchiefs, or tinder-boxes; as these farther Bushmen do not know money. But they love knives.

Cobra poison

The name of the poison which is in the two glands *//khwi /nan* [*//khwi* a Cobra; *//khioi /nan*, snake's head]. The Boer's name for this snake is '*Capell*' [Cobra]. The Bushmen cut out the two poison glands and afterwards put them to dry. This poison is good for shooting: one can eat the game after it. The flesh round the wound becomes black where the poison has gone and is cut out. To get tomorrow what they mix with it to make it black – some part of a plant with a white flower. This poison is mixed with another (*!kanna*) before it is used to poison the arrows. Therefore the flesh of the animal shot becomes black round the wound.

!Guken or Puffadder

This snake's poison is also good for shooting food with. The Bushmen cut out the poison glands and put them to dry. This poison causes the flesh round the wound to become white.

!Kanna

This is mixed with the *//khwi /na* poison. A plant with a white flower and a short stem; it has a round bulb in the earth, with a very short root below that; the part that they use for poison is the bulb. They peel the bulb, which has a hard skin; the inside of it is white. They burn the peeled white bulb in the fire, that it may become black. They cut off a piece and pound it fine, and mix with it the poison from the *//khwi /na*. They do not work the *!kanna* with their hands, but with a stick (also with a knife) on account of its being poisonous. They use the poison, so mixed, for their arrows. It is black.

NOTE

1. Editor: *Boom-Gift* is Dutch for 'tree-poison'.

Stone artefacts

≠Kasin
L.C. Lloyd's paraphrase of his account

L. IV. 1. 3481
10–11 NOVEMBER 1873

//kurru, pl. *//kutten-//kutten*. Klaas says that the stone of which the /Xam-ka !ei make them is not to be found down here. They make little ones from white stones, which they split, and make the split pieces into arrow-heads. There are large red stones from which they make arrow-heads, and also knives. Some of the *little* stones are also red inside.

Flints are, Klaas says, to be found at his place, at least stones such as two flints he shows me, which come from a stone he picked up by the sea; but the stone, from which they make their *//kutten-//kutten* is different.

Porcupines

Meat-sharing is a San practice on which numerous ethnologists have commented. It is a mechanism for ensuring that everyone in a camp is fed, even though hunting is a chancy affair and a man may go for months without a kill. Food avoidances are also of interest. *Kum* 15 shows that an unmarried girl was subject to certain food restrictions. The link between pubescent girls and the rain is taken up again in *Kum* 54.

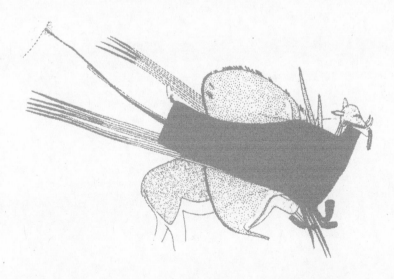

Sharing porcupine meat

/Han≠kass'o
From /Xabbi-an, and from personal observation
of Tssatssi, //Kabbo, ≠Kabbe, and ≠Nein!khe

L. VIII. 16. 7409–7417
10 SEPTEMBER 1878

We /Xam-ka !ei cut up a porcupine like this: we take off the porcupine's side, we put it down. We also cut off its other side; we put it down. Then we slit the porcupine's back. We cut away one side of the skin of the back, then the other side; and we put them down, for we want the meat to be plentiful, for there are many people. Then we cut up the porcupine's sides and we do the same to its other side, we cut it off too. We also cut off its tail for we want there to be plenty of meat, so that everyone may get porcupine meat, for the people are hungry.

Then a woman cooks the porcupine meat because it is plentiful. When she has finished cooking the meat and it is done, she takes one thigh and gives it to another person. She also takes the porcupine's forefoot and goes to give it to someone. Then she takes a bit of the skin of the back and gives it to someone. She comes and takes this thigh and gives it to someone. She comes and takes the porcupine's forefoot and gives it to someone. She takes the other bit of the skin of the back and gives it to someone, while she eats a bit of the skin and the porcupine's tail.

We men gnaw the porcupine's backbone; for we want our wife to give more to the children who are crying with hunger. So we men merely gnaw the backbone.

Then our wife cuts up the rest of the skin of the back for the children. She eats a bit of the skin and the tail, while we gnaw the back.

The porcupine's tail

/Han≠kass'o
From /Xabbi-an

L. VIII. 16. 7408 REV. AND 7409 REV.
10 SEPTEMBER 1878

A girl does not eat the porcupine's tail. She eats only its body, because a place in the porcupine's tail is white. That piece is what men call a danger signal.[1] It is white, its skin is white. People say: The danger signal beats for us, as it is grazing. A girl does not eat a porcupine's tail because such things are what the rain seeks. The rain snatches at them. That is why old people eat these things. When a girl gets her own hut and is married, then she eats the porcupine's tail.

NOTE

1. Editor: The *Bushman Dictionary* gives *!gwe:*, here translated, 'danger signal', as 'a letter, picture'. 'The Bushmen's letters are in their bodies.' This statement probably refers to a trembling in the body that the /Xam took to be a presentiment. See Bleek and Lloyd, 1911: 330–339.

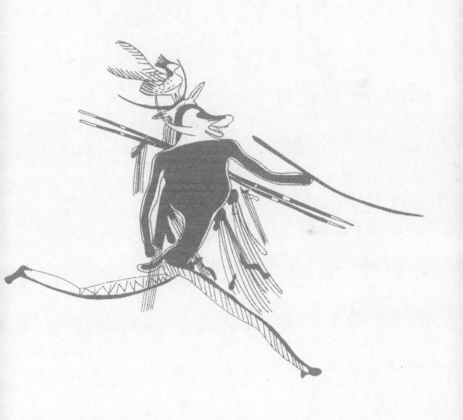

The Koranna

The Koranna mentioned in the following *kukummi* were marauding bands driven into San territory by the advance of the colonists. Like the /Xam-ka !ei, their society was also being destroyed. More fanciful texts (*Kum* 35, *Kum* 36) show just how disturbing relations with the Koranna were for the /Xam-ka !ei.

The escape of /Kannan
from the Koranna commando

/Han≠kass'o
From his mother, /Xabbi-an

L. VIII. 26. 8269–8285
15 FEBRUARY 1879

When /Kannan went to seek food, she was digging there. She espied people, a commando. She returned home. She came to tell the people.

She exclaimed, 'People are standing upon the vlei! You must make ready so that we can escape.'

A man said, 'The children of ostriches are always eating on Kuammata's vlei.'[1]

/Kannan exclaimed, 'They are real people! You must make ready so that we can escape.'

The man contradicted /Kannan. He said that /Kannan was speaking falsely, 'It is the children of ostriches that are always eating on Kuammata's vlei.'

The man said, 'My goodness! Why is the old woman obstinate about it? I am accustomed to see the children of ostriches eating on Kuammata's vlei.'

/Kannan replied, 'They are real people, real people; you must allow us to escape quickly.'

The old man said, 'It is the children of ostriches that are always eating on Kuammata's vlei.'

/Kannan said, 'They are real people, real people. You must allow us to escape quickly; for the sun seems to be about to set, while all the people are at home. The people do not split up at home, so that one part of the people may escape, while the other part of the people remains at home.'

The man said, 'They must be the children of ostriches, those which I am accustomed to see; they are always eating on Kuammata's vlei.'

/Kannan said, 'We ought to escape; they are real people.'

And the sun set, while /Kannan was pleading there, telling the people that they should allow them to go. She [*untranslated word*] the people, but the people would not listen to her. The people said she was deceiving them. Therefore the sun set, on account of it. They slept, while the Korannas, travelling in the darkness, reached them. The Korannas slept opposite to them. On the morrow, the Korannas attacked them. The Korannas shot them, shot the people; ran in among the people, so that they could shoot them.

And /Kannan exclaimed, 'You do not seem to have seen these people! For you contradicted me.'

The old man who had contradicted /Kannan exclaimed, 'I ought to have agreed with /Kannan; for /Kannan spoke truly.'

As /Kannan sprang away, she exclaimed, 'You do not seem to have seen these people! When I told you about them, I said that they were real people, but you contradicted me.'

She ran away, ran fleetly away. The Korannas could not overtake her. She ran, ran, ran, ran. They could not catch her; she was not a little fleet. Therefore the Korannas were weary because of it. The Korannas could not get near to her.

She stood still. She exclaimed: 'O Korannas! You may stand still, for you will not catch me. You may stand still over there.'

When she had thus spoken, she ran away. She went afar off and stood still. She exclaimed, 'O Korannas! You may stand still; for you will not at all equal me.' Therefore the Korannas stood still. They felt killed by fatigue.

All the people were slaughtered, slaughtered behind her, those people whom she vainly advised, they were those who were slaughtered. The Korannas killed them, while /Kannan was the one who lived, alone lived.

NOTES

1. I do not know the place where they lived; for I merely listened to the people. Editor: *Vlei* is Dutch for 'marshland'.

How the approach of a commando was foretold by the mist

Diä!kwain
From his father, Xa:ä-tin

L. V. 16. 5199–5205
11 AUGUST 1875

At a time when the people have not yet come to attack us, when they were still intending to attack us, there is a morning mist that sits there. It is our mist.

They shoot at us in the mist. We make clouds. Our blood is smoking. It feels that the people are shooting at us in the mist. That is why we make clouds before the people have come to us. Therefore the people who know exclaim, they say, 'A fight[1] appears to be coming to us today.'

My father used to tell me that I did not seem to know that our mist settled there when a fight was coming to us. The people fought us in the mist. When the people had finished fighting us, they went away and left us. When they had finished fighting us, they went away.

The mist did this: when the people went away and left us, it also went because it felt that our blood had flowed out. That is why our mist went away; it felt that our blood, which had been making clouds there, had flowed.

NOTE

1. Editor: The *Bushman Dictionary* gives /ā as 'fight, harm, curse'.

Relations with colonists

Some of the most painful *kukummi* deal with relations between the /Xam-ka !ei and white colonists. The alienation felt by the San is evident in the following texts: on all sides they were confronted by the invincible power of the colonists. *Kum 20* gives another of //Kabbo's dream experiences, here juxtaposed with the daily work he was required to perform. The magistrate is probably one with whom he stayed on his journey to Cape Town. *Kum 21* shows why many San preferred to die from starvation or to be shot by a commando rather than work for the colonists.

Sir Bartle Frere[1] returns to Cape Town

/Han≠kass'o

L. VIII. 28. 8474–8485
7–8 June 1879

The people were turning about; they were turning about![2] They stood still, stood in rows. The other people stood together. They watched what the people were doing. The children gathered themselves together; they looked at what the people were doing, looked at the people who arranged the people in lines, so that the people might stand quietly, keeping in lines, the people standing behind.[3] The children stood upon the parade[4] because they did not have place where they could stand. They stood upon the parade because they did not have a place where they could come to stand. Therefore, when the cannon fired,[5] the people who had been where the train stops came running. They ran, coming among the people who had been standing. They also stood.

A dog came in among the people; it looked about for a place[6] through which it could go. It went in among the people; it went among the people, people, people, people. It went in among the people, went through the people and came out yonder, behind the people. And then he came back again, because the children frightened him back: he came back again to the people. He went in among the people. He came out on this side of the people.[7] Then he took the road. He seems to have returned home, for I did not see him again.

When the great white man was passing along between them, the people went forward, while the people felt that they were following the great white man. And the people who were riding followed the people who were red (i.e. the soldiers). And other people followed them in the middle of the street, the people with white caps (i.e. the volunteers).[8] And the people who played, followed them. The people whose caps were white, they were those who went in front (of the volunteer cavalry and band), because they were those who followed the great white man. The people who were riding (the volunteer cavalry) followed them. And the people who played, they too followed them. And the people went forward altogether; the people were no longer there.

NOTES

1. Editor: Sir Bartle Frere was Governor of the Cape Colony at this time.
2. Going in and out among and around the other people.
3. I feel that the people were numerous, hence I say the people standing behind.
4. '*Vlei*' is the translation which the narrator gives of the word used here, but the parade is meant. Editor: The Grand Parade is an open area next to the Cape Town railway station.
5. The guns (that is, cannons) were many.
6. Looked for a passage, a place which stands open.
7. i.e. on the side nearest to the narrator.
8. They (that is the volunteers) went out from the people who were black (i.e., the civilians, Europeans, Malays, black people, etc.).

Letter from Diä!kwain to his sister
!Kweiten-ta-//ken and her family[1]

(Copy of attempt at translation of D.H.'s letter, sent to Dr H. Meyer, Calvinia, for transcription to D.H.'s sister Rachel, etc. Finished 27 Aug.)

Charlton House,
Mowbray,
Nr. Cape Town.
20th August 1875.

I have been wanting to say, why can it be that Rachel and her family do not send me a letter? That I might hear whether they went to the place to which they intended to return; if they had returned, they would have sent me a letter. Therefore, I am thinking that I want to hear whether they have returned; for, if they had returned, they would have told me, that I might know that they had got home: they must please speak to me.

Will Dr Meyer, when he has become well again, be so kind as to despatch a letter to Middlepost, to Gert van Wyk; at whose place my sister 'Griet Lynx' (or Springbok-skin) used to live? That one of them (i.e. of his relatives) may let me know, whether they are still well there. They must let me know why it is that they do not seem as if they remembered me, that they do not speak to me, (and) why Rachel has not told me that she has returned home well; for a silence reigns, if she has returned. Therefore, I know not why she has not told me, that I might know, that she has returned. Therefore, I desire that Dr Meyer, when he has become well again, will, at his good pleasure, allow Rachel and her family to know, that they may acquaint me, that I may know what has happened to them.

For I had thought to return. My master, he was the one who told me that I should first wait a little, as he did not yet desire that I

129

should return (home), going away from him; for I had thought of returning. He, in August's Moon – that was the one in which he died – leaving us. Therefore I know not what I shall still do about it; for my mistress still weeps; – this is why I still sit melancholy on account of it.[2]

They (his family) must let me hear what they say. For, I still behold my mistress; therefore I want them to let me know. For I do not wish yet to leave my mistress, while she still weeps. For a husband/man to give his consent (to my going) is not with my mistress.

So, these things they are those on account of which I first yet a little behold what she will do.

NOTES

1. Editor: When Wilhelm Bleek died on 17 August 1875, the future of his and Lloyd's researches was in doubt. The quandary in which the whole household found itself is reflected in this letter that Diä!kwain dictated to Lloyd three days after Bleek's death. His sister, !Kweiten-ta-//ken, had left Mowbray on 13 January 1875 to return home.
2. i.e. on account of what has occurred.

Dreams of home, and life with the magistrate

//Kabbo

L. II. 22. 1949–1964
24 AUGUST 1872

I dreamed of a lion that talked.[1] They talked to their fellows. I was listening. I saw them. They were black. Their feet resembled the feet of a lion. I was afraid of them. Their legs were many. They had hair. Their tails were long. I was afraid, startled awake. I looked because I was startled awake. I lay there watching carefully. Their tails had black hairs on the top. They were shod with hairs.

Going along, they told their fellows that they would hold on to the spoor and follow the springbok. For it was springbok spoor that went along. These lions went to the flat land.

I was startled awake. I saw the springbok spoor about which the lions had talked to their fellows. I saw that the springbok were numerous. I saw their footprints. I was startled awake.

I slept again. I dreamed that !Kwabba-an was staying at the house of people who were different. She asked me for tobacco. She asked me to give her something to smoke. I told her that I had smoked all the tobacco. I gave her the pipe which is here; she smoked it.

She asked me, 'What pipe is this?'

I told her that I had bought the pipe when I was with the magistrate. He took me to a white man's house.

She asked me where I was staying. That is what she said.

I told her that I would stay with my magistrate. She told me that I was not returning to her. She asked if I was still working; if that was why I had not returned to her.

I told her that I was not working. I have been teaching here.

She told me that she had seen springbok. Yet she was not eating springbok.

I told her that I had been waiting for her. /Hari≠kafsho was to have brought her to me. That is what I said. I talked to her.

Then the cow knocked with its horns in the house. I was startled

131

awake. I lay there watching. I stopped dreaming of /Hari≠kafsho. My daughter and my son lay there watching while /A!kunta milked the cow.

The day has dawned. The place is light. It is time to work. We must work nicely in the house.

/A!kunta turned the cow loose, while I lay there awake. He brought the milk to the house. He will wash the milk-pail, while I get into my trousers. I shall drink coffee. I shall take the broom.[2] I shall sweep the stoep nicely. I work nicely on the stoep.

Then I put the broom down and go to the cow's house. I take the rake and clean the path. I shall clean away little pieces of wood from my [*27 August*] house, so that my house will be nice and I shall walk over ground which is nice. Then I shall not fall down in the darkness, when I come to eat. I shall be able to walk over a place which is nice because I go to my magistrate in the darkness. I might fall down.

I also work for the cow in the darkness. When the place is dark, when it is night, I go to get water for the cow; when I cannot see the ground. I do this so that the cow can drink in the darkness, so that the cow will be full of the darkness's milk. The cow sleeps in the house, while she stands fastened. She ate grass which was green; which was wet. She can now drink water.

NOTES

1. There were two lions.
2. The /Xam-ka !ei sweep with bushes, J.T. (i.e., //Kabbo) says.

Gui-an and her mistress, Trina de Klerck

/Han≠kass'o

L. VIII. 19. 7657–7670
18–20 DECEMBER 1879

We were sleeping in one place, one house. When Doortje[1] got better, she told us that Trina[2] had beaten her because she had not washed the dishes, that she had not washed the dishes, so that Trina could give food to the people. There were two people, two men. They were Piet Rooi and Hendrik.[3] I am the one to whom Trina said that Doortje had struck her.[4] Doortje was the one who said to me that the mistress had beaten her about the dish-washing. The mistress had stood on her; the mistress had trampled her.

And Doortje came to the house. She became insensible because the mistress had beaten her. The mistress stood on her. The mistress had been trampling her. She had arisen, while she was still warm. She came home to her house. But when the wind was cold, she became cool, she became insensible, insensible. We lifted her up. We put her in to the house, while she was not breathing.

And the place became dark as she lay there, while she could not breathe.

Koos cried there, but the mistress said that Koos was deceiving. She said that Doortje did not want to work. She was lying down simply because she was lazy.[5] I was there, I saw that Doortje's breath was gone; her heart had fallen.

She was insensible. She was not breathing. When the night came, she recovered her breath; when night came.

[*20 December*]. The first beating that they gave Doortje. Sara said it was a thing with which Trina beat Doortje; and the white man (Jacob de Klerck) was the one who was beating Doortje with a reed.[6] It was the thing with which the white man was beating Doortje. It was the thing that caused Doortje to faint. Sara was the one who said so; she was there.

I was not present at the beating, when they beat Doortje. It was the beating about which Doortje said that she did not see well.

Doortje also said her master beat her on the veld because of a sheep about which she did not know. That was why her master beat her in the veld; he thought she had taken the sheep away. She did not know about the sheep, for the sheep there were not few, for the sheep were many. When her master went out into the veld, he saw the people sitting eating the sheep. And her master went for the [*untranslated word*]; he went to look at the sheep. He went to her because he saw that the sheep was fat. Her master went to her, he went and beat her. She also said that she fell down. She was at home.

NOTES

1. 'Doortje', whose youthful name was Wi!ta, was the wife of 'Koos Toontje', and the daughter of !Kau-/kutten (male) and Kebbi-an (female). The name of her father's (paternal grandfather's) place was /Kau or 'Jagspan'.
2. The wife of Jacob de Klerck of Klerksfontein.
3. The mistress did not wait for her, for she was still drying the mistress's things; for she also did not see nicely that she could quickly take up the things; for she looked well that she might take a thing up nicely, that she might not take a thing, while one thing stood upon another thing, and the things break, on account of it – the cups.
4. It was not true; for the mistress was ashamed before the wife of 'Klein Koos' Klerck who scolded her about 'Doortje'. Old 'Koos' Klerck also scolded his son's wife. 'Trina' did not a little beat 'Doortje's' child.
5. When a person does not work, the /Xam-ka !ei say, 'Our elder brother takes no notice of us (of what we ask him). He is one who does not work.'
6. A reed which is large. It is the one which people call //hui!kaka!nwa; that reed to which the white men say 'Bambush' (bamboo).

Hunting ostriches and bartering
their feathers for tobacco

//Kabbo

L. II. 7. 737–778
27 OCTOBER – 2 NOVEMBER 1871

The /Xam-ka !ei also hunt the ostrich. A /Xam-ka kui takes the ostrich; the ostrich runs away. He says to the ostrich, 'Ke! He!'

Another man says to him, 'The ostrich runs away over there.' The other man says to him, 'The ostrich seems to run out of the thorn bushes which are here.'

The other one says to him, 'Look at the place yonder.'

The other one says to him, 'The ostrich's house seems to be here. The eggs are here.'

The other one says to him, 'We must make a screen of bushes near the ostrich so that we may kill the ostrich.'

They make a screen near the ostrich. The other one says to him, 'The ostrich is coming yonder.' The other one asks him, 'Does a female ostrich come yonder?'

The other one says to him, 'A male ostrich[1] is coming yonder.'

The other one says to him, 'You must look out for it so that we may kill the male ostrich that is coming yonder, so that we may eat him as well as his eggs.'

The other one says to him, 'O Brother! you must truly shoot the male ostrich for us that is coming yonder, so that we may get its feathers. You will take its feathers to the white man yonder. He will give us tobacco, and we shall smoke.'

The other one says to him, 'You must watch for the male ostrich which is here, so that we may truly kill it, because we do not have feathers. [*28 October*] You will be able to take its feathers to the white man yonder, so that he may give us tobacco and that we may smoke.'

He said to the other one, 'I am the one who will kill the ostrich.'

The other man said to him, 'I am the one who will kill the ostrich that is coming yonder.'

The other man said to him, 'I am the one who will kill it.'

The other man said to him, 'I will kill it when it comes to me.'

The other man said to him, 'You must shoot it.'

The other man agrees with him: 'I will do so, for it appears to be coming to me.'

The other man said to him, 'I will do so.'

The other man said to him, 'Yes, my brother.'

The other man said to him, 'It now seems to be coming to me.'

The other man agreed with him, 'It does so.'

The other man said to him, 'You must lie nicely, you must not shoot the ostrich with an old arrow.'

The other man said to him, 'It seems to me that the bird is coming.'

The other man said to him, 'You must await quietly, so that it may come to the house, so that it may come quietly to the eggs. Then you must shoot it when it is standing in its house, when it [*untranslated phrase*][2] the eggs. You must aim at the ostrich with a new arrow.'

The other man said to him, 'I have not got a new arrow which feels nice.'

The other man said to him, 'I wish the ostrich was coming to me because you behave as if you are going to miss the thing.'

The other man said to him, 'You seem as if you will scold me when I miss that ostrich.'

Then the man lies down nicely. The ostrich first walks to the eggs. The ostrich stands. The ostrich looks at the eggs. The ostrich comes. The ostrich reaches the eggs, while the eggs are in the house. The man shoots the ostrich. The ostrich runs away, while the arrow remains in it. The ostrich runs away. The arrow falls down, but the poison is in the ostrich's flesh. The ostrich goes to lie down.

The men put the ostrich's eggs into the net. They drink the yolk. They carry the eggs, they carry them away to their wives. They go unloose the burden at the house. Their wives put down the ostrich eggs. They break the other eggs. They beat them up. They pour the yolk into two pots. They stir by twirling the implement between their hands. They stir the yolk with two gemsbok tails' hair brushes. They drink the yolk.

The wives ask their husbands, 'Did you not lie in wait for us at the ostrich's house for its meat?'

Their husbands said to them, 'We did lie in wait. It returned to the house. Your husband shot the ostrich. The arrow stuck in the ostrich. The ostrich was wounded in a bad place. The ostrich went to lie down.'

Her husband said to her, 'I did so.'

His wife asks him, 'Was the poison warm with which the ostrich was wounded?'

Her husband said to her, 'The poison was warm. We will follow the ostrich tomorrow.'

His wife said to him, 'I think that we cannot smoke. Therefore I was right, for it seems to have been a male ostrich.'

Her husband said to her, 'It was a male ostrich.'

She agreed with the man, 'Yes, my husband.' That is what she said.

They lie down. They go early on the morrow. They go to get its spoor. They follow it. They spot the ostrich which is lying down. They go round the ostrich. They go round, thereby coming close to the ostrich.[3] Hitting the ostrich, they turn it over. They take hold of the ostrich's head. They twist and break the ostrich's neck while they hold the ostrich's beak. The ostrich kicks with its legs. The ostrich dies.

They strip off the ostrich's feathers. They tie up the feathers. They put the feathers into the arrow-bag. They put down the bag with the arrows in it. [*31 October*] Then they strip off the ostrich skin which is black. They cut up the ostrich with their knives. They cut open the ostrich's belly.[4] They clean the ostrich bowels.

They roast the ostrich liver after they have made a fire. They make stones hot on the fire. They remove the stones with a stick.[5] They roast the ostrich's thighbone upon the heated stones. They roast the ostrich heart. They put the ostrich meat in the nets, which are numerous. They fasten the nets with sticks.[6] They tie the net strings. With a stick they lift out the ostrich meat. They knock the fire's dust off it.[7] They place it on the bushes to cool. They cut up the meat which has been cooked. They put it into their bags ready for their wives. With their knives they pick the bones clean of the little pieces of meat.[8] They leave the bones.

They put the cooked meat in the other side of the net, so as to keep it away from the raw flesh. Their wives will eat soon. They also save the ostrich bones for their wives, so that they will be able to eat out the marrow, so that they may eat roasted meat together with fat. [*2 November*] They carry away the raw ostrich meat. They put roasted meat into the bag. They go to their wives at their house.

The wives say to each other, 'Our husbands are coming yonder carrying meat.' They also say to their children, 'Your fathers are coming yonder carrying meat.'

The children say, 'Our fathers are coming yonder carrying meat.'

The fathers of the children arrive at the house carrying meat. They unloose the nets in which the ostrich meat is. Their wives untie the nets. They put the ostrich meat on the bushes. They eat the roasted meat. Their children eat the roasted meat. They eat the marrow from the ostrich bones. They cut[9] up the meat and put it in the pot.[10] They put the pot on the fire. They pour water in the pot. They make fire. They put the ostrich meat into the pot. The water boils. They stir the pot with the gipp's-hair stick.[11 & 12] They drink with the gipp's-hair stick. They drink soup. They drink fat, for they take up the fat.[13] They also dip into the ostrich fat with the roasted ostrich meat.

[*28 October*] The other man says to him, 'O brother! You must take the ostrich feathers tomorrow with the eggs. You must barter them for tobacco. We will come and smoke for we are craving tobacco.[14] For I will also seek ostrich eggs for us tomorrow.'

The other man takes the ostrich feathers and eggs early. He goes to the wagon.

The white man sees him as he comes. The white man says to the mistress, 'A Bushman seems to be coming yonder to bring us ostrich feathers and ostrich eggs.' The white man says so.

The lady also says so. She says to him, 'Let us wait for him, so that he can come and we can see him.' The man comes up to his cart, while the cart stands still. The Bushman salutes[15] him. The man salutes the white man; the man salutes the lady. The man salutes their children.

The Bushman begs him: 'Give me to smoke.' He says to the man,[16] 'I have not got tobacco.' The white man says to the Bushman, 'Give me ostrich feathers and I will give you tobacco to smoke.'

Then he gives the white man feathers. The white man thanks him. The white man gives him tobacco. He thanks the white man; he smokes. After he has saluted the white man he returns to his house. He also salutes the lady, he has saluted their children.

NOTES

1. Editor: It was the feathers of male ostriches that were valuable for trading.
2. Flaps its wings over the eggs, strikes them with its beak.
3. 'loop om drie, so, loop rond'. Editor: Dutch for walk around. This text gives a good idea of how Lloyd used //Kabbo's knowledge of the Dutch/Afrikaans language.
4. 'Op schnie' the 'pence'. Editor: Dutch for 'cut open the stomach'.
5. 'hal uit de klippe'. Editor: Dutch for 'take out the stones'.
6. Two long sticks.
7. The ground together with ashes.
8. 'Schnie kleine flesh (vleis) de been'. Editor: Dutch for 'cut small pieces of meat from the bone'.
9. 'Schnie'. Editor: Dutch for 'cut'.
10. 'ground pot' (earthen). Editor: For an account of how /Xam clay pots were made, see Bleek and Lloyd, 1911: 342–347.
11. 'gipp sein achter haar, he dick haar', which I understand J.T. to say, they put on a stick, and call /ku /ga =ka. [Editor: A more literal translation of the Dutch would be 'The gipp's back hair, it is thick there'].
12. /gi = the aardwolf, *Proteles cristatus*, a member of the hyena family.
13. They take up the fat from the pot by turning the stick with hair wound all round it, about on the surface of the soup. Editor: For an account of how these brushes were made, see Bleek and Lloyd, 1911: 348 and pl. 21.
14. The /Xam-ka !ei say his heart 'secht lusst de tabac' (J. explains). Editor: Dutch for 'I long for tobacco'.
15. Say 'morning'.
16. The Boer people.

PART II

Myth, ritual and belief

/Kaggen and his family

/Kaggen, the trickster-deity of the /Xam-ka !ei, features in a number of *kukummi*, most of which Dorothea Bleek published in *The Mantis and his Friends*, a book that has, unfortunately, never been reprinted. Although the name /Kaggen is usually translated as 'the Mantis', he is, except in one or two rare episodes, a man, not an insect. His wife is the Dassie (the rock rabbit, *Procavia capensis*), the Mother of the Bees. Their adopted daughter is the Porcupine, and she is married to /Kwammang-a, who comes from a family of meerkats (or 'pawed-creatures').

The Porcupine and /Kwammang-a have a son, the young Ichneumon (i.e. the mongoose, *Herpestes ichneumon*), who enjoys a close alternate-generations relationship with his grandfather, /Kaggen. /Kaggen's creation of the eland was a key, richly symbolic episode in southern San belief (see also Orpen, 1874). The tale records the creation of the supernatural power that San shamans harness and that permeated the entire San cosmos. /Kaggen was himself the original shaman (Lewis-Williams, 1996, 1997).

The Mantis also plays a role in *Kum* 30. Here /Han≠kass'o is at pains to emphasise the positive side of the Mantis's character.

How the Ichneumon discovered what the Mantis (/Kaggen) did with the honey

Diä!kwain
From his mother

L. V. 1. 3608–3683
27 DECEMBER 1873 – 7 JANUARY 1874

Editor's introductory note: *Portions of this narrative are included in Dorothea Bleek's composite 'First Version' of 'The Mantis makes an eland' (D.F. Bleek, 1923: 2–5). The complete narrative is published here for the first time. Diä!kwain's telling of the story is disjointed, and he switches from third to first person. Lloyd added an explanatory note (Note 1, below) to clarify the order of events. The cause of the apparent confusion may be partially explained by the circumstances that Lloyd describes in her Note 2. The confusion of this tale gives a good idea of the difficulties that Lloyd's /Xam-ka !ei teachers faced when they tried to sustain their dictation of a tale over a long period.*

The Ichneumon is a child. He went with the Mantis. When the Mantis cut honey, he intended to give it to the eland. He gave it to the eland on a flat, hollowed stone. When he had called the eland, he gave it to the eland. He had called the eland from the middle of the reeds in which the eland was, so that the eland would come to eat. The eland went back into the reeds, so that he could stand in the middle of the reeds when he had eaten the food. He went to stand in the reeds.

The people did not know that it was an eland to which the Mantis was giving the honey. Therefore they sent the young Ichneumon to see what the Mantis was doing with the honey. The people sent the young Ichneumon so that he could see what the Mantis was doing with the honey, so that he could tell them about it. The Mantis had told them that the honey was not fat. When he returned home, the Mantis said that the honey was lean.

That is why the Ichneumon will see what he does with the honey.

The honey which we cut is not usually lean. The young Ichneumon must look, for I did not believe the things which the Mantis told us.[1] Therefore the young Ichneumon must look at the man to whom the Mantis was giving the honey.[2] When the Mantis comes, he will tell us about it; he will deceive us, telling us that the honey is dry. Therefore the young Ichneumon must look, and I will know if it is true that the honey was dry; for the Mantis came and told us that the honey was dry. The young Ichneumon will himself see whether it is true that the honey was dry.

The young Ichneumon went with the Mantis. And the Mantis cut honey, while the young Ichneumon watched. The Mantis cut, filling the bag while the young Ichneumon was watching. His people had told him about it. When the Mantis was not listening, they had spoken stealthily to him about it: he must watch the Mantis to see what the Mantis was doing with the honey. The young Ichneumon should come to tell them about the Mantis, whether the honey was dry. Then we shall believe, because of the Ichneumon's report, that the honey is dry, if the young Ichneumon comes to tell us about it. I shall believe on account of it. Now I do not believe because it seems that the Mantis is deceiving us. If the young Ichneumon tells us that the honey was dry, we [*29 December*] shall believe on account of it.

When he had seen that the honey was fat, the young Ichneumon came to tell his brothers [his cousins, the Meerkats] that the honey was fat and that the Mantis had cut it, filling the bag. That is what the young Ichneumon came to say: he told his brothers that the Mantis had cut, filling the bag with liquid honey. They asked him what the Mantis had done with the honey, [*30 December*] and he told his brothers that the Mantis had given it to the eland.

And they questioned him about the place where the eland was. He said that the eland was in the reeds, and that it had come out when the Mantis had called. It had come to eat. The eland ate up the food. Then he told the eland to go into the reeds again. The young Ichneumon was looking through a little hole in the sack in which the Mantis had put him, so that he should *not* see. He saw through the hole in the sack which he had made by cutting it.

The Ichneumon's brothers questioned him about how the Mantis had called the eland. And the Ichneumon told them what the Mantis had said, how /Kaggen had called the eland. He called the eland.

His brothers then said, 'You must show us it, for these are things which the Mantis is hiding from us. We must see.'

When his brothers asked what the thing was like, he said, 'The thing is black; it is large.'

His brothers then said, 'You must go and show us so that we can see what it is.'

And the Mantis went away again for honey. They told the young Ichneumon not to go with him. The Mantis ordered him to go with him. The Ichneumon thought about it. His brothers told him not to go with the Mantis; they thought that he should take them to the eland. They told him not to go with the Mantis so that he might take them to the eland. These things must have been the reason why the Mantis had not been bringing honey.

The Mantis thought about it, that he had been obliged always to give honey to the eland. That was why he had not been bringing the honey home.

'When the Mantis has gone, the young Ichneumon shall take us to see if it is true what he said about a real eland.'

The young Ichneumon told them that it was an eland. They then said, 'We will go, so that we can see, for it appears to be truly an eland. It seems that the Ichneumon spoke truly. We will now go and see the things at the place to which the child shall direct us.'

And they went after the Mantis had gone. They reached the eland and sat down outside the reeds. And they questioned the young Ichneumon because they did not see the eland, for the eland was in the reeds. They questioned the young Ichneumon about where he had sat, where he had been in the sack into which the Mantis had put him. That was why he had cut a little hole: so that he might look at the thing to which the Mantis was giving the honey.

And the Mantis took up the bag, he took the bag to the flat hollow stone. And he poured in the honey.[3] He called the eland, and the eland came out of the reeds, while the young Ichneumon lay watching. And the eland came to eat. It returned to the reeds when it had eaten the honey [*5 January 1874*]. The Mantis arose from the flat stone when the eland had finished the food and went to take the young Ichneumon out of the sack. [*6 January*] And they returned home.

Those at home questioned the young Ichneumon about what the Mantis had said, how he had called the eland. And the young

Ichneumon told them about it, what he had said, how he had called the eland, and how the eland had come out of the reeds.

While the Mantis was in the veld seeking honey for his eland, they all called the eland. And it came out, on account of it, while another man sat holding a bow because he wanted to shoot the eland as it walked up to the flat stone. And the eland walked, coming up. The man shot it. And the eland, staggering, ran away, and fell dead. They went up to the eland and cut it up, while the Mantis was going to the honey.

When the Mantis arrived at the honey, it was dry. When he got there, he looked to see why the honey was dry on that day. He suspected that the young Ichneumon was the one who had done this, that he had taken his brothers. The young Ichneumon must have seen the eland through the hole in the sack. The Mantis did not know that the Ichneumon was cunning. It seemed as if the eland's blood was coming out.

'What is making the honey lean? It is not always like this. The honey is not always like this; for it is always fat; it seems as if a fight[4] has come into me (my home). Therefore I shall look for other honey, so that I can see if it be the truth, that a fight has entered me because of it, at home.[5] I shall leave the honey so that I can go to see. It seems as if the young Ichneumon is the one who has done this; he did it.'

The Mantis arrived at some other honey, and again he cut it out. This honey was also dry. He took up his quiver because of it and slung it on. Then he said that he would go so that he could see for himself. He went himself so that he could see, because he felt his body.[6]

'These things must have been the reason why the young Ichneumon would not go. His brothers must have put him up to it; that is why he would not sleep with me. He thought that, because his brothers had told him about it, he should not sleep with me. They wanted to question him. These are the things that I shall go to see; for it seems as if the young Ichneumon is the one who has done this. I shall go so that I can see if the eland is alive.'

And he went. He had no honey. He put down the quiver. He reached the flat stone.[7] He called the eland, but he received no answer.[8] He became angry. And he called again, but the eland did not come out.

He now said, 'Why is it that I do not always wait so long when I

call here? Why am I now calling for a long time? The eland will not
come out. The fight must have been true, it entered me (my home).'

He looked at the flat stone and noticed blood on it, where the
wounded eland had staggered. The Mantis turned back because of it.
He wept. He took up the quiver and ran along the eland's spoor as he
cried. He ran, going out on a little bank; and he saw the people standing and cutting up the eland. The young Ichneumon was with them.
And he slung the quiver over his head,[9] because he saw the people. He
saw the young Ichneumon with them.

Then he said, 'These are the things that I told them about, what
the young Ichneumon must have done. This is what he did; for the
people are standing here cutting up.'

He took out an arrow because he wanted to fight the eland's fight.
He ran up to the people because of it. He planted his foot and shot at
the people. And the arrow came back.[10] The arrow passed over his
head, and he dodged it. The Meerkats continued to cut up the cooked
meat,[11] feeding themselves with the eland's meat which they were
cooking. They knew that these arrows would not kill them. Therefore
they continued at rest.

Then the Mantis said, 'There is still an arrow here, standing in the
quiver, with which I will shoot you. It will hit you.'

He ran near and shot, but the arrow came back, passing over his
head. He saw that he would kill himself. He let alone the arrow[12] and
ran to the people. He thought he would beat them with the knobkerrie. And he ran up to the people while they continued to stand and
eat, cutting meat to feed themselves. He ran, coming up. And he
asked the Meerkats why they were doing what they were doing, and
why they had killed his eland.

And he put down the quiver and took out the knobkerrie. He
planted his foot; he intended to beat the Meerkats.[13] But the Meerkats
snatched the knobkerrie from his hand. He put down the knobkerrie
and took hold of the Mantis[14] [*7 January*] and beat him, laying him
upon the eland's horns. And the Mantis jumped up and ran away
because he had slipped out of the other man's hands.

And he called the quiver, so that it would follow him, it and the
veldschoens. As he went running, he called the things so that they
would follow him. The quiver went after him to the house, and the
veldschoens.

And a man asked him where his things were. He told the man that the Meerkat was the one who had beaten him. Therefore he had fled, leaving his things. His things had themselves followed him to the house, those which he had called. For the eland's fight was that which had come upon him; the eland which he possessed, its fight had come upon him. Therefore the people wanted to kill him upon the eland. He said that on another day he would get the Meerkats when they were alone because they had killed his people. The Meerkats had beaten him violently on the eland's horns.

People asked why had he taken the young Ichneumon with him. Did he not know that the young Ichneumon was cunning?

The Mantis said that he had thought that the Ichneumon was a child, that he was not cunning. But the young Ichneumon was cunning. 'Therefore I took him with me. I wanted him to hold the bag for me, so that I could put in the honey when I had cut it. He should hold the mouth of the sack open for me. He went to tell his brothers that I had given the honey to an eland. The young Ichneumon went to tell his brothers that the Mantis had given the honey to a large thing. And his brothers said that they would go to take the eland out of the reeds, the place where I had put it.

'Therefore the young Ichneumon took his brothers to show them the place where the eland was, the place where I had put it. I put him into the sack. I do not know through what part of the sack he saw the eland. I had put him in before I called the eland; that is why I did not know that he had seen the eland. He was already in the sack. That is why I did not know that he had seen the eland. That was why he was willing to go with me. He must have refused. I[15] should have realised this at the place over there, to which he was willing to go with me. That was why I suspected. I had continued to call him, but in vain. I saw that he was unwilling to go as he usually did. He did not always behave like this. I left him at home because I thought he seemed as if he would do thus.

'Today, I saw the young Ichneumon doing this. Today he behaved differently from his usual behaviour. That was why he was unwilling to go with me. That was why he refused. I suspected that he must have heard a story from his people; for when I came back from the veld, he was unwilling to sleep with me that night. The darkness had come out the honey's cutting.[16] It was the night on which he was not willing to sleep with me. I suspect that that night was the one during which the young Ichneumon told his brothers about the eland. I think that was the night during which he told his brothers. For he did not come when I called him to eat. He said to me that he was going to eat at his brothers' house. He was not going to eat the Mantis's food. He would eat the food which the Mantis was willing to give him another day. Therefore the Mantis suspected that the young Ichneumon had heard a story which his people told him. That is why he behaved differently from usual: he did not sleep with me. The place over there is where I saw the young Ichneumon when he was with the Meerkats.

'These are the things that the Meerkats must have told him about the eland: what he should do when he went out with the Mantis. He should watch me to see what I did with the honey and to what thing I was giving the honey. These are the things which they must have put the young Ichneumon up to; that he would watch to see what I was doing with the honey. That was why the young Ichneumon took his brothers to the eland. He went to show his brothers the eland. That is why they went to kill it, when he took them to it.

'And they killed the eland. They also fought me about the eland when I fought the eland's fight. Therefore the Meerkats struck me violently upon the eland's horns. The other people continued to stand and cut up the meat to feed themselves.[17] They continued to stand, watching while the Meerkats struck me violently upon the eland's horns. I ran away because of it. I told the quiver to come, it and the shoes, that they might follow me to the house where I went to wait for them.'

The shoes arrived, they and the quiver; they reached him at home, as he sat at home. The Meerkats, carrying meat, came to their own house. They went to eat the eland, to eat it up.[18]

NOTES

1. David H. tells me that when the /Ni-opwa (the Ichneumon) went the first time (having been put into the sack by the Mantis before the eland came out of the reeds), he saw nothing; so when he returned home and told his brothers that he had seen nothing (having been put into the sack by the Mantis), they advised him

to take a small stone knife or splinter in his mouth (the next time he went), so that he could cut a small hole in the sack with it, and see. This he did, the second time he went, and returned home and told them about the eland. The third time he went with his brothers to show them the place, and they killed the eland.

2. [*6 January 1874*] David H. told me the tale this way, the first time he told it, but not when he dictated it to me – so I note the right story here. It was difficult for him to dictate at first, which is probably why I could not get this properly, as he first told it to me – I have now heard again that this *is* the right story.

3. The stone was concave in the middle.

4. Editor: The /Xam word /*ā* can be translated as 'fight' or 'curse'.

5. Where the eland lived, not /Kaggen's own abode.

6. That his body was not right, D.H. says.

7. A broad flat stone, with a hollow in the middle.

8. The eland's usual reply was to come out of the reeds, not to call.

9. His arms were now more free, and he could draw out the arrows with his right hand from the quiver which was now on his back on the right side.

10. This is the custom of /Kaggen's arrows. Editor: The Meerkats had acquired the power of the eland (Lewis-Williams, 1997).

11. D.H. explains, that /*Kwai an-ka en* is flesh cooked with hot stones. They were not afraid of him, because they knew that his arrows would not come to them.

12. One that remained still in the quiver, D.H. says.

13. He intends to beat one *xara* (Meerkat).

14. By the lower part of his legs.

15. /Kaggen is now talking to /Kua about it.

16. When he (Mantis) had returned home, D.H. explains.

17. With baked flesh, i.e. flesh cooked with hot stones.

18. Another adventure of /Kaggen's comes here [Editor: The next tale in the note-books concerns the mythical being with eyes in its feet, also called the *Will-o'-the-Wisp*; Bleek 1924: 13–15] which happened afterwards, when he had been at home recovering from the fight about the eland. This was also related to D.H. by his mother.

The Mantis's fight with the Cat and the Ichneumon's rebuke

//Kabbo

L. II. 9. 966–1005
DECEMBER 1871

When the Mantis saw the Cat he fought it, and the Cat fought him. That is why the Mantis grew feathers and flew into the water. He spoke to his things. He said that his things should of themselves follow him because he went forth first. He spoke with his mouth, and his things felt that they always listened. Of themselves they rose up. They followed him while he flew along speaking. He did not walk along the ground so that he could pick up his things because his head had been broken in haste.

For the Mantis always used to speak to his things. The Mantis felt that his things always used to speak. His things understood why he was acting so, as his head was badly broken.

For our friend beat Cat-head. The Cat puts his head into the earth. We beat his tail; but we miss our stroke. He puts his head out of the ground and he beats our head. We beat, hitting his tail. His head is in the earth, because he has hidden his head. He hides it in the ground. He puts his head out of the earth. He beats and he scratches us with his nails.

The Mantis says, 'O Ichneumon! You must wake up, you must not sleep, for I really am dreaming of the morrow. Morning will quickly break for me. I shall quickly go and do as you say, for I did not see Grandfather[1] (the Cat) well. I saw him disappear, for he hid his head. It was the Grandfather who beat my head. Grandfather's head was in the ground. For Grandfather thought that he was clever. I am not as clever as Grandfather. I must understand as he does, for he understood me. I was foolish.'

Ichneumon says to him: 'You really must let me sleep. You were foolish to start a fight because you do not fight well enough. You must never again get into a fight. I really will quickly dream of the morrow.'

153

The Mantis did so: 'My head wounds do not ache; I shall sleep. My heart is not sweet; my heart feels as if I fought too quickly. Grandfather Cat must also get wounds, because I have wounds.'

The Ichneumon says to him, 'You really are one who does not fight well. You fear a fight. You fight as if you could not see your adversary. Whenever you meet someone, you fight. You also fought !Gwe-!kweiten-ttu here. Then you fought the Cat even while your head was still festering from the fight with !Gwe-!kweiten-ttu.

'Then you fought the Cat here. Your head will again be festering because the old wounds on your head are still festering. You fought again. You did not see the Meerkat go to skin the eland which /Ki-ya-//kos shot. So you started another fight. You do not listen, as an old man should. You keep on starting fights.

'While my grandmother[2] waits for you at the place where you were, you keep on starting fights. Whenever you see folk, you start a fight. You do not bring food home even though you are close to food. You do not bring ostrich eggs; all you bring home are your wounds. Your skin does not seem to ache, because your skin seems to feel cool. You seem to shoot an arrow with a bow. You will be killed if you start a fight. Your ears do not seem to hear about starting fights. I will no longer be still. I am talking to you now, but I shall keep quiet in future.

'You will have to watch with your own eye. You are obstinate even though I talk to you. You feel as if you are in the middle of a fight. You do not listen. You close your ears to my talking. You do not pay attention. I speak to you, you hear, but then you start a fight. You come home with wounds. You come screaming to lie down in the house. I question you. You tell me that you fought. I question you. You tell me that you did not fight well.

'You dreamed of the day; you said so. Then again, you went to fight a man. You did not fight well. You flew away because you did not fight well. Then you fell silent. You must not dream again of the morrow. You must really allow me to sleep while you stay at home, while you remain in the house.

'You must not again go looking for a fight with a man. You should come home carrying food, but you bring nothing home because you keep on fighting. I thought that you were seeking ostrich eggs, but you did not think of looking for ostrich eggs. You seem to think only of a fight.

154

'You do not think that you will be hungry. You will still become fat with this fat. You will not be hungry. You should imitate your friends. Your friends seek food for their children. But you are not finding food. Instead you start fights. You should look for ostrich eggs for your wife. You should bring them to her as she sits waiting at home for you. She does not eat people; ostrich yolks are what she eats. You do not bring food to the house; because you do not do right. You seem to hear, but your ears are shut. Then your thoughts are not with us.

'Even a little child becomes wise because he tries to understand; he understands a little. I am merely a child; I understand what people say. [*2 December*] I feel that we who are little children have our thoughts. A little child can merely drink milk nicely, because he tries to look at his mother's breasts. He tries to get the milk. He sucks from her. He is still small.

'We who are grown up should always understand. Then we seek meat. We hunt the springbok. We hunt the ostrich; we will shoot the ostrich; we will eat meat. We shoot the springbok; we will eat meat. We will look for ostrich eggs; we will eat them. We do not hunt other men in order to get into fights with them.

'We go to hunt meat; we do not eat other men. Meat is what we eat, when we know that it has hair. That is what we shoot. We carry meat to our children. We will shoot meat. We will cook it on the hunting ground. We give our children meat that is cooked. They will come to us to eat because we really give it to them. That is why they grow up. They will be with us when they are grown up because we have brought them up. They will grow up. Then we will have many people.

'You put aside your shoes when you ate the Proteles's meat.[3] You moistened it and put it on to roast. Then in the middle you thought that you would eat the other. Then the Proteles's mother put you on to roast; because you turned your back when she had already given /Kwammang-a another little Proteles. You turned back as we were returning. You seemed to go halfway in front. He said so himself, but he thinks that you would not listen.

'You pretended to have warmed your foot by the fire. You put aside your shoes. You sat eating. And we walked away. Then you missed the shoes, you mislaid the shoes. You spoke to me about it. I told you that you must go back. You told me to pick up your shoes because you had forgotten them. But I told you to go back yourself. You should go and pick up the shoes because I was returning home.

'That is why you got burnt while you were lying next to the fire. The fire burnt you. Then your arms grew feathers because you were lying burning by the fire. [15 December] You flew out of the fire because you were burning. When you were writhing in the fire you got feathers. You flew out of the fire so that you could quickly go to cool the fire's blisters. You flew into the water. You wet your flesh. You became a devil lion⁴ when you were in the water. Your arm's feathers were washed off. You became a new Mantis (devil lion).

'You seemed as if you had been carrying your belongings all along because the things themselves went to you. Talking, you came to the water to wet and loose the feathers.⁵

'Then your wife asked me if you had been with me. I told her that you had turned back for your shoes that you had forgotten. You put the shoe into the bag. You said that the shoe had been left behind, while you had the shoe with you. You stood talking about the shoe because you were roguishly deceiving us. You returned for the other Proteles but the mother Proteles was cross. Then she went to peep at you. /Kwammang-a did not turn back.

'When the sun set, you turned back. I told your wife to wait a little because you had turned back in the dark to the Proteles's house. You must have gone back and got burnt. You turned back in the dark after the sun had set.'

NOTES

1.   Editor: Because the Cat is a 'pawed creature', he is probably a member of the Mantis's son-in-law's family and hence grandfather to the Ichneumon, the Mantis's grandson. The Mantis, in accordance with San custom, has a more informal relationship with his grandson than with his son-in-law, /Kwammang-a. That is why the Ichneumon is able to scold the Mantis. This tale is therefore probably one of the many that deal with social stress between affines (Lewis-Williams, 1997; Lewis-Williams, 1998).

2.   Editor: The Porcupine, the Mantis's wife.

3. Editor: The following paragraphs evidently refer to another Mantis myth that Bleek and Lloyd did not otherwise record.
4. Editor: Lloyd here uses the old translation of /Kaggen, 'devil'. A 'mantis-lion', a literal translation, was probably related to concepts of shamans turning into lions. See Lewis-Williams (1997, 1998) for more on the Mantis as the original shaman.
5. Wash off, I believe.

The Ichneumon argues with the Meerkats

≠Kasin
From his mother

L. IV. 2. 3520–3533
NOVEMBER 1873

[*15 November*] The Meerkat was the one who shot an eland. He went out early on the morrow.[1]

He found the eland's spoor because he was looking for it. He spotted the eland as it was lying down. He went to the eland. He went to put down his things. For he was going to cut up the eland.

They (the Meerkats) took out knives.[2] They sharpened them. They then flayed the eland with them. They finished flaying. They cut up the meat.

One stood upright. He saw the Ichneumon coming. The Ichneumon walked towards them. The Meerkat who had seen the Ichneumon told the other Meerkats that the Ichneumon was coming to them. The Ichneumon was alone. The Ichneumon came.

The Ichneumon said that the Meerkat should not cut up the eland, because the Meerkat was a child. The Meerkat was silent. He continued to cut up the eland. The Ichneumon walked up to the Meerkat. The Meerkat now looked at the Ichneumon.

The Ichneumon now said, 'You, the Meerkat, are a grown-up man.'

The Meerkat told the Ichneumon that he (the Meerkat) was not a grown-up man; for the other one, [*17 November*] the Ichneumon, had said that he (the Meerkat) was a child. Therefore, the Meerkat told the Ichneumon that he (the Meerkat) was not a grown-up man. The Ichneumon said that the Meerkat should not talk, for he, the Ichneumon, now saw that the Meerkat was a grown-up man.

The Meerkat continued to talk about it. The Ichneumon had said that he, the Meerkat, was a child. The Ichneumon should let him alone about it.

The Ichneumon insisted on saying that he would fight the

Meerkat. The Meerkat insisted on saying, 'What is it that you (the Ichneumon) want to fight about?'

The Ichneumon said, 'I do not want to fight. You do not understand me.'

The Meerkat said that the Ichneumon was the one, he who was the Ichneumon.[3] Another Meerkat should take hold of the Ichneumon so that he could throw his head against the ground.

The Ichneumon now said that he would take hold of him. But the Meerkat took hold of him and lifted him up. He threw his head on the ground. The Ichneumon ran away, on account of it.

The Meerkat now asked why the Ichneumon was running away. Another Meerkat now said that he now was surprised[4] that he did not stand his ground, [*19 November*] that he ran away, because it was he who had been talking about fighting. He who was the Ichneumon, he was the one who did not stand so that he could fight.

Another Meerkat said, 'Let him alone about it, for he spoke like a man about it.[5] Let him go on his way.[6] The other people must finish so that they can go home. For, they (the Ichneumons) fight on the hunting ground when they seek food; while they are not here while they are good. The Meerkats see the place seems thus. They see where they can be or live. This place was not comfortable when they were at it. The other one, the Ichneumon, seems to do that which the other one (the lion) did to the jackals. He seemed as if he would take up this thing (the eland). Therefore he looked.

It seemed as if the people should seek food for him. He should look at what the people are doing: [*untranslated paragraph*]. When they see that there is fat they fight, for they are men. They do not seek food; they are as if they were men. They seek people who are different, their food. They do not seek so that they may feed themselves by shooting (game).

NOTES

1. He did not follow it up at once, but went back to the house, because the sun went down.

2. The *xara* [Meerkats] were now numerous, in order to cut up the eland; he was alone when he shot it on the previous day.
3. i.e. he was the one who had first wanted to quarrel.
4. 'verwundert'. Editor: Dutch for 'amazed'.
5. i.e. spoke like a man who can stand the fight.
6. 'He can *mal loop*'.

/Kwammang-a is found by crows

/Han≠kass'o

L. VIII. 2. 6147–6157
JANUARY OR FEBRUARY 1878

The crow went, it went and ate up the piece of fat halfway on its journey. So the people sent another long-necked crow, *xurru*. They hung around its neck a piece of fat. Again, it went and ate up the fat. It turned back and finished the fat halfway. Therefore the people hung the piece of fat round the neck of the pied crow, *!kagen*. That is why the pied crow was the one who took the fat to the place at which /Kwammang-a was. It arrived at the place where /Kwammang-a lay. He lay fallen at it.

Thus it came flying. It said, 'Ga, ga! Does /Kwammang-a go, while you go?'

And /Kwammang-a spoke. He said, 'You must go and say that grandfather's people must come to take me out, for I am hungry as I lie in here.'

Therefore the pied crow flew away, while it still had the fat round its neck which the people had hung round its neck. Therefore the fat lay white against its neck while it felt that it was the one who had taken the fat to the place at which /Kwammang-a was. It still had the fat round its neck. Therefore it took off the fat. It took back the fat. Hence the people of the house espied the fat which it still had round its neck. That is why the fat, altogether white, covered up his neck. He was the one who brought the fat home, for he did this to the fat: he had it round his neck. Therefore the part of the fat that was on his breast remained on his breast, while the piece of fat that was lying on his neck lay white on his neck.

That is why we who are Bushmen say the pied crow is *!kagen*, for we think that the feathers are white on his neck; they are white on that part of his neck where the fat formerly lay. Therefore we say *!kagen* to him.

Animal tales

The Bleek and Lloyd Collection is rich in tales about animals in which the material and spiritual realms merge. Often, animals behave as if they were people, and shamans (both female and male) intervene in daily life. Some tales, such as *Kum* 27, end with a moral. Many other tales deal with social tensions, especially between affines. *Kum* 31, like *Kum* 2, is remarkably long and shows how a /Xam narrator could develop and dramatise a tale.

The lion and the jackals[1]

≠Kasin

L. IV. 1. 3485 REV. – 3492 REV.
11 NOVEMBER 1873

A jackal went out two days running and on both days shot an eland. Both times the lion came and deprived him of it. Twice the jackal went home and complained about it, and the people at home were hungry.

The first day the sorceress[2] told them not to talk but to be silent. On the second day the sorceress advised him to remain at home the following day, which he did. She caused the bushes and water on the earth below to vanish away, so that an eland would come right up before the house. She did this by her power. The jackal shot it close to the front of the house while the sorceress was looking on.

Then she made a tall mountain, the eland rising dead upon it at the same time. (This */kou/*[3] was a long, tall mountain with a round flat top upon which she put the houses and water.) The houses were many upon it, also the people. They all went up on it, as it rose up.

The lion came on the ground below and looked and saw no bushes and, on looking further, found that there was no water, and also no stones. He looked about and saw that the jackal people were on the mountain far above him.

He walked about and sought water round the mountain. He asked the jackal for water to drink. The jackal deceived him and said that he had no water. The lion asked again for water, but the jackal again said he did not have it and that he was without water.

The lion was very thirsty and asked again. The jackal said that they had no water, and that the lion could see for himself that the earth was dry. The lion asked again for water. The jackal again said that he was without water.

The lion asked, 'Why do you make such a great fire if you have no water?' He saw the fire up above them, like stars.

The jackal showed him eland fat in a dish. The lion wanted it to

165

be poured into his mouth. The jackal said no, because it was for the children.

The lion asked again that the fat should be poured into his mouth. The jackal said he would do so, but that the lion must wait a little.

He went and said to the other jackals, 'The lion is asking us for fat.'

The other jackals told him to get a stone and heat it. Another jackal took a stone, and they all heated it. The first jackal went and told the lion to wait. He went back and asked the others if the stone was heated. The others said yes.

They took the stone out of the fire. The others told him to take fat from the pot which was on the fire and to fill up the dish.

The jackal again showed the lion the fat. He said to the lion, 'You must not look (for fear the fat should go into his eyes). You must shut your eyes and open your mouth.'

Another jackal held the wet eland's skin. He held the stone with it, so that his hands would not be burned by it. The first jackal held the dish of fat. He drew back and told the other one that the lion had closed his eyes.

The other jackal dropped the stone into the lion's open mouth. The lion sprang back because the stone had burnt his throat in going down, as well as his mouth. He ran away, burning in his inside, his chest and cavity of his ribs. He died while he was running away.

The jackal looked, which he could do well as the place was bare of bushes, and said to the others, 'The man lies dead.' All the jackals stood and looked.

They said that the lion was a strong man. How was it then that he was not strong with fire? The jackals said that he had seemed to be a strong thing, but he was really only a little thing who had not been able to resist a small stone. They said that they, the jackals, are little things, but the lion has a large body. That they are like a little stone.

Notes

1.   An English translation of the story of the Jackals and the Lion (taken down quick-

ly from Klaas in /Xam chiefly; and a little in Dutch in the way of explanation, which I could not understand well). Editor: Guenther (1989: 149–151) gives the longer version of this tale (L. IV. 1. 3485–3515).

2.   Editor: Bleek and Lloyd translated *!gi:xa* as 'sorcerer'. The word means 'shaman', 'healer' or 'medicine person'; literally, one who is full of *!gi:*, supernatural potency.
3.   Editor: The *Dictionary* gives /kou as 'ridge, kranz, overhanging cliffs'.

A gemsbok becomes a lion

*/Han≠kass'o
From his maternal grandfather, Tssatssi*

L. VIII. 31. 8775–8782
31 AUGUST 1879

He[1] used to stalk, to lie in wait for gemsbok. He went to lie in wait. He went to put down the arrow. He went to put down poison. He stalked the gemsbok when it was grazing there.

Stealing along, stealing along, he came, came, came, came, came, crouching he came. He saw that the gemsbok was grazing at a place that was bare, where there was no bush that he could go to hide behind; for the gemsbok was feeding at a place that was bare. So he walked away. And the gemsbok saw him, and the gemsbok did this: when the gemsbok saw him standing, it became a lion. When the gemsbok saw him standing there, the gemsbok, afraid, turned from him and became a lion. The gemsbok behaved in this manner: the gemsbok went.

When the gemsbok was a lion, the man walked along looking at it. He did not look where he was treading when he was walking along, for he was walking along watching the gemsbok, and he saw the thing which was a gemsbok become a lion. The gemsbok had no horns which the gemsbok had had.

He stepped on an arrow, for he was walking and looking at the gemsbok. He trod, placing his foot on an arrow [*untranslated line*]. The poison of the arrow tip stood upright. [*Fragmentary translation*] The poison stood poisoning his wound.[2]

NOTES

1. I do not know his name, for it was his brothers whom I knew. /Khokengu was the younger, /Karru was the elder. His younger brother was /Khoku. They were Berg Bushmen. 'Klaas Streep' was his grandfather. His brother-in-law, Willem Streep, was !Khwo!ku. His other name was !Kabbi !Koin.
2. Editor: The rest of the story is untranslated, pages 8782–8788.

The old woman who was carried off by a hyena

/A!kunta or Klaas Stoffel
From his mother

L. I. 2. 151–158
AUGUST AND SEPTEMBER 1871

[*11 August*] The hyena carried the old woman away on his back, as she lay in the house. The hyena carried the old woman away to the mountain. The hyena went to throw her on a pointed rock. The old woman sprang to one side; she sprang and sat on this side. She got up and beat the hyena.

The old woman went to get fire. She returned to singe the hyena. She cooked the hyena and ate it. She sang, she went away, singing about the hyena.

The hyena had carried her away, as she lay in the house. Her children heard her, as she came singing about the hyena. The children said, 'The hyena carried away my mother.'

Another child said, 'The hyena, he carried away my mother, as she lay in the house. The hyena carried her away to the mountain. The hyena went to throw her on a rock, but she sprang to one side. She stood up; she beat the hyena. She went to fetch fire. She came to singe the hyena. She cut up the hyena and cooked the hyena. She ate the hyena. She returned to her children, for she was fat. The children said, "Look, Mama is fat!"'

The mother said, 'The hyena carried me off. He carried me on his back to the mountain. He went to throw me on the rock. But the hyena himself, the hyena killed himself. I arose. I beat the hyena. I killed him. I broke off a piece of rock. I cut up the hyena with a stone knife. I cut up the hyena. I cooked the hyena in a pot.[1] I ate the hyena's meat. I cut the meat for myself. I cut off the hyena's meat. I drank the soup. I roasted the hyena's head. I put the fire over the hyena's head. They burned. I took them out of the fire as they roasted. I cut up his head. I ate them. I carried the hyena's meat.'

She went along singing, for the hyena had carried her away, as she lay in the house. The child heard her, as she came, singing about the hyena. The hyena carried her away, when she was in the house. The child said, 'My mother comes singing. She comes singing about the hyena. [*11 September*] The hyena carried her off.'

The child said, 'The hyena carried my mother. The hyena carried my mother away to the mountain and went to throw her on the rock.[2] She sprang and sat on one side; she turned. She stood up. She threw the hyena's head on the rock. The hyena lay dying. She dashed the hyena's head on the rock, as the hyena lay dying.'

[*16 September*] The old woman sang, going along singing. The old woman went singing about the hyena. The hyena lifted up the old woman from her house. The old woman sprang aside. She did not just sit there. [*18 September*] She arose. She beat the hyena. The hyena himself, the hyena killed himself.[3]

NOTES

1. The old pot, the children having taken away the good one.
2. The pointed rock on the mountain, where the rock was split into needle rocks.
3. By casting himself violently on the pointed rock, where he had intended to cast the old woman who was on his back, who sprang aside, and saved herself.

The /Kain-/Kain, the girls and the Mantis

/Han≠kass'o

L. VIII. 3. 6271–6303
FEBRUARY 1878

My mother /Xabbi-an told me this story. As her father Tssatssi had told it to her so she told it to me. So I tell the story.

The /Kain-/Kain[1] used to go up to a girl when she lay ill.[2] Then he told the girl how to get up. The girl should put *!kau !kauiten*[3] upon him. When the girl had got up, he stabbed the girl's breast with a knife. Then blood poured from the girl's nose. He picked it up. Smelling it, he put it on his own nose. Then his nostrils went red.

Then they went away while the girl lay there. They went to seek another girl, another hut.[4] They went up to another girl. He told the girl to get up and that she should put *!kau !kauiten* upon him. He stabbed the girl's breast when she got up. And the blood of the girl's nose poured down. And he took it up and smelt it. Then they left that girl.

They came near the house where the Mantis was. The Mantis had dreamed of them, that they, the /Kain-/Kain people, were coming to molest the girl. The Mantis did this: early next day he instructed the people that the girl's mother should give the girl a sharp knife. She should let the girl lie down with it. For the Mantis dreamed that the birds were coming to molest the girls. That is why the girl's mother should give her a sharp knife. He had dreamed that the birds would come the next day. Therefore the girl's mother gave the girl a sharp knife. She who was the girl's mother gave it to the girl.

The girl's mother spoke to her about it. She said: 'You should not play with the birds, for you must listen to what Grandfather Mantis says to us, that the birds have come to molest the girls. Grandfather Mantis said so today. Therefore you must not play with the bird when it comes to the hut. You must stab the bird to death when you feel that the /Kain-/Kain is coming in to smell you. For the bird will kill

171

you if you play with it.'

Therefore the girl lay down with the knife. Then when the bird came, the girl lay holding the knife, ready to stab. She did not look, she listened to how the bird came rustling. She was listening to it. And she felt that the bird came to sit down here; then the bird spoke.

The bird said that she should get up, she should put *!kau !kauiten* on the bird. Then she stabbed the bird. She plunged the knife into the bird's *!kau !kauiten*. Then the wounded /Kain-/Kain went away.

Then, returning, the people came together. They said, 'You see the bird is as Grandfather Mantis told us. You see the bird as it lies there. The wings seem to have crashed into the ground.

'That is why it behaved like this and came early, avoiding us whilst we had dispersed to gather [*unintelligible word*]. Then it flew down because it came early to avoid us. That is why it has flown down. It did this. Therefore you can see that the /Kain-/Kain people are scattering because of it.'

For the thing there seems as if the girl were stabbing them all, as if they had been going about[5] together. The /Kain-/Kain people are those whose feet are running away in all directions. They are afraid of the child even though she does not run after them. For she stabbed the bird. She lay down. They run as if the child were pursuing them, as if the child were not lying down. But the child is not pursuing them. They are running; they go in fear as if they had gone about together. They are those whose feet run away from the child. I think that the child has done this: she has stabbed one of them so that they might stop killing the girls.

Our brothers[6] flew[7] after the molesters when they left them, that they could kill going and coming[8] to the girls. Therefore our brothers flew after the girls. The girls were fetching water for their mothers. They kill, letting them disappear. They have come to kill us, as if they feared having molested the girls.

The people say, 'That is why I want you to behave nicely to Grandfather Mantis. For he is the one who thus dreamed about it and told us. He dreamed about the people, and he told us about it. He spoke the truth.[9] Although he teases, he speaks the truth. We can now really see what he told us. The people say that he lies. People seem to think he does not act like this (i.e. tell the truth) when he teases. He sounds as if he were lying. He speaks like this because he is a man who teases. That is why he seems to be a liar. But he really spoke the truth, for we have seen what he told us about. People are accustomed to say that he lies, but we have seen what he told us about. He is not deceiving us now. He has told the truth. We have seen the thing which he told us about, that he had dreamed about. Later, we saw the thing that he had told us about earlier. Later we saw the thing that he had told us about in the dark, early in the morning. We saw it in the afternoon.'

Notes

1. Editor: The *Bushman Dictionary* (p. 297) gives */kain-/kain* as 'a certain bird with black beak and breast, red bill and legs'.
2. Editor: A girl at puberty. See also *kukummi* 52–56.
3. Editor: Lloyd was unable to find a translation for this word.
4. Editor: A hut in which a girl is secluded at puberty.
5. Editor: It seems that Lloyd translated the /Xam word *tin* (*Dictionary*: 203) here as 'advance' (p. 6292 & p. 6294) but prefaced it with a question mark. The *Dictionary* translation has been followed here as it is more idiomatic English.
6. Editor: Lloyd translates '*kanni*' (p. 6295) as meaning brothers, but prefaces her translation with a question mark. The word appears not to be listed in the *Dictionary*.
7. Editor: The phrase '*!goe ya*' is translated as '? flew after' (p. 6296).
8. Editor: Lloyd was not sure how this phrase should be translated (p. 6296). The sense of it seems to be 'that they could kill them as they drew near and left the girls'.
9. Editor: This is one of the tales in which the Mantis, contrary to popular, present-day perceptions, is beneficent. This is therefore a highly significant account of the Mantis.

The first /Xam man brings home a young lion

//Kabbo

L. II. 26. 2320–2504
L. II. 29–30. 2597–2779
L. II. 31. 2780–2873
JANUARY–JULY 1873

Editor's introductory note: It is not clear why sections of this very long yet coherent tale were left untranslated. Perhaps Lloyd found them repetitive. In any event the tensions of the story are unimpaired, even though the narrative sometimes doubles back on itself. The notes were added by more than one informant.

The first /Xam man, !Khwe //na ssho !kui,[1] was the one who went and spotted the lion's children. He lifted up in his arms the first little lion. He held it in his arms and brought it to his house. He came and put it down.

His wife asked him, 'What little dog is this? It looks different. That is why its head is like this; its ears are not long.'

He said to his wife, 'My younger brother gave me the dog which is here. He thought that I should feed it and bring it up; he said so, he spoke to me.'

His wife said to him, 'It is a young lion which is here.'

He said to his wife, 'You must not speak like this of my younger brother's dog.'[2]

His wife said to him, 'You must not say that because this is a young lion; its head is large; its feet are different; its hair is red.'

He said to his wife, 'This is a young dog [*untranslated and obscure line*].'

His wife talked softly to the children and they agreed with her.

He said to his wife, 'Because we do not eat young gemsbok, you must feed the young dog. He is here nicely for us, so that he may run and catch young gemsbok for us; that we may eat meat.'

His wife said to him, 'The mother lioness will follow your spoor because you have brought her young lion to our house.'

She said to her little son (her eldest son), 'Oh! Child! This is a young lion.'

She said to her husband, 'You must bring wood for us so that we may lie down next to a fire; when you have put down this young dog.' She thought that she would talk to the children.[3] Her man agreed.

Her husband went to get wood, while she thought that she would talk to all the children so that they would understand. She thought that, while her man was still collecting wood there, she would quickly talk to the children so that they would understand, so that the children would know that the animal was really a little lion. Her husband agreed and went to get wood.

She said to the boy, 'Look at your father!' She asked the boy, 'Is father near?'

The boy looked in the direction of his father and said to her, 'He is not near.'

She said to the boy, 'I thought that your father could hear me speaking to you.'

The boy said to her, 'You can speak to me, because I am now standing so that I can watch for him. He is still getting wood over there. I am watching him so that you can speak to me.'

His mother said to him, 'I feel that you think that the animal is not a young lion. Its head is like this.' His mother said to him, 'Look at its eyes: they are large. Its eyes are yellow and shining.'

The young lion looked at the child's mother. The mother said to her child, 'Look at it! It looks at us when I speak its name.'

The young lion looked around.

She said to her little son, 'You will be afraid when you are out with your father. Father has deceived us into thinking that this is a dog. It is a young lion; its mouth is large. I came and told your father to tie up this dog, to put it away, for I do not know this dog that your father brought us. Its head is like this. [*7 January*] I never saw a dog like this, for this dog is the one that your father brought us.'

The mother lioness called, and the young lion suddenly raised his head. It listened. The woman pinched her son: 'Look! This is a thing which is different.' She was speaking softly to her son; her son was also speaking softly to her: 'I am now afraid. Now I understand.'

She said to her son, 'Your father has stolen a young lion; yonder

175

its mother calls. She is asking, seeking her child.'

The boy's mother said to him, 'You think that the young lion will not run away when it has grown up; but your father has deceived us. He is a foolish fellow. That is why he brought us a young lion. The mother lioness will continue looking for it, and come to us.' She said to the child, 'You must therefore wait to see what happens.' The child agreed.

She said to the child, 'Your father will feed it and rear it. You seem to disagree, but I speak the truth.'

The child agreed, 'You speak truly. I understand. This is a thing that walks by night. It is different: a dog's feet are white; a young lion's feet are hairy; a dog's feet are not hairy.[4] The backs of its ears are black; the tips of its ears are not long; they have short points. This is because its parents eat people.[5] Therefore it understands that it is still a little lion. You see that it listens, even though it is little because it understands. It is still a little lion. It knows that it is the night's little thing. Therefore it listens. It listens nicely to its mother. It listens because its mother is the one who used to call like that when it was with her. Therefore it listens nicely. Its mother must be looking for it. That is why its mother cries, trying to find it.'

She (the woman) asked her husband, 'Oh! My husband! Why did you bring to us a young lion?'

[*8 January*] Her husband said to her, 'This is a dog that my younger brother gave me. I asked him for this dog. Why do you stare at the little dog as if you do know what it is? You do not look nicely at my younger brother's little dog. The dog's father looks like this; that is why the little dog resembles its father: it feels that it is a little male dog.'

His wife said to him, 'This is the dog which you dreamed about. It will become angry with us. I am afraid of it.'

Her husband said to her, 'The dog's mother looks like this. She will come so that you can see her when my younger brother goes with her.[6] He told me that the dog's mother kills gemsbok.'

She said to her husband, 'You are deceiving me so that I will think that this is a dog. This dog will kill me. The dog's mother yonder, over there, is calling; it makes a noise like a lion. What I hear is a lion. It was a lion that used to do this when I was still living with my parents. A lion does thus: the lion cries. I can see that this is a little lion.'

Her husband said to her, 'You are the one who is saying that I dreamed about this dog. But I did not dream like that. I asked for it so that we could own a dog.' Her husband said to her, 'I shall take this dog out with me. It will chase a young gemsbok for me.'

He slept. The little dog watched as they lay in the house, they and his wife. The little dog made as if it would spring upon them. The man scolded the little dog. His wife continued to pinch her son because she had said that the child should lie down with her so that she could pinch him so that he would lie watching and not sleep. She held the baby under her arm.

The young lion got up and went away. It went and sat upright. It lay down.

Her husband arose first; his wife got up after him, when he had made the fire. He picked up his quiver and slung it over his shoulder. He took out the knobkerrie and put it under his arm. He called the dog's name and it went with him.

His wife said to the child, 'The young lion goes yonder. You can see that it pretends that it did not look angrily at us, but it does look angrily and it does smell our scent. It feels that it is a thing which goes by night. It kills people. It eats people.'

The young lion went stealing up to her husband, but he spoke very angrily to it.[7] The young lion let him alone. The young lion truly went and killed a young gemsbok.

The man ran up to the young lion. The young lion came forward to meet him. He spoke very angrily to it, and it cantered back. It growled as it went. Trembling, the man reached the young gemsbok, [*9 January*] and the little lion lay down. The man dragged the young gemsbok away; he dragged the young gemsbok away to the *!khui*[8] (a large tree).

He laid down the young gemsbok, and the young lion looked at him. He scolded the young lion. He called the young lion's other name, the one which he had given it. That was the young lion's name with which he made a dog of the young lion, so that he could always use it when calling the dog. The young lion listened to its name. The young lion knew that it was a young lion. It heard its name which was !Kui-sse-!khwi-/ku.[9] It lay looking at the man who had carried it off when it was little. The man called its name. The man called, enticing it, so that it would listen to its name.[10]

The man took up little bushes so that he could put the young gemsbok on them, so that he could cut up the young gemsbok and its meat on them. He cut out the young gemsbok's lungs. He called !Kui-sse-!khwi-/ku. !Kui-sse-!khwi-/ku galloped forward. He threw the lungs to !Kui-sse-!khwi-/ku. !Kui-sse-!khwi-/ku caught them and swallowed them. !Kui-sse-!khwi-/ku looked steadfastly at him. He scolded !Kui-sse-!khwi-/ku. He took the young gemsbok's heart. He called !Kui-sse-!khwi-/ku. He gave the young gemsbok's heart to !Kui-sse-!khwi-/ku. !Kui-sse-!khwi-/ku caught hold of his hand, caught hold of his hand together with the heart. He quickly snatched his hand away from !Kui-sse-!khwi-/ku's mouth, as !Kui-sse-!khwi-/ku swallowed the young gemsbok's heart.

He said, 'Why is it that this young dog is catching hold of my hand?'

He cut off the young gemsbok's neck and gave it to !Kui-sse-!khwi-/ku. !Kui-sse-!khwi-/ku came and caught hold of his hand. Again he hastily snatched away his hand. He picked up his stick and threatened !Kui-sse-!khwi-/ku. !Kui-sse-!khwi-/ku sprang away with the young gemsbok's neck.

The man thought that he must go away before he had cooked any of the meat. He talked to himself. His thoughts[11] talked to him. He said to himself with his mouth that he must go away because the young dog did not look nicely at him. He feared that he would be thrown down and held, because the young dog had behaved in that manner. It had come, catching hold of his hand.

He said to himself, 'I ought to go away because this young dog was snatching at my hands with its mouth. I sprang aside, in front of the young gemsbok on account of this young dog. It behaved like that. It seemed as if it wanted to throw me down and hold me in the darkness. I shall return home while the sun is up so that I myself may watch the young lion.'

He quickly prepared his load so that he could lift up the young gemsbok quickly and so that he could watch the dog as he went. He put his arms into the skin of the young gemsbok's feet. Standing up, he lifted it up.[12] He took up his quiver and slung it on. He called the dog's name as he walked away. He called the dog as he walked. The dog cantered across to him. The man trotted forward.[13] He stopped trotting and walked. He trotted with the one leg; he walked forward with the other leg. He looked at the dog and thought that it would catch hold of his back. He grasped his stick so that he could beat the dog. He went, dragging his feet along the ground. He saw his house. The dog saw the house.

The woman said to the child, 'You must look around for the lion. You must put long pieces of wood in the fire. We will throw fire at the young lion. For it was a young lion which father brought to us; it has grown up.'

The young lion saw the fire and galloped back.

Her husband went calling after it. The child heard his father as he called so that the woman would stand up. His wife said, 'Listen! It sounds like a man calling.'

The child got up and saw his father. 'My father is the one who is coming there. He comes dragging his feet along the ground as he carries.'[14]

His mother said to him, 'You must watch for that dog [*10 January*] so that you will be able to see it and throw fire at it while it is still coming. It must come running into the fire. I shall hold the shovel[15] so that I can throw fire at it.'

The child spotted the young lion coming galloping. He said to his mother, 'It is truly the one which is coming there.'

His mother said to him, 'You must pick up fire so that you can stand, holding the fire, so that we can throw fire at it. You must hurl fire-sticks at it. [*11 January*] We must throw fire at it so that it will spring and turn back. We must drive it away from the house. It must lie down for us so that your father may first come to us, he who brought this dog. For this dog has not behaved well. It is the one of whom we must be afraid so that we may first spot it over there. It looks like a thing which we eat. You must listen to your father. He is coming, calling to us.'

The child said to her, 'He is coming near.'

His mother said to him, 'You must take the fire because a lion is coming over there. You can see its face; its face is yellow. It is the one whom we must greatly fear; for it is a lion who is like this.'

Her son said to her, 'You must scoop up the fire so that you can quickly throw fire at it. I will throw a fire-stick at it so that it will quickly turn away from us, so that it will first lie down,[16] so that father may first come to us and may drive away the dog. It must allow us to eat first. We were afraid there, next to the young gemsbok. [*13 January*]. That is why we did not eat it. You heard father coming and calling so that we would know that the dog is coming. We must stand up so that it will see us. The dog seems to be coming to attack us. You are the one who heard father.'

Coming to attack, the dog reached them. The child said to his mother, 'Throw fire at it! I shall throw fire-sticks at it as it goes past. I shall throw fire-sticks at its body so that I shall hear the stick strike the lion's body, while you throw fire into its face. Then it will spring back. Your little boys will now throw fire-sticks at it. You can hear it coming, growling angrily. It must jump back opposite to us. Your husband must come first. He is the one who always calls its name. I now hold two fire-sticks.'

He asked his mother, 'Oh my Mother! Have you put the small child on your back so that the fire will not burn it when we throw sticks of fire at the person coming over there? It is now near. It now comes close by.' He said to his mother, 'You must scoop up fire because you have now taken the little child on your back.'

His mother agreed: 'I have now done so. You must stand outside so that it will pass you. I am the one who must stand in front of the house, by the door. I am the one whom it must see, as I stand.'

Her son said to her, 'The animal that your husband brought was a lion. My uncle's dog did not behave like this.'

The young lion came up to them. The boy called to his mother, 'Quickly, throw fire at it so that I can hurl my fire-sticks at it.'

His mother threw fire at it. The young lion sprang away. The boy hurled sticks of fire at the young lion, while his mother scooped up the fire. His mother threw fire after the young lion. The boy also hurled fire-sticks after the young lion as it sprang away to leeward. It cantered across in front and lay down. It lay in the shade. It lay growling.

Then the boy's father came to his mother at the house. Standing, he talked to his wife. He said to his wife, 'While I was cutting up this gemsbok, I was afraid, because of the dog that is lying here, the one that your brother-in-law[17] gave me.'

The woman scolded him: 'You were the one who brought us this dog, because of your foolishness. You behave as if your mother had not taught you so that you would understand. You are the one who went and took up a young lion. You came and deceived me with it; you said that it was a dog, but it was really a young lion. It was always like this when you deceive me. The young lion here will kill a child of mine, for it watches while we are lying in bed in the house; it does not sleep. I was the one who lay looking, while it sat upright above us. That dog is the one which is here; you brought it because of your foolishness. You did not see my brother-in-law; you deceived me. My brother-in-law is with his father. You are speaking falsely to me so that I will believe a lie, but it is really a deception. It is the one with which you have deceived me. You carried off the child of the mother lioness. The mother lioness is the one who is looking for the young lion which lies here.'

The young lion looked at the woman who had called its name, which was 'young lion'.

The child said to his mother, 'Oh! My mother! Be silent! The dog is looking at you.'

His mother said to him, 'Do you not see? You seem to think that this is a dog. Father did not broil meat for us because he was afraid; he feared the dog that is lying over there. He was afraid there, next to the young gemsbok which is now here. That dog is the one that my husband has fed. It is the one that will kill him.'

Her husband said to her, 'This dog met me, while the young gemsbok lay on the ground.'

His wife said to the child, 'Listen to your father [*14 January*] talking about this dog. What did your father's thinking-strings do so that he thought so wrongly? He brought a young lion to us. He was the one who said that !Kui-sse-!khwi-/ku was here, a lion which eats people. It understands the eating of people; it feels that its parents eat people. That is why it smells that the scent of people is like this.'

The man said, 'I kept myself alive by throwing something at the young lion, at the dog lying yonder. It thought that it would kill me, laying me down next to this gemsbok before I had gone to it. It was driving me away from this gemsbok. I thought that I am a man, hence I hit it with stones. It left me. Then it went and lay down opposite me. I went to the young gemsbok. That is why I did not cook; I first returned home hungry because I felt that the dog which lies here was watching me very closely today. It was the one to which I was obliged to speak very angrily, while I was cutting up this gemsbok. I

felt that lion used sometimes not to dream nicely; for the dog seemed
to be angry with me. That is why the dog went and thought about
killing me.'

The woman said to him, 'A young lion is here.'

He said to the woman, 'You must not speak like this about my
younger brother's dog.[18] He will be angry with me because I spoke
about the dog that he gave me; while you do not keep quiet for me. I
am the one who must speak about the dog.'

He poured out water and set down the water at a little distance.
The young lion looked at the water, while the man held a stick. The
man went back. He called the lion's name which was !Kui-sse-!khwi-
/ku. The young lion cantered forward; it cantered up to the water.
The young lion drank; it looked at him. He looked behind him at the
young lion; he looked behind his back. He went to sit down in the
house.

His wife said to him, 'Why is it that you do not cut up that gemsbok, so that we may eat its meat? You are the one who did this; you
did a bad thing, that was not handsome. It is ugly. I now have to
throw fire.'

Her husband said to her, 'The dog did this; the dog resembled its
father; that is why it did this.'

His wife was winking at the child, her son who had thrown fire-
sticks with her.

Her husband said to her, 'I thought that I would call as I came, so
that you would hear me, because it seemed as if the dog would kill
me on the hunting-ground. I saved myself by throwing stones.'

The dog looked hard at them.

She nudged her son with her elbow and said to him, 'You see! The
dog over there is looking angrily at us, while the lying man sits there.
He is the one who lied to us. [16 January]. He cheated us. He wanted
us to think that this is a dog, but it is really a lion. That is why you
fear it. You know that the lying man who sits here deceived us; he
brought us a young lion. I must have married a liar; he was the one
who brought a young lion. I am afraid, sitting next to this gemsbok;
that is why I do not eat.'

She went on saying to her husband, 'Oh lying man! Quickly cut
up the gemsbok so that we may soon eat, so that you can throw bones
to the dog lying over there.'

Her husband replied, 'I have already given it the lungs. It swallowed both of them. Then I threw it the gemsbok's heart; it swallowed it. It continued to look strongly at me. Then I cut off the young gemsbok's neck; I gave it the neck. I quickly snatched my hand from inside its mouth; its mouth felt hot. Therefore I menaced it with the stick; it sprang away on one side because it feared the stick. It still looked, waiting for another piece of meat. It continued to watch me as I was returning home. That is why I came along calling out so that you would stand up.'

His wife said to him, 'Are you the one who did not see that it was a lion that you brought, with which you came to deceive me? Therefore I spoke to this child, so that he would be very much afraid of this dog; for it is really a lion. I am the one who sees that it is a lion. It is the one that is usually like this. Its hair of its legs will be black when it becomes a grown lion. It is still a young lion. You thought that I would not realise, but I was always one who understood. I am an understanding person. I am one whom my mother counselled. I knew. I always recognised the lion. I saw the lion's hair; for I am truly a grown woman. I am not a young child, that I might be foolish. You tried to cheat me, I who am grown up. You are deceiving me. You seem to think that I did not really know you, that you were trying to cheat me so that I would not know, but I always knew you. That lion, it is the one which is lying down.'

She said to the child, 'I want you to be with your father so that you can watch him. You must stay at a little distance and come softly behind him so that you can watch the dog when it has killed a gemsbok. And then you must sit hidden so that you can watch your father when the dog has killed a young gemsbok. Then, when your father is by the young gemsbok, you must come forward because the dog will catch hold of you while father is looking at the young gemsbok. You must therefore find an arrow, so that you can stick in another arrow.'

[*Untranslated from page 2426 to page 2438.*]

[*18 January*] The man said to the dog, 'Sit down over there!'

The dog walked back and sat down.

The child said to his mother, 'I am now watching.'

His mother said to him, 'You must not sleep; the day must break while you are still lying awake. You must watch the dog sitting over there, that which is not a dog.'

Her son said to her, 'It is a thing that walks by night. It looks at us, killing. That is the animal with which my father deceived us. It may kill us.'

[*Untranslated from page 2440 to page 2458.*]

[The mother is speaking] '... The dog thought that it would go early and hold him down so that it could eat him. The dog thought that it was hungry. He was the one who scolded the dog. Therefore I thought that you should be with him early. You shall see tomorrow when you go; and then, you must come to tell me so that I may know. And then I shall speak to you, for an untruthful man has deceived us.'

The child agreed: 'I now think that when morning ... [*7 lines untranslated*].'

His mother said to him, 'You must keep behind him. You must walk after him. As he goes along, you must keep yourself to one side. So that you can watch the dog. And then you must stick in the arrow. You must always remember that it is a young lion, so that you may kill it. You know that it is not a dog. It is a lion that the lying man brought to us and of which we are all afraid.'

The day broke and her husband arose. He made the fire, while the young lion was sitting upright. It sat looking around. The man made the fire. The child sat holding the bow. His father prepared to leave so that he could go. He put the things together; he put the things together. The child also got ready. He slung on the quiver. The man went out of the house, and the child went with him. They both went, going out of the house.

They went near to the river. The young dog went down into the bed of the river and went along, keeping in the river bed. The child ... [*untranslated page*]

[*3 February*] The young dog approached them stealthily. The boy said to his father, 'Why is it coming towards us?'

[*Untranslated from page 2466 to page 2490.*]

The man said to the child, 'You must come and run near to me, because the dog is going over there. It seems as if it has smelt the young gemsbok. For the young gemsbok is now crying.'

The young dog was catching hold of the young gemsbok and biting it. The man called to the child, 'Oh! Child! You must run and come near, so that you can run after me, so that we can both go to the young gemsbok. The dog has bitten it and thrown it down.'

The child thought that his father was deceiving him and that they might all die. The child took an arrow. His father, running, looked back at the child. He saw that the child had set in an arrow in his bow. He called out to the child, 'We do not shoot the dog's gemsbok; we beat it and kill it with a stick.'

The dog bit, killing the young gemsbok while the man was still running along. The dog looked towards him, when it heard his foot rustle, while he came. [*untranslated line*] He spoke very angrily to the dog. [*untranslated line*] The dog cantered back away from him. It went to lie down. It lay [*untranslated word*] its tail. It looked back at the child who ran and hid. The child, watching, went past him. They reached the young gemsbok and dragged it away.

The father said to the child, 'You must watch the dog because I am cutting up meat; so that I may cut up quickly.'

The child watched the dog. The man finished cutting up the young gemsbok. He cut off the young gemsbok's heart and called the dog. The dog galloped up to him. He threw the young gemsbok's heart to the dog. The dog caught at it with its mouth and swallowed it. The dog stood [*untranslated word*] its tongue. He cut off the young gemsbok's neck. He threw it to the dog. The dog snatched it together with his hand. He sprang to one side.

He said to the child, 'We must go. You see this dog; because of it I have had to spring aside next to the young gemsbok. That is why I have not eaten.' The child agreed.

They made ready the load and went. The man called the dog. The dog cantered slowly. The dog was listening to him. The child thought that he recognised the shape of the dog's ears; that is, that it was a young lion; for a grown lion was like this. They drew near to the house. The dog was listening to the house. The dog was cantering stealthily up to the house. The father called to the child's mother.

She stood up. She said to the children, 'It sounds as if that dog is coming. Your father is calling to us. You must help us to make up the fire because the dog is coming. We must do so, so that we can throw fire at it, for it is a lion that is coming. It cannot be a dog. A lion behaves like this.'

The child ran along next to his father. They continued running. They ran, being loaded. The young lion reached the child's mother, and she threw fire which was burning at it. The young lion sprang away. It went to lie down. It lay down lashing its tail. It lay watching. Running, the boy's father reached the house; he was weary. He unloosed his load.

The child said to his mother, 'Oh! my mother! We have been afraid because of the dog lying over there. It is not really a dog. It is not like a dog, for it is like this.'

His mother said to him, 'It must be a lion. It is like this, it has tear furrows.[19] You must look: his eyes are yellow. His ear tips are short. You must look: his ears are in the hair.'

Her husband said to her, 'What are you saying about your younger brother-in-law's dog? The dog looks like its father. The dog is angry like its father. Your younger brother-in-law told me that the dog's father behaves like this. That is why I am afraid of the dog. You too must fear the dog. You must throw fire at him, so that he will fear fire; for he is an angry dog. I must be among you, I who know his name. Saying his name makes him lie down. I am still while he lies, listening to his name. He looks up. He looks at me.'

His wife cuts up the young gemsbok's meat and puts it into the pot. The dog walks, coming.

The man says to the dog, 'Stand over there!'

His wife says to him, 'Cut the meat quickly, so that you can throw it to the dog.'

The man cuts off some meat and throws it to the dog. The dog jumps across in front of the meat as it flies through the air. He catches the meat and takes it away in his mouth. He goes to lie down; he eats lying down. He swallows the meat whole.

The woman winks to her son. The man sits watching. She seems to look past the child so that she can wink at the child. She points stealthily with her arm and says to the child, 'You must watch the lion. It is still a young lion. You must wait for it to grow up. You must watch it when it kills gemsbok. You must be afraid when you are with your father because this is a lion which was stolen out of the bushes. This deceiving man was searching for ostrich's eggs which the hyena seemed to have hidden. He saw a little lion, while the lion cubs were sitting together. He picked up a little lion. It has grown so that he could teach it to recognise his scent.[20] The little lion must smell his scent so that he can know him by smelling. In the absence of a dog, he possessed a lion cub, so that he could feel as if he had a dog. In fact he possessed a lion cub.'

The child said to her, 'Oh! Mother, the dog runs and stands next to your husband. It looks as if it will come when it has grown up. It looks as if it will kill the little gemsbok together with the man.'

His mother said to him, 'That is why I am talking to you about it, so that you will know that it is not a dog. It is a beast of prey that was stolen. It was stolen out of its mother's house when its parents were away. You must look at its face.'

The child said to her, 'Oh! Mother, the dog thinks that your husband will give it meat. The dog is moving its mouth. The dog is behaving as if it is angry with your husband. It is looking strongly at him.'

His mother said to him, 'I thought that you ought to look at the dog so that you could see the dog's face for yourself. The dog's face is yellow, its hair ... It is different from a dog. It behaves like a thing which kills people.' [*10 February*]

[*Untranslated from page 2614 to page 2687.*]

[*13 May*] The child's mother said to him, 'You must go so that you can be with father, because a little child is one who talks. You must go closely behind father's heel and watch carefully on each side. You must watch the dog, and when its sees a gemsbok, you must run to stand close behind father as he drives the young lion away from you all. For the dog ran, nearly catching father; it sprang past father.'[21]

The child said to his mother, 'Oh! Mother! I was startled and sprang behind father's back. I stood trembling on the other side of him, because I thought that the dog had turned. It ran away, jumping, as we arrived at the place where the young gemsbok lay dead. [*15 May*] The young lion passed in front of us and then lay down. That is where it lay, lifting up its head to watch us. I looked steadfastly at it, because I thought that it was going to come. I thought that it would catch me at the back of the neck, throwing me down, if I did not hold the young gemsbok's legs for your husband.[22] I looked around for my bow. I thought that I would take up the bow and jump away. I shall shoot, for this must be a beast of prey. I know its eyes; its eyes look through its hair. They are large. Its nose is large. Its mouth is round. It seemed as if the lion would swallow us. Our feet would slip down into its throat as it swallowed us whole. And then it

187

would catch another person. It would swallow him down too, for it seemed as if it would do so. For it swallows the young gemsbok's neck whole.

'This is a dog which was stolen. It is a thief's dog. That is why it does not eat its parents' food, which its parents eat at night. They think that they walk about in the darkness. They catch things by night. They eat them. [*31 May*] By eating people's food, it will cause itself to grow. Father cheated us into thinking that this is a dog, but it is really a beast of prey stolen out of the thick bushes. It takes the place of a dog because he did not have a dog.

'He saw the gemsbok's children with his eye.[23] He did not run and catch them because the legs of the gemsbok's children are many. They run away swiftly. He has only two; that is why he left the gemsbok's children alone. He returns hungry; hunger is here. He searches around among the bushes so that he can bring home a young beast of prey.

'I, his son, was not with him and did not see him; for he was alone. I was not with him and did not follow the young gemsbok's spoor with him so that we could shoot it. [*6 June*] He looked around for the spoor of the gemsbok's children. He came home. He lies down hungry. He bound the net round his body. He does not drink. Therefore he is peeping about among the large trees. He appears not to fear.

'We will wait in vain for him when he is eaten up, when the beasts of prey have eaten him, when his bones are dry, when a mother beast of prey drags him into the bushes. For he does not understand. He is a rogue because he cheated us. He thought that we did not know him. He deceived us. He believed that we would think that this is a real dog, he who is an old man. We have indeed seen grown beasts of prey that kill people. They bite people, so that they can eat them. This dog runs towards the lion when it roars.'

His mother said to him, 'The mother lioness calls, seeking the cub. That is why you saw the cub run towards its mother. It went to sit down. When its mother was silent, it listened. Then it cantered back. That is why it sat upright, staring steadfastly at the place where its mother roared for it. Its mother must be looking for it. She roars because she smells the scent of a man's foot. She smells the cub's scent, where the man picked it up. The man took it away.

'First he went to look for ostrich eggs, but he did not bring us ostrich eggs. Instead, he brought a young lion. We are afraid here. Our parents think that we are at peace, but we are afraid, here in the darkness and solitude, for we are not among people. [*9 June*] The people who lived together with us for some nights in various places saw the things that we saw, what father brought to us. They saw it with us, the things that he himself did.

'He saw the lions in the bushes as he walked about among them. [*10 June*] He was the one who brought the dog at which we now stare. It lies looking, watching and thinking about killing. It does not listen and watch for jackals; it watches us inside the house. It lies thinking about catching a man. That is why my dish, made of the breastbone of the ostrich, was near by. It was near the fire. Father must fetch thick pieces of wood so that he can make a big fire, so that it will be red, so that the dog will see the fire, so that the fire will not go out, so that it will remain alive. The dog may catch us and lift us up in the darkness when we are sleeping. Father must place the stick next to him so that it can lie near him; so that he will be able to snatch it up quickly, so that he can beat the dog for us and make it jump away. I shall stand up and dip the dish into the fire. Then I shall throw fire at the dog so that it will burn the hair on its head. For the hair on its head is thick. Then it will spring away.

'You must first pick up the bow so that you can shoot, even though you do not think that this is a real dog. This is not a real dog. This is a beast of prey. Father deceives us with this beast of prey so that it will eat us. You must know because you talk with understanding. You are grown up. That is why you talk with understanding. You yourself, you understand, you talk well. That is why you understood about this dog.

'You must sharpen the arrow-heads. You must go, holding the arrows in your hand. You must lay them upon the bow so that you can shoot quickly when you see the dog spring between you at the place where you lie hidden. When you see the dog catch hold of father, you must run away so that you can tell me. You must escape from it when it bites and kills father. You must keep behind the tree at your back, the one behind which you lay flat on your back.[24] [*12 June*] You must run away so that you may run quickly, springing behind the other bushes. You must also spring behind the little hill.

The hill must lie behind the little child's back, as he runs in great haste, so that descending, he can run quickly. That he may come quickly to tell us; for the beast of prey is used to chasing a little child, if the little child runs slowly.

'That is why the little child must hurry. He looks behind him so that he can run and turn back behind the hill. Then the beast of prey will pass behind him while he runs hidden behind a little hill. That is why he will still be alive and will be able to tell us what happened when he returns. He knows that *he* is the one who returned running, while the beast of prey turned back. It returned quickly to the thing which lies there behind it.

'The lion thinks that the man will go away when he comes to life, but the man does indeed lie dead.[25] The lion also thinks that the vultures will eat his man. Therefore he hastens back. He first gallops a little about looking for the child's spoor. Then he turns back; so that he can go quickly to carry the man away from the ground which the blood has soaked; so that he can go quickly to hide the man under a large tree. Then he fetches another thing, so that he can carry it back to the large tree.

'Then the lion will be angry in the tree, angry with the jackals which scent him and come to him, so that they can watch him. They arise; they walk around. The lion looks and growls; then the jackals sit down. The jackals bay, begging the beast of prey for meat, because they are jackals. One jackal begs; it yelps when it begs, and the beast of prey becomes angry with them. The beast of prey catches a jackal and kills it. [*16 June*] He carries it to the other place so that he can put it alongside the other thing, so that they all can lie under the bushes.

'He will become hungry as he lies there. He became thirsty while he guarded the jackal and the gemsbok. So he first lies down, making himself hungry. Afterwards, he will eat. Then he will look for his parents; listening, he will look for them. He remembers that he lived with a man. That the man was the one who stole him and picked him up. The man made a dog of him. Therefore, the lion ate people's food; that was what he grew up on. The young lion did not grow up on the food of darkness, that which his parents ate; he truly smelled people's scent.

'He thought of his parents, that their scent was not like this; for this is like people. Their scent is like this. The scent was different. His parents' scent smelled of things of darkness, because they are beasts of prey that lie in the darkness. They lie under the bushes. They lie in the shade under the bushes. Therefore they smell of bushes' [this particular bush's] scent.[26] They have hair; therefore they do not have fire. They are things which stealthily approach and carry off people by night while the people are asleep. Running, they also take people away by night. They bite, holding a man in their mouth. They softly steal up to a man, so that they can kill him and they can eat him.

'This young lion, he who is here, father made a dog of him. Father cheated us. He found it at the lioness's house. We shall wait for father, but he will be in the lion's stomach. He will have been swallowed, while the sun is still up. We shall wait for him, because we shall think he is cutting into slices the gemsbok that he shot dead. But he is eaten up. For the lioness, whose child father stole, will come to the man; she will catch him, while the sun is up. She will bite him dead.

'The lion comes to her while she is eating there after she has carried off the man. She carries the man away to her house so that the lion's children can eat with her, so they can all eat. The he-lion also comes to eat. They all crunch the man's bones. And they all go to the water because of the bones. [*17 June*] Then they go to sleep in the water's reeds, so that they may sleep, lying among them.

'That was the lioness about whom father deceived us when he stole her child. He thought that I did not think properly. In his thoughts, I was foolish and he was the one who understood. Therefore he deceived me. But he is foolish; he is cunning; he is a man who is cunning, on his other side. He is foolish in his thoughts. He is a liar; therefore he lied to us about the lion about which we know the truth. Its ears look as if someone had cut them when it was already a grown lion.[27]

'Therefore I want you to be with father. Then you will be able to talk nicely to your grandparents because you know that you were the one who saw, with your own eye, what the dog which father gave us did to him on the hunting-ground when he was not at the house with me. I could not see what the dog did to him. For my husband came and told me that. I did not think of his (living) body, that he appeared likely to live on the hunting-ground.

'I thought that this dog would kill him on the hunting-ground.

For it seemed as if the dog would spring and catch hold of us while we sat eating the young gemsbok's meat. Swallowing, it looked at us, while it swallowed down the back of the young gemsbok. It did not break it by biting it. He swallowed it down while it was still whole. This dog swallows down things which are big; it is here.

'It thinks that it lived in the bushes. The dog was stolen, while the mother lioness was hunting. She left the child at the house so that she could kill a springbok and bring it to the child. The lion's children which are grown-up, they themselves hunt; they kill and feed themselves. A small lion-cub is the one that sits alone waiting at the house for its mother. It does not yet walk. Its brothers are those who hunt with its sisters; they all go out. Its mother is with the male; they hunt together. The children play around their parents, springing about and catching hold of each other, so that, playing, they can go together when they kill a springbok. They eat; then they go to sleep together.

'And when the sun cools down, they come out of the shade with cooled bodies, when the evening's shadows are long. They play as they go to the house, while their parents are still far off. [*18 June*] Their parents return to them carrying a springbok so that the small lion-cub, who lies hungry at the house, can eat.

'Therefore father went and picked it up while it was waiting for its parents. Father was the one who saw the old lions' spoor. His thoughts [or thinking channels?] were closed. Therefore he brought us a /aken-sse, so that it will kill us all when it becomes a grown-up lion. Therefore our grandparents will not know about us, because they do not know how father brought this young lion to our house, the one with which father deceived us. He said that his brother-in law gave us this young dog. He was the one who gave the dog.

'Father gave the dog this name[28] when he was alone and thought that you, my son, were not with him, so that you could listen to him. He was going along alone when he called the name. He thought that he would say the name when he came to the house. Sitting there, he would call the name to teach the dog so that the dog would know its name, so that the dog would listen to its name. Uncle did not give the dog this name, for my brother-in-law does not have dogs like this. This is a dog which came out of the solitude which it inhabited.

'Now it is here. We look hard at its eyes: it resembles a thing of terror. That is why we fear. It does this: it intends to kill us, it wishes to eat us. You will not be able to shoot it, because father will prevent you. You shoot because you think that it is not our dog, for it is a dog of darkness that came out of the darkness which it inhabited. There it did not see people with a red skin. Instead it saw its parents who have hair and who have four legs. We are the people at whose house the dog will smell fire. He was stolen out of the darkness which he inhabited. He would have grown, lying in the darkness and never seeing people. He would have lain sleeping with his parents had he not come to us so that he might raise himself up and kill us in the house.

'Father does this: he scolds the dog, as if he were not the one who had done this foolish action. His thoughts were closed about it. His people do not appear to have instructed him about his foolishness, [*19 June*] so that they might have driven away his foolishness by talking to him. It is his foolishness which deceives us here. The dog will come and throw him down.'

The child said to her, 'Oh mother! The scent of the dog's mouth smelt yesterday; I sprang to one side, round your husband. He scolded the dog which he thought would throw him down, while the young gemsbok lay far away. The dog came straight towards us. That is why we thought that we would die today, because the dog did not 'turn back. Your husband struck at but missed the dog, as it sprang past him. The dog cantered[29] like a great beast of prey. He galloped, going to a thornbush. He went to sit upright next to the thornbush. He sat angrily. Your husband scolded him as he sat next to the young gemsbok. He thought that it seemed as if the dog would come.

'Do you think that I wanted to go today? I trembled and did not broil meat. I returned hungry. I was afraid there, while your husband cut up the young gemsbok. Your husband was also afraid. That is why we came calling as we carried the meat. We wanted you to hear us so that you would first stand up, so that you would talk to little daughters, so that you would hold the children by their wrists,[30] so that you could take the ostrich-breastbone dish and put it into the embers and throw fire at this dog, for he did not stop galloping round; so that he might turn away from us because it seemed as if he would really come in to the house. The fire made him turn back.

[*23 June*] 'I shall be with your husband today, so that I may watch.

193

Frightened, I shall first stand behind a tree while your husband urges the dog towards the gemsbok. When I see that they are full-grown gemsbok, I shall go forward.'

His mother said to him, 'You must do that.'

The father and son went. They urged the dog towards full-grown gemsbok. The dog caught hold of a full-grown gemsbok and threw it down, biting it and killing it. The frightened child stood behind the thorn-tree; his father ran towards the gemsbok. The dog ran straight forward, coming to meet him. He scolded the dog as it came. The man scolded. The child stood thinking that he felt as if this is the morning on which his father would die.

'The dog came and I stood frightened behind the tree so that I could run away to mother. For that is what mother said.'

The dog caught hold of his father. The dog held him and threw him down, while the gemsbok lay yonder. The dog stood biting his father. The child went softly straight back. He ran hard and looked back as he ran. It looked as if his father had been bitten dead. For the dog stood there alone, and his father lay quite still. The child must run with haste, for the dog may come forward to him. The dog came forward.

The child said to himself, 'It must be a lion because it comes yonder. I remember the advice that mother gave me that the lion would behave like this when he had killed father. It seemed as if the lion would catch me if I ran slowly and did not go to mother at once. I think it seems to turn back.'

The lion, running about, turned back.

The child looks back and says, 'I thought that he would first do this, so that I could go to the house and tell mother that, frightened, we must go quickly, for the man lies yonder.'

The lion ran to his father. [*23 June*] As the father lay dead, the lion took him up and bit him; he was quite dead. The lion left him. The child thought that he would first stand still so that he could watch, so that he would not mislead his mother. The dog ran to the young gemsbok lying some distance away, the one that was a young adult gemsbok. The dog went to take it up. [*June 25*] The dog bit it. The dog bit it, testing it. The dog tried to find out if it were indeed dead. The dog cantered back to the man; he went to take up the man. He bit, trying the man. He quickly snatched up the man and bit the man's neck.[31] He threw the man on his back. The child watched from afar, standing above. The dog bit and threw the child's father onto his back and took him to where the gemsbok was lying. The dog laid down the child's father.

The child's thoughts said to him, 'Father has been bitten yonder, thrown up onto the lion's back and carried away. That thing which ought to walk by night, it was the one that killed him, that thing which he brought to us and with which he deceived us, we and mother. Father is over there. A lion is the one that laid him down at the place where the young gemsbok lay. The lion stands over there looking around. He appears to be standing because of fatigue. I must stand and watch, for he seems to stand looking for a large tree so that he may pant away his fatigue. There are two lying there, he and the young gemsbok. I must look to see what the dog will do when it sees a large tree; and I shall tell mother, even if she does not believe me.'

The dog saw a big thorntree that stood far off in the bushes. Biting, the dog threw the child's father on its back, while the child stood watching.

The child said to himself, 'Father is over there, bitten and thrown up upon the lion's back and carried away. He is long; he is red because he does not have a coat of hair. He is being carried away to the thorntree that stands over there so that the lion may put him into the thorntree. I stood watching because the dog did not see me, for I hid behind a thorntree. I ran away while he was biting there.'

The lion carried his father away to the thorntree which was in the bushes. The lion went into the thorn tree.[32] The lion laid his father underneath the tree. The lion then jogged along, coming back; it jogged along, coming to the young gemsbok. The child still stood watching. The lion quickly snatched up the young gemsbok and dragged it along, making a noise on the ground.

The child said to himself, 'The young gemsbok is being carried away.[33] It is being carried away over there. It went into those bushes. I think that I must go away so that I can go and tell what I have so clearly seen: the dog cannot be a dog. He was the one who carried twice into the bushes over there. I was not with the man with whom I used to be. He went first, and he was carried away into the bushes. Afterwards, the gemsbok was carried away; it too went into those bushes over there. I think that I must run, for I have seen clearly. I shall say this. I shall tell when I reach the house. I think that I must run quickly so that we shall not go in the darkness. For father was thrown down today, when he did not go straight to this gemsbok. The dog who is not a dog is the one who went to meet and stand in front of father. [*26 June*] This is the creature with which father deceived us. He said that it was a dog; but we knew it to be a lion. He did not appear to see the lion; now he is the one who was thrown down. He was carried away; he was laid down and hidden. The dog which hid him is not a dog. I shall say thus: I shall tell my grandparents, when we go in the dark to them.[34] It is not a short path that we shall travel in the darkness between the two houses.'

He ran towards his mother. His mother said, 'This child, is he not one who comes running? His father is not with him. He seems to have run away afraid. He is doing what I foretold. For the dog must have caught with his mouth, sniffing the child's father. The child is here. This is what I told them would happen. He comes to tell me so that I may know, so that I should not wait here, while death has been done by this dog; I truly knew it. When it was very little, its eyes resembled those of a beast of prey. It grew up and its eyes were so.'

Running, the child reached his mother. He said to his mother, 'Oh! Mother! Were you at peace, while I was afraid? This dog, that is not a dog, did this: he went towards your husband and stood in front of him. Your husband scolded him. The dog came. Frightened, I stood behind a tree; the dog sprang upon your husband. Springing upon him, he threw him down. I ran, keeping myself upright, while your husband was held down. The dog ran, looking for me. I thought that I must run quickly. I went to watch, standing on the hill over there. [*7 July*] Running, I came to the top of it.

'Then I came to you to tell you, so that we can go quickly, while the sun is still high, for I think that the dog will come to our house. It feels that it has not yet eaten. He went back. First, he lifted up your husband so that he could carry him into the bushes. When I saw him do this, I knew that he must be a lion. I want you to put together our things, so that we can go, while the sun is still high. We shall go closer to grandfather's house; for we are not near to my grandparents. We must go quickly to the house. We shall have to travel the space between the houses in the darkness. That is why I want you to place the child on your back quickly, so that we can go quickly forward. We must leave our old things. We must travel lightly and not heavily burden ourselves. We must go hastily, for the lion seems to be eating there. It came back to lift up and carry the young gemsbok. You seem to think that it was a young gemsbok; but it was actually a young fully-grown gemsbok; its horns were long. Its hair was white. While the dog was biting it, its tail was like a lion's tail; while it was biting the young gemsbok.'

His mother agreed with him. 'It must have been a lion. It was the one who killed father. I thought that the lion would do this; for father told me about the smell of its breath as it sprang, going past him. You must say this when you talk to your grandparents. The lion will fetch its parents so that it can bring them to come and eat with it. The gemsbok is with the man. It ran to listen to its parents when they roared there. Father was the one who, calling, brought it back.'

They went. The child said to his mother, 'Oh Mother! You must jog along[35] so that you can jog along, going near; for we must go fearing. You must tell your daughter over there to run.[36] Her younger brother must also run. For they seem to think that I am not exhausted with fear. I did not stop so that I could walk and recover from my fatigue. I shuddered with fear, while my heart was startled when I saw that your husband appeared to have died today. For he was silent.'

They went, going in the darkness between the houses. The child said to his mother, 'We must go in the darkness to find the footpath so that, travelling in the darkness, we may reach the house, so that we may tell my grandparents in the darkness. Then they will know in the darkness; they will hear in the darkness. They will be afraid in this dark place. We shall all be afraid here. They must make a big fire; for it is not quiet. We are now afraid.'

Travelling in the darkness, they reached the house. The child's mother called out, 'Are you asleep?'

The dogs barked. The child said to his mother, 'The dogs are barking.'

His mother said to his grandparents, 'Drive away that dog over there. I have come in the darkness to rouse you at this place in the night, because of the dog which arrived at my house carried in the arms. I brought it up giving it a share of food. It did not bark as this dog does; it barks at us because it is a real dog. It watched us stealthily. You were not the one who gave us the dog, the dog which was like a dog which had lived in the darkness. My husband told me that you gave him the dog. [*8 July*] Therefore I want you to tell me about the place where my brother-in-law saw you. For I do not know if you saw each other on the hunting-ground, when my brother-in-law did not come to you at the house and you gave him the dog at the houses.'

[*9 July*] Her younger brother-in-law spoke to her; her younger brother-in-law denied it to her: 'I did not see your husband because I remained here. I did not see your husband. You are the one I saw when you came in the darkness to this night's place. I have not seen your husband. I saw that you came alone, when you came in the darkness. The children were those who were with you.'

His brother's wife said to him, 'The dog which you gave is the reason why I did so. I came alone because of it. I was frightened because of it.'

Her younger brother-in-law said to her, 'I have not yet seen your husband. Your husband was to have come to my house so that I could give him a young dog.'

His brother's wife said to him, 'I saw brother carrying a little dog in his arms. The young dog looked strongly at us when he was little. Brother told me to respect the dog because you gave him the dog. Brother knew the dog's name, when the dog was little.'

Her younger brother-in-law denied it to her: 'I did not give it; my dog is still standing here. Its coat of hair is like this. Its ears are like this; they droop.'

His brother's wife said to him, 'The thing which brother brought, its ears were not like this. Its ears were short; they were not long.'

Her younger brother-in-law said to her, 'Your husband was the one who brought you a thing which had lain in solitude. It did not smell the scent of the fire. Your husband had it because of his foolishness. Foolishly, he brought it. He did not behave as our mother taught us; he was foolish. That was why the lions roared when your husband took away the lioness-mother's child. He brought it to your house. You must have been afraid there.'

His brother's wife agreed with him: 'Brother did do so. He brought me a young fighter. It looked knowingly. It looked as if it wanted to fight. Its eyes looked as if it had been in the dark solitude. I want your grandson to be the one to tell you. He was the one who was with his father. He himself saw what the dog did there. You seem to think that the dog's hair was not yellow. The dog had a long tail; hair stood on the tip of its tail. The roots of the dog's ears were black; the tips of the dog's ears were as if people had cut them with a knife.'

Her younger brother-in-law agreed with her: 'It must have been a lion. Lions are like that. Dogs are like this.'

His brother's wife said to him, 'The animal which brother said was a dog was not like this. Its head was covered with hair, hair which concealed its eyes. Its eyes made us afraid. When it came to me at the house, I at first stood afar so that I could keep my grandsons together as he came angrily. [*10 July*] I was the one who barred its way and drove it away. My scolding of it was why it stopped and turned back and sat looking at us, while I stood holding the fire (in a dish). It feared the fire. It walked back while brother jogged along to me. The children stood behind me as it walked back. It laid down; it lay watching.'

Her younger brother-in-law agreed with her. Her elder brother-in-law also agreed with her: 'It was a lion that did that.'

His nephew said to him, 'Oh my Uncle![37] The dog which brother brought was very little. It was the one which killed brother over there. Brother said that you were the one who gave it.'

His uncle agreed with him: 'Father deceived you so that you would think that it was a dog. Indeed, father behaved foolishly even when he lived with us. His brother who is sitting there taught him so that he would behave with understanding; for he was always a foolish person.'

The child said to him, 'Oh my Uncle! I remembered what mother said to me when I went. That is why I was frightened and stood behind so that I could run away. The dog would have come to kill all of us if I had not run away. For the dog ran about looking for me. I ran through many bushes so that they would conceal me so that I could first tell brother's wife, who is my mother, she who spoke to me when I went. She said that we would be frightened this morning and come to you.'

His uncle said, 'I thought that that was what you did. A little child does that when he is clever so that he may tell all the people so that they may get the story and know. We did not know. We sat peacefully because we did not see anyone who could have told us. I thought that mother was doing this because she thought that the young lion would not go to fetch his parents, for he knows the Bushman's house at which he grew up and where he ate food and grew up. When he has eaten up father, he will think of the house, that he did not see the other people, those whom he thought he would destroy. He will first go to fetch his parents; and his parents will smell the scent of the man's blood on the cub. They will go round in front with him intending to eat so that they may first finish the bones. Then they will go to the house where they think the other people probably are. For it used to know the other people.'

His nephew said to him, 'You seem to think that I did not come so that your sister could tell you and that we could go away early, fearing, so that, fearing, we could climb the mountain, the one which you will descend. You must go softly to look at the house. And then, carefully watching, you must go to the house so that you can look around. I shall be with you so that I can take you, and then we shall go carefully. You must not go quickly. We must go gently to the house so that we may first look well. For the dog seemed as if it would go to bring its parents to the house.

'If we do not see the lion at the house, I shall take you to show you the place where I stood frightened. I shall show you the place where the dog threw down the young gemsbok. I shall show you the place where your brother ran along. The dog met him as he was running along. The dog caught hold of him before he had gone near to where the young gemsbok lay. He was grasped and laid down midway. He did not go near. That is the place from which I ran away while brother was held down there. I did so. I went to tell, to rouse them to listen. Then, frightened, we came here. We did not sleep at the house because we were afraid there.'

His uncle agreed with him: 'Fearful, we shall go early, and climb the tall mountain standing over there. We shall do what you say. And we shall go carefully to the house because of the lions. We shall go and look.'

[*11 July*] The child said to his uncle, 'I have said so.'

Fearfully, they went early to climb the mountain. They slept on the mountain. Waking, they came down from the mountain. They went to the house so that they could look around. Looking carefully, they quietly climbed the hill near the house. They looked around.

They did not see the lions. Carefully, they approached the house.

The child said to his elder relations, 'You must come, walking carefully so that we can first see well. Then we shall look about, but we shall not see the lions at the house.'

They went quietly to the house. They spotted the lions' spoor.

His uncle said to him, 'Look! This is the spoor of the lion that was looking round here.'

The child said to him, 'They must have come to the house, for over there the sticks of the house have been broken apart.'

His uncle said to him, 'I want your uncle over there to look at mother's spoor, the scent of which the lion found on the night's place here. They seem to have finished the bones, as you told us.'

His other uncle said, 'I hope that my nephew will see the lion which sought their scent at this place. For his father did this: he brought them a young lion. He came to feed it and bring it up. You can see that the spoor of the young lion's father is here. His son brought him so that they could come to the other people. He watched them stealthily.[38] Mother was the one who behaved with understanding. Frightened, she went while the lion was eating there. She was the first to go away frightened. You are the one who behaved with understanding, you who are a child. I know what you did: you stood frightened, so that father could run forward alone, and then you returned.'

The child said to him, 'I did this because your brother's wife told me that she thought that father had behaved foolishly. She was the one who understood. She was the one who said correctly that it was a lion with which father had deceived us. She told me to fear it.'

His uncle agreed with him: 'Mother spoke truly.'

They look around about the house for the spoor.

His uncle said to him, 'Look at the sticks of the house; the lions have disarranged them.'[39]

The child said to him, 'The cub's spoor is here. His father's spoor is the one which is here. The cub's spoor is this. His mother's spoor is the one which is here. His brother's spoor is here. His sister's spoor is the one which is here. His other brother's spoor is here. His sister's spoor is here. His other sister's spoor is the one which is here. We must go. We must go to see the place where he killed father. I shall take you to the place so that you can see where, biting, he laid down father. And then I shall take you to the young gemsbok, at the place where the young lion threw it down. Biting, he killed it.'

His uncle agreed, 'We shall do so. We shall go, watching carefully. Afraid, we shall go to the trees for they are great, great trees. The lions appear to have gone to the water. We shall go and look around, and, when we look around well, we shall pick up father's arrows. We shall take up the bow, for the bow is probably lying there.'[40]

They went forward. The child showed his elder relatives. 'This is the place where I stood watching and from where I ran away. That is where I stood watching when your brother was carried away. He was carried away to the bushes over there; a large thorn-tree stands in them. They are the bushes to which the dog went, carrying your brother, while I watched, standing at this place. The young gemsbok was also carried away to the bushes when the dog came to lift it up. That was your brother's dog.'

They walked to the place where the child's father had been. The child showed his elder relations: 'This thorn-tree is the one behind which I stood frightened. I ran away from this place. This is the place from which I ran away. My spoor is here. The dog's spoor is the one that is here.'

His uncle agreed with him: 'I wish that father's younger brother had seen the lion whose spoor is here. But your father made a dog of it. But our house still stands, we who have real dogs.'[41]

They went to the place where his father had been. The child showed his elder relatives: 'This is the place where the dog came forward and met father. The dog came back from the young gemsbok while it was lying over there. The arrows lie yonder. The bow lies over there. That place over there is the one from which your brother was carried away. I want you to take up the things. These bushes are the ones which I came to show you. That is the thorn-tree over there. We must turn back so that the scent of our spoor may not become abundant. We must go quietly away. We shall go to tell the people at the house. They will see the arrows. The dog which was here has brought his parents. Their spoor is here; it is abundant because he ran to bring them. I want us to go away frightened. Frightened, we must go away to a different mountain.'

Fearfully, they went away to climb another mountain. They did indeed go away.

NOTES

1. Said to be the first (or one of the first) /Xam man.
2. 'Munnie praat so mein broers sein hundjes'. Editor: This is //Kabbo's Dutch (Afrikaans) translation of the /Xam sentence.
3. i.e. when the man was out of the way.
4. This means, D.H. (i.e. Diä!kwain) explains, that a dog's feet don't have long hair.
5. i.e. because it is a beast of prey, D.H. says.
6. Explanatory note by D.H., Feb. '76. 'Call the dog which (?) goes with you (?) that it may scent about, that you may see if it will/may not perceive a thing which it can smelling, put up?'
7. Expl. note by D.H. 2 March 1876. Her husband said, 'Tta tta tta tta tta!' to frighten the lion. He, in another way, he says, 'Yonder man, what is it that he wants to do? that he does thus there? It seems as if he were stealing up to me.'
8. 'Wolle doorn' a great tree, D.H. says, but brittle and not strong. It is like the 'Kokker boom' of which the men make their quivers. Editor: This could be a large species of aloe, *Aloe dichotoma*, the '*kokerboom*' (the Afrikaans '*koker*', meaning 'quiver'), from which quivers are known to have been manufactured by /Xam men.
9. This is his name as a dog.
10. The man thought to make it love him, D.H. says. The man thought that his dog would love him, when it heard him calling its name. The man did what we always do: when we hear that a dog growls at us, we call the dog's name.
11. Lit. 'thinking strings'.
12. That is, arose with his load on his back, D.H. says. He had lain down upon the load, to slip his arms through the gemsbok's feet, which he had fastened together, two and two.
13. This load being too heavy for him to run, D.H. explains. */kaoun/kaoun* 'to go slipping the feet along the ground'.
14. Explanatory note by D.H. 'My father went slipping his feet along the ground, while he felt that he was carrying a load. Therefore he went, slipping his feet along the ground, on account of it; while he felt that the things which he was carrying, or with which he had loaded himself, were heavy. Therefore he did not run. For he went slipping his feet along the ground; because he felt that the things which he was carrying did not admit of his running. This was why he continued to go slipping his feet along the ground.'
15. Sometimes made from the breastbone of the ostrich, and sometimes from an ox's horn; also from the tortoise, and turtle, D.H. tells me.
16. D.H. thinks that the son would have said *tata* here.
17. J.T. says that Charlie is Wilhelm's *!khwi opua*. In this instance the man is talking to his wife of his own younger brother who is *her* brother-in-law.
18. *N.B.* I think that it means *literally* 'Thou dost therefore speak thus' (as an angry exclamation), but both Jantje Tooren and David Hesar translate it much as I have done.

19. 'The path where the water runs out of its eyes.'
20. By rubbing his hand under his arm, and letting the cub smell it.
21. J.T. says that all this took place on the previous day.
22. The child, being afraid, does not hold one of the gemsbok's forelegs for his father, that the latter can cut open the gemsbok's chest.
23. [*7 June*] The men say to one another when telling one another to look at game, 'Oh! Beast of Prey! direct your eye to yonder place.' The women use this same expression when asking their husbands to fetch wood, 'Oh! Beast of Prey! fetch wood for us, for I did fetch wood, I do not desire/want that I should fetch wood.' A man says to another, 'Oh! Beast of Prey! come up, you must look, that you may look in all places, that you may seek in all places.'
24. This means, as they explain it, that the boy must, in running away, keep trees (this tree, and others) between him and the lion; so that the latter may not perceive him.
25. The lion thinks that the man pretended to be dead and will get up and go when it (the lion) is out of the way.
26. *!koa-ken* (*!koa!koa* pl.) a bush which is in /Xam-ka !au, by a river, or rivers; it has yellow flowers.
27. Its ears have apparently not grown correspondingly to its body. Great lions' ears are also short as if people had cut them.
28. A name which the /Xam-ka !ei have for the lion; what the meaning of it is, I do not yet know. J.T. explains that it is a thing which kills people; that is why it has this name. */aken-sse ta tchuen* – A name for lions. *!kui* – Another name used (for many lions together). *!ku ttu /i* – A name for a lion with great paws – If he were to put a foot on the fire, the latter would be put out. *!koa!koa-ssho* – This name (of a girl) means the same as counting sheep, J.T. says.
29. Speaking of a horse, Stoffel tells me that one says *ssuken-i*, to trot; *//kuarra*, to canter; *!kuxe*, to gallop.
30. The mother, J.T. tells me, takes hold of her children's wrists together, in one hand, putting and holding them behind her for their protection, and with the right hand she lades up fire with the ostrich-breastbone and throws it at the lion.
31. Note added Feb. 21 1876. *!Kui-sse-!khwi-/ku* – D.H. calls the young lion's name thus; he heard the story both from his mother and from his paternal grandfather !Xugen-ddi.
32. He went through the bushes among which the tree stood, to its stem.
33. Because it is a big gemsbok, the lion carries its chest, and the after-part of its body drags along the ground, making a noise as it is dragged along. And the lion, being young, cannot carry it entirely on his back, as a fully-grown lion would have done.
34. J.T. explains that they would journey all the time that the sun was light; then they would still go on, and it would be dark when they got *near* the old people's house.
35. This is a movement when one jogs along *carrying* something.
36. This child is a little behind.
37. *!Koin*. It really is used for *Uncle* here; but it seems to be used for several older male relatives.
38. As a cat does a bird, J.T. says.

39. Thrown away from each other by the lions' entrance into the house.
40. 'He dink de bog is lay daar.' Editor: Another of the half-Dutch, half-English translations given by the informant.
41. Their house has not been broken by lions.

The Early Race

Many texts in the Bleek and Lloyd Collection refer to the Early Race of people who lived long ago when the rules of the present-day material world did not apply. //Kabbo told Lloyd that the people of the Early Race were stupid and did not understand things well. The /Xam-ka !ei also spoke of a time when people were animals. It seems that these pre-people were in fact the Early Race; the idea of people having formerly been animals has captured the popular imagination. The notion springs largely from a note that Lloyd added to a left-hand page: 'We who are Bushmen were once springbucks, and the Mantis shot us, and we really cried (like a little child). Then the Mantis said we should become a person, become people because we really cried' (L. VIII. 4. 6365 rev.).

A man put into a mouse skin turns into a lion

/Han≠kass'o
From his mother /Xabbi-an, who, he thinks,
had it from her mother ≠Kammi

L. VIII. 17. 7527–7541
20 SEPTEMBER 1878

The children[1] once cried 'Upp!' to the fieldmice.[2] They shot at them. They saw that they were not fat mice.

The other person was a youth. They plotted to put him into the fieldmouse skin. They cried 'Upp!'[3] to the fieldmice. They shot at the fieldmice, and they killed a fieldmouse. They skinned it. They put the other person into its skin. Then they saw that he did not go in well, for he stuck out. He would not fit in.

Again they cried, 'Upp!' They shot at the fieldmice, and skinned a big fieldmouse. They skinned it. And they put the other child into it; they held him very firmly, and said, 'Trot away.' And he trotted away and became a lion.

And they said, 'Lie down over there. Then you will stand still for us.'

The other one lay down. And, because he feared the other one, he said, 'O my companions, let us take out our brother.'

And someone else said, 'We must leave our brother alone for our brother's sister-in-law mocked him. She has been scolding our brother.'

And the other one threatened them. They ran away, and he chased after them.

They said, 'It is ourselves, it is ourselves.'

And one said, 'I told you to take our brother out for us.'

But another person said, 'We must leave brother alone. Our brother's wife did this: she scolded us. She was plaguing our brother. She will see.'

The other one (in the skin) went into the reeds, while they went home. And the other one's brother's wife said, 'Look over there! Look

209

over there! Where are the people?'

And the children said, 'We left our friend while he was in the reeds. He did not stand still, but it seemed as if he wanted to kill us.'

And the other's brother's wife said, 'Look over here! Look over here! Our friend seems to be here.'

And they led his brother's wife to the reeds into which he had gone, while all the people went together. And the children called out, 'O people, you should really go out to a flat place, because our friend no longer seems as he used to be.'

Then his brother's wife[4] said, 'Come out, come out, come out of the reeds there into which you have gone.'

Then her younger brother-in-law darted out of the reeds. He charged those people who had come. At first he did not see his brother's wife. Then he saw his brother's wife. He went up to her. He ran up to her. He sprang, seizing his brother's wife. He threw her down and bit her head. He broke it, while the people[5] cried out, 'Why have you done this to our friend? Are your brothers not gentle? Is that why you put our friend into a fieldmouse skin?'

The child carried off his brother's wife. He carried his brother's wife off to the reeds in which he had been.

NOTES

1. They were children of the Early Race. I do not know their names.

2. The fieldmouse does not have another name, for it is a 'mouse'. Its holes are many in a flat place. The mouse resembles a lion. It is wont to wave about with its paws, (holding up his two hands in front of his chest). It sits on its hind feet. It says 'Tssi, tssi' when it waves its paws. It eats bushes; its teeth are like a porcupine's; it is wont to 'gnaw' (?) off the bushes.

3. Explanation of *!kuppen*. They say 'upp, upp, upp', making a noise in their cheeks by closing their lips, swelling out their cheeks, and suddenly drawing them in. They do this with the hand, agitating the right hand very quickly; the bow being meanwhile held in the right hand. They say 'upp, upp, upp' when they startle fieldmice and, when the fieldmice have gone out and want to go in, they call 'upp, upp, upp, upp'. Then the fieldmice sit listening quietly, and as the fieldmice were turning back they sit quiet.

4. She was an 'ackeldos' lizard, a red lizard. The 'ackeldos' lizard was once a man, he is red, he is long. It is about the length of Jantje's hand, with the forefinger extended.

5. The people who had gone to see the child. They were those who scolded their sons.

People of the Early Race hunt lions

/Han≠kass'o
From his maternal grandmother, ≠Kammi

L. VIII. 18. 7551–7588
23 SEPTEMBER 1878

Long ago people hunted lions. They went out and spotted a lion. And it charged them. One man threw a bone, striking a lion's face. His younger brother also knocked down that lion. And they cut up the lion.[1] They carried the lion's meat. They went to cut it up.

Again the two of them hunted lions. They went and found lions' spoor. They saw that the lions' spoor was fresh; they followed it right up. They followed the lions' spoor to the lions. Then a lion charged them. And one man knocked down a lion, while his younger brother knocked down a lioness. They cut up the lions and carried them to the hut. Carrying the meat, they reached the hut where they unpacked and sliced up the lions' meat. They dried it.

And they hunted again. They went hunting. They went and saw lions, and the lions charged them. And one man threw, hitting the lions, while his younger brother also knocked down a lion. And they cut up the lions. After they had cut up the lions, they carried them home. And they unloaded the meat. They sliced it, and dried it.

When day broke, they went hunting again. They went hunting. They hunted. They went and found a fresh lion's spoor. They tracked it. They followed it, and they followed it to where the lion was lying. The lion charged them, and one man knocked the lion down, while his younger brother also knocked that lion down. And they cut up the lion. They cut up the lion. They carried the meat home. They brought the meat home. They unpacked it. They sliced it.

And when day broke, they hunted lions. They went hunting. They went and found lions. The lions charged them when they came up to them as they lay asleep. And the lions, charging, ran up to them. And when a lion tried to seize him, he hit the lion's face; he beat it through. And his younger brother also knocked down a lion.

211

Then the elder man stayed at home, while his younger brother went hunting alone. His younger brother went hunting. He did not say he had seen a lion. He went hunting, went hunting, went hunting. He went and found lions, but the place was not nearby. He went and saw lions. And the lions charged him. And he tried to do as he always did, to throw a bone, hitting the lion's head. But the lion jumped towards him. The lion seized him. The lion killed him.

And his brother waited for him. Then his brother sang there. He said his younger brother's wind was like this, for he seemed to have killed a lion. The children said that their father's wind seemed to be like this, for it seemed that the lion had killed him. After many nights had passed without their father returning, the children went away with their mother. That is why they went away, while their uncle stayed alone at home.

Then he sang,

> O my little brother!
> My little brother's wind feels like this,
> When my little brother has killed a lion.

And he said, 'Brother, brother, can these be stars?'
When the lion's eyes were shining as it approached him, he sang,

> My younger brother's wind feels like this,
> When he has killed a lion!

He said, 'Brother, brother, what can this be? Stars must be shining above me.' He sang. He said: 'Brother, brother, why is it that stars are shining above me?' The lions' eyes shone as they approached him, for there were two lions.

Then the lions walked up to him. The lions seized him. He cried, 'Ai, ai, ai! Auuuuu!'

A lion dragged him out of the hut and bit him to death. And the lion carried him off; it took him away; it went and ate him up. When it had finished him, it went away.

He had said, 'Oh my younger brother! My younger brother's wind is wont to feel like this when he has killed *//kuamma*.'[2]

But the children said, 'O Father, Father's wind feels like this when a lion seems to have killed him.'

And their uncle said, 'O hi! You there! Oh dear! Leave off! Why do you speak like this? Father does this when there are two lions. That is why he does not come. He is still slicing lion's meat, because he wants it to dry. He will come.'

Then the children's mother said, 'We will go away because a lion must have killed father. You see that father is not coming; a lion must have killed him. Therefore let us go. Uncle will stay quietly there. We will go. He can stay there quietly at the hut.'

Then the lions followed up the younger brother's spoor. They followed the younger brother's spoor. They followed his spoor right up to the hut in which he had lived. And the lions heard him singing there. And as he was singing and looking out there, he saw the lions' eyes shining, approaching him. Then he said they were stars. The lions seized him, while he thought that they were stars.

They are thigh-bones, and they make knobkerries of them because they have many of them.[3] That is why they make kerries of them, and they hit a lion with them. They knock down a lion because they feel they will do so when a bone has broken the lion's head. They will do this with another bone. They will also knock down a lion.

The lion would not have killed his younger brother if he had been there, but the lion did so because he stayed at home. His younger brother also behaved foolishly. He had only ostrich bones which were not hard. Therefore they broke, broke, falling off the lion's head. Hard bones are the ones which knock down a lion, hit, striking the lion's head. Then the lion does not get up again after it has fallen. They had knocked him down with a giraffe's bone. They knocked him down with it. While the other man knocked the lion down with a giraffe's thigh-bone. Then the lion died, because the head of the giraffe's thigh-bone of which they had made the knobkerrie, struck his skull. Then the lion stayed dead. Then he stood hitting the lion, beating him to death.[4] He saw blood come from the lion's ear. Then he stopped.

At that time they carried elephant's bones. They hunted with them because they had also hunted with giraffe's bones. When they took the elephant's bones, they put them away at home so that they could knock down a lion with them. These bones are hard. They also knocked down a lion with them. Then when a lion charged them, they threw the bone, hitting the lion on its head. The elephant bone hit the lion's head. His younger brother also hit, striking the elephant's bone on the lion's head. Then they cut up the lion.

NOTES

1. They seem to have cut up the lion with knives.
2. The Early Race of people were those who called the lion's name with *//kuamma*, when they hunted lions; they killed the lions and ate them. Therefore, they said *//kuamma* to them, as if they hunted lions every day. Editor: *//kuamma* seems to be a 'respect word' used in special circumstances. The more usual /Xam word for lion was *//khâ*.
3. Because they have ostrich bones and giraffe bones.
4. Struck him, kept striking him, for he thought that the lion might be feigning death.

About a moth called by *!kum !kum (Aloa amasis Cramer)* and said to pour lice upon them

Diä!kwain
From his mother, ≠Kammi-an

L. V. 18. 5374–5389
OCTOBER 1875

The /Xam-ka !ei tell us that the *!kum !kum*[1] is a thing that has lice. Lice are what it pours down over us when it keeps hovering over us. Lice are what it pours on us. Therefore people do this when they hear it as it hovers above them: they say, 'That person, I want it to go away from me. For lice seem to be pouring on me. I want it to go away from me.'

The people drive it away because people used to say that it has lice. It used to have lice. Lice used to go about at the place where it walked. Lice walk one behind like scent [? Lloyd's question mark] for the smell of the lice it is that the lice walk with the scent. It pours, making lice from itself because it wants lice to be with us, so that we may also have lice like it.

That is why people do not want it to come and stand hovering above them. This is what they do; they blow with their mouths, driving it away because they feel that it has lice. Therefore people do not want it.

[*6 October*] People speak, they say, 'You yourselves can see that there are lice. You see them. They are with the *!kum !kum*. The *!kum !kum* seems as if it has dust on it. These are the lice that it produces out of itself.'[2]

People tell us that the lice have a shell,[3] a louse shell. That shell is what the *!kum !kum* pours on us. This is what it used to do.

The moth was a man. It used to talk with the man, but it kept putting lice on the man. The man would be thinking that the moth was talking nicely with him, but it talked to deceive the man, so that it might pour [*7 October*] lice onto him.

This is what the man did when we walked away from him. He saw that he was full of lice. The man spoke and said, 'This must have been why the *!kum !kum* did not want to sit away from me. He must really have poured lice on me while he was talking with me. I thought that he was talking nicely with me, while he must have been deceiving me so that he could pour lice on me. That really must be it. I see what he must have done. He cheated me. I see that there is a mass of lice.'

Other people speak. They say to the man, 'Do you think that the *!kum !kum* is a friend? It is one to whom we do this: when we see it, we do not sit down near to it because it is a mass of lice. Therefore people do not let it settle. They do this when they see it: they blow at it because they feel that it deceives a man who does not know it because it wants to pour lice on him.'

NOTES

1. Oct. 4/75 *!kum !kum* – moth caught at Mowbray Oct. 3/75 said by D.H. to be found in /Xam-ka !au, in trees.
2. Editor: The 'dust' and 'lice' referred to here are probably the urticaceous scales of this kind of moth, which cause irritation and itchiness on human skin.
3. Editor: The *Dictionary* does not list 'shell' as one of the meanings of the /Xam word '*ka*' that is used in the text.

The fox[1] and the Koranna commando

/Hanǂkass'o
From his maternal grandfather, Tssatssi

L. VIII. 18. 7593–7595
AND L. VIII. 18. 7602–7607
27 SEPTEMBER 1878

The fox was once a person.[2] He felt he was one of the Early Race. The fox once said, 'You are thinking. You are awake.'

Some people thought they heard; other people did not hear him. 'You are thinking. You are awake. You are thinking. You are awake.'

Another person was eating there when he said, 'You are thinking. You are awake.' He said, 'You are thinking. You are awake. You are thinking. You are awake.'

Then the Kora man, who should have lain watching the pitfalls[3] fell asleep as he was lying there watching. He shut his eyes while another man lay watching for him alone. He stayed, stayed, stayed there. He stayed, stayed, stayed there, while he felt that he said, 'You are thinking that you are awake.'

Therefore the Kora, who had lain watching for him, shut his eyes. He slept. When he saw that the Kora was asleep, he did this: he took away the Korannas' knives. He carried them together on his breast.[4] He carried them away. He went to tell the other people that a war party was sleeping at his home.

The other people acted quickly. They quickly took other knives so that they could go quickly to stab the Korannas while they were still asleep.

Then they gathered together. They crept up to the Korannas. Then they stabbed the Korannas. They killed the Korannas with the Korannas' own knives. The Korannas remained dead. As they lay asleep, the foxes stabbed them.[5]

NOTES

1. The bat-eared fox, *Otocyon megalotis*.
2. The beasts of prey were once people. They became beasts of prey because of the lynx and the anteater. These were the ones who did this. They cursed each other because of the little springbok's doings. They cursed each other. All things were once people.
3. Editor: The /Xam word used here is '*puoin*', probably another spelling of '*puin*', given in the *Dictionary* (p. 684) as possibly deriving from the /Xam '*pwai*', meaning game animals.
4. Carried them on his breast (left) for he felt they were not light, for he felt they were many.
5. I think that they seem to have been the blades of which the [black people] now make assegais; for the Korannas also used to have them; when the white men had not travelled there, (namely) to our place. The Korannas bought guns with cattle; while they felt that they had not a little cattle.

The youth of the Early Race who warned those at home of the approach of a Koranna commando

/Han≠kass'o
From his mother, /Xabbi-an

L. VIII. 25. 8251–8268
TRANSLATED AROUND FEBRUARY 1879

The parents sent a youth of the Early Race to the water, when the Korannas had descended to the water. He put ostrich eggshells into a bag. He went for water. He went to the foot of the water's little hill. He came to the top of it. And, when he came to the top, he spotted the Korannas down at the water. At the same time, the Korannas spotted him.

He became small. Swaying about, he descended to the water.[1]

A Koranna exclaimed, 'Pity! Oh! How is it that the people send him to the water, while a grown person does not scoop up water?'

He sat down and took out an ostrich eggshell. He put down the ostrich eggshell into the wet mud. He dipped up mud. He soiled the ostrich eggshell with mud.

So a Koranna exclaimed, 'Dip up nicely for him.'[2] And a Koranna dipped up water for him, dipped up water nicely for him.

And another Koranna exclaimed: 'We ought to knock him down because he will go and tell his people.'

And the other one replied, 'We ought to let him alone because he does not seem as if he will tell. He is a foolish person.'

The other one exclaimed, 'You are obstinate. We ought to kill the child, so that we can follow his footmarks.'[3]

The other one exclaimed: 'You will not listen when we say that we ought to leave him alone because he does not seem to understand.'

And they stopped the mouths of the ostrich eggshells for him.[4] They put the ostrich eggshells in the bag for him. They took hold and helped him to pick up the load.[5] Taking hold, they helped him to pick

219

up the load. Holding him, they raised him up. Thus, he went along swaying. They were laughing at him.

Swaying about, he descended the hill. He went and became a grown-up youth at the back of the hill. He went quickly to the house and said:[6] 'Those people have bound on war's [*untranslated word*].[7] Those people have bound on woodpigeons' tails. Those people have tied on war's [*untranslated word*]. Those people have bound on woodpigeons' tails. Those people have tied on war's [*untranslated word*]. Those people have tied on woodpigeons' tails.'

He arrived at home.[8] He exclaimed: 'Why is it that you are keeping quiet? The Korannas are down at the water. A war party (commando) has tied on woodpigeon's tails. They have also bound on war's [*untranslated word*]. You must make ready so that we may escape.'

And they made fire.[9] They made fire with stumps of trees.

The women went away, but the men were those who still remained at home. They thought that the women should climb the mountain first. They would soon go away. And they climbed the mountain, while the fires' stumps smoked at the houses.

Thus the Korannas thought that the people were still there, even though they had gone away. The Korannas surrounded the houses, still believing the people were at home. The Korannas missed the people.

A Koranna said, 'I want you to see. For when I said, "Let us kill the child," you said that the child did not understand, that he was a simpleton. But he was the one who told his people. We are those who have missed the people at their house, just as if I had not counselled rightly.'

NOTES

1. He walked like a little child, he was swaying about.
2. They pitied him. While he felt that he spoke to all the Korannas. Therefore another Koranna, who also beheld (and), pitied him, arose, he dipped up nicely for him.
3. The other one, he wished them to kill the child, that they might follow the child's footmarks with which he came out of the house.

4. Stop the mouths of ostrich eggshells with grass; grass which is surpassingly beautiful.
5. They, grasping, lay the eggshells on his back; they, grasping, help him to load/carry putting his arms into the bag's strings.
6. While he went along singing about the people whom he had seen.
7. Because the things were black.
8. His people's houses, he went to his mother's house, at which he lived.
9. All the fires, the fires of all the houses. They desired that the people should think that they were all at home, while they had gone away.

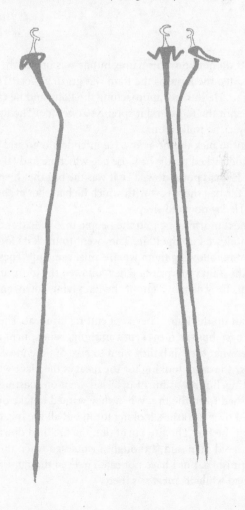

How the rain in the form of an eland was shot by one of the Early Race of people[1]

/Han≠kass'o
From /Xabbi-an, who, he thinks, had it from her mother ≠Kammi-an

L. VIII. 17. 7461–7472
16 SEPTEMBER 1878

A man – I do not know his name, but he was one of the 'Early Race' – once hunted the Rain, as the Rain was grazing there. The Rain was like an eland. He hunted, approaching the Rain, and he came and lay down. He shot the Rain, and it sprang to one side. The Rain did this: it ran away, as he walked on.

He went to pick up the arrow. He intended to go and put it back. He went and picked up his bag, the bag which he had taken hunting with him. He had put it down. That was the bag that he picked up. He put in the bag the arrow with which he had shot at the Rain. He returned. He lay down to sleep.

Early next morning he told the people that he had shot the Rain. And they followed up the Rain. They went to track its footprints.

They were following them when a mist came up. They continued to follow the Rain's footprints. They followed the footprints right up to the Rain. They caught sight of the Rain lying down, and they went up to it.

They cut up the Rain. They kept cutting off meat. They kept putting it to roast, but the meat kept vanishing, being burnt up in the fire. This is what they did: they went to take out the meat. They turned over the ashes looking for the meat at the place where it had been roasting, but it was burnt up. They went on roasting, and all the meat vanished from the fire. When they wanted to take out the meat, they turned over the ashes, looking for it, but all the meat had been burnt up in the fire. The fire burnt out; the fire died down.

Then an old man said, 'I thought I would go when this eland's meat was finished, but I have not eaten it, even though I roasted it. So now I will go while its meat sits there.'

And another answered, 'We will all do so, because we did not know what sort of eland it was. Let us go, because it is an eland whose meat we do not eat.'

As they walked away, the Rain shut them in. When the Rain saw that they were preparing to go, it shut them in. The Rain's navel[2] shut them into the hut, while they said that they feared the hut. The Rain's navel shut them into the hut, and they sat waiting for the Rain's navel. And they worked[3] at a pond. They worked. They became frogs. They hopped away while the people of the hut became frogs. They hopped at the hut, the people who had followed the spoor hopped away. He made a pond; he had been on the hunting-ground; he worked, making a pond.

NOTES

1. Editor: For more on /Xam beliefs about a Rain-animal, see Lewis-Williams, 1981.
2. Editor: For more on the Rain's navel, see *Kum* 50.
3. Editor: *Tabba*, here translated 'work', can also be used to mean to influence things by supernatural means, as in 'They had put away the *so-/ōa* at home that they might work upon (influence) the things they were shooting' (*Dictionary*: 187).

The woman who was killed by the baboons

Diä!kwain

L. V. 25. 5993–5997
18 FEBRUARY 1876

The woman who lived with them was the one whom they killed and ate. They used to say that it was young hunted animal's flesh,[1] but it was a girl's flesh. Because they saw that the girl was not a little fat, they killed her because of it.

My father and mother used to say to me that the quagga, when she was a person, resembled a boulder[2] as she went along. That is why the baboons, beholding, fearing her greatness, killed her.

My father asked me if I did not see what the quagga was like. Even though she was game, her flesh stands one (piece) above the others.

Therefore the baboons planned her killing. They killed her because they felt that the quagga was like a boulder when she stood among other people. That was why their hearts were not comfortable when they saw the quagga. All the people[3] looked at the quagga. The baboons thought that they would get rid of the quagga by killing her.

The time when game were people was the one when the quagga also resembled us who are people.[4] We are like it. That was when the baboon[5] was also a person. It looked like a man.

NOTES

1. Editor: In the original manuscript Lloyd translates !*khwai* as meaning 'gemsbok's flesh' (*Dictionary*: 431). The word also means 'game, or hunted animal', probably a better translation in this case, as the *kum* is about a woman who was a quagga.
2. A hard, round, smooth, great stone.
3. All the people, not only the baboons all the kinds of people.
4. Editor: this note appears on 5993 rev. at the beginning of the *kum*.
5. It means all the baboons, D.H. says.

Ritual relations with animals

/Xam beliefs about animals ranged from detailed knowledge of their behaviour to beliefs about their supernatural powers. As a result of these beliefs, hunting was accompanied by various ritual observances, the most elaborate of which seem to have pertained to the hunting of eland (Bleek, 1932: 233–249). The following texts give further observances, including those of the hartebeest, which, after the eland, was the Mantis's favourite animal.

The Mantis tries to save the hartebeest

Diä!kwain
From his father and mother

L. V. 17. 5257–5300
SEPTEMBER 1875

This is what our mothers did when the Mantis came to us. The Mantis came and mounted father's quiver. He stood on it. He stood, pointing to it. When our mothers saw the Mantis, as he stood attracting attention, they exclaimed, 'Look! The Mantis is standing on my husband's quiver.'

Our mothers said, 'The Mantis stands attracting our attention. He says that the man whose quiver this is will be the one to shoot a hartebeest.'

Our mothers told us that, when a man is afar off on the hunting ground and shoots a hartebeest, that is when the Mantis comes to do this at the hut. The people at the hut do not yet know that the man has shot a hartebeest. [*14 September*] The Mantis is the one who tells them that a man has shot a hartebeest. The Mantis is making the hartebeest's skin ache with the things that he shows, because he wants the hartebeest to live. He does not want the poison to kill the hartebeest. [*15 September*] This is what he wants the people at home to do when they see him: he wants them to kill him so that the hartebeest will recover. That is why he behaves in this way.

A woman who knows what is happening tells the other people about it: 'You must not drive away the person over there. You must leave him. We shall see why he has come to us today. The people who are hunting have not returned. We shall go and listen to what they are saying, as they return from hunting. For this thing is showing us. It really knows that one of our men is shooting a hartebeest. The Mantis is a thing which is a hartebeest's thing. He is with the hartebeest.

'The old people used to tell us that the Mantis does this when a man is going to shoot a hartebeest. He approaches the hut. He comes to look around, seeking the hut of the man who is shooting the hartebeest, because he wants the woman of the hut to do this when she sees him. She will say that she thinks that something is the matter, that something bad has happened. This is why the Mantis is standing on these things: so that she will catch him and throw him away because she does not want the Mantis to come into her hut.'

This is what the Mantis does when he sees that the woman is throwing stones to drive him away: he flies away. When the woman has driven him away by throwing stones, he goes to the hartebeest and speaks to it thus: 'You are writhing there for nothing because the wife of the man who shot you has thrown me away. You must get up. You must look for things that you can eat. You are writhing there needlessly. Although you see that the people have not respected[1] you, you can get up, you can walk.'

The man is still on the hunting-ground. This is how the Mantis behaves [*16 September*] when he comes to look at us because he wants to see whether we want the game to die. This is what he does when he sees that we respect the game. Even though he had tried to deceive us so that we would do something bad to him, he sees that we have understanding. For we do this: although we see him, we behave as if we had not seen him. We appear to take care of him.

That woman has told the other people that the Mantis behaves like this when the men are returning home.[2] The men tell them that a hartebeest has been wounded. She then tells the other people. She wants the other people to be silent. But they disbelieve her when she tells them about the Mantis, when she tells them that the Mantis knows. That is why he behaves like this. The Mantis looks for the man who has done this to the hartebeest. He means to go and search his hut. This is what he will do when he sees the hut of the man who shot the hartebeest. He will sit on his quiver.[3] By standing there, he will show the woman whose man has shot the hartebeest. He means to show this woman that her husband was the one who shot the hartebeest.

People do this when they see that the Mantis behaves like this. They look at each other, standing among their fellows. They merely speak to each other with their eyes. That is how they talk to each other when they have seen the Mantis, when they see that the Mantis behaves like this.

The women do this when they hear that the hartebeest has been wounded: they tell each other about it. They say, 'You must not allow the man over there to smell the scent of the pot.'

[*17 September*] This is what the Mantis does when the sun sets and the people are sleeping. He goes to the man who shot the hartebeest. This is what the Mantis does when they are asleep there. The Mantis does this. A little child is the one who is pinched. The Mantis pinches it because he wants the little child to cry, so that the child's cry will enter the ears of the man who shot the hartebeest, because of the things which the Mantis did to them.

He wants the crying of the child's mouth to enter the father's head. The hartebeest wants it to seem as if it heard. It will stand up when it hears the little child's crying. The man who shot the hartebeest is the one who hears the child's crying. Therefore the hartebeest also seems to hear when the man has heard the child's crying. That is why the woman looks after the child. She wants to prevent the child from crying so that the child's father will not hear its crying. This is what she does when she hears that the child sounds as if it were going to cry: she quickly puts her breast into the child's mouth because she does not want the child to cry. She does not want its father to hear its crying because of the things which the old people told us about what the game does, that we should look after the game if it is to die. If we do not look after it, it will not die. For it seems to know what we do when we are in our home and it is on the hunting-ground. It seems to know what we are doing there.

Therefore the women are afraid that the man who has shot the hartebeest will smell the scent of the pot. They think that the hartebeest will do this if the man who shot it smells the food. The hartebeest will also perceive the scent when the man who shot the hartebeest smells the scent of the pot. The hartebeest will also smell what the man has smelt, and the poison which the man has shot into the hartebeest will become cool. It will not be strong enough to hold the hartebeest dead. [*Untranslated line*] If the poison becomes cool, the hartebeest will live, for it feels that the poison is not strong. The scent of the pot is what cools the poison. The people do not want the man who shot the hartebeest to smell the scent because of what the poison's thing does to them, to the people who shoot game with poison. Then they respect the game because they feel that the poison's thing wants it to live, so that it will get up and walk like a thing that is not wounded. The things that a person smells act like this.

Then people do this when they follow up the spoor of the hartebeest. They pick up his footprints, smelling scents. They will see it lying there dead. They see that he has walked as if he were well and as if he had not been poisoned.

And people say to each other, 'Look what has made the hartebeest not take the poison. [*22 September*] Although our brother shot the hartebeest and told us just now that the hartebeest was writhing there, that it was thoroughly poisoned, it has not taken the poison.'

Another one says, 'Our brother must have smelt the scent of the pot. The pot's scent has this effect when we smell it. For I have seen the traces where the hartebeest was lying before our brother had not reached home. The time at which our brother reached home was when the hartebeest behaved like this. The hartebeest was writhing not a little until our brother was nearly home.'

NOTES

1. Editor: For more on /Xam 'respect' (*!nanna-sse*) customs, see Bleek and Lloyd, 1911: 182, 271–285.

2. Editor: After a San hunter has wounded a large animal with a poisoned arrow he returns home for the night. The next morning he and a few companions track the wounded animal, the poison having taken effect during the night. For eland hunting observances, see Bleek, 1932.

3. Editor: San men sometimes left their quivers at home and placed their arrows in leather bands around their heads, arms or waists. This practice made the arrows more accessible.

The killing of a white springbok

/Han≠kass'o
From his maternal grandfather, Tssatssi

L. VIII. 22. 7994
NOVEMBER 1878

People do not kill a white springbok. They merely look at it. They feel that the springbok will disappear altogether. The springbok will not come to a place where a white springbok has lain dead. All the springbok go away altogether, completely. Therefore the people merely look at a springbok which is white, even if it is near to them.

The springbok's tongue

Diä!kwain

L. V. 25. 6025–6030
FEBRUARY OR MARCH 1876

Our mothers told us what would happen if we ate the tip of the springbok's tongue. Our mothers told us about it.

As we walked along, it would be as if someone had hit our toe with a stone. Our toe would stumble on a stone if we ate the tip of the springbok's tongue.

Our mothers told us that we should therefore cut off the tip of the springbok's tongue and that we should leave it and not eat it. For we would hurt our feet with loose stones. Springbok tongues make our feet stumble on loose stones[1] if we eat the tip. Our toes hurt us because we have hit our feet on loose stones that cut.

That is why we who are children are afraid to eat the tip of a springbok's tongue. We feel that our mothers were those who told us about it, that the springbok's tongue would do this to us. That is why we are afraid of it. When we want to eat it, we fear it.

NOTE

1. 'Feet stamp *tuin* the *klip*', D.H. says. Editor: The informant's half-English, half-Dutch translation.

When game has been shot

Diä!kwain
From his mother, ≠Kammi-an

L. V. 21. 5680–5697
December 1875

We feel that the stars are things that do not go to a place near at hand, for they do not stand still. We are afraid to look at them because we feel that the game will do this even if it feels ill: it will not grow worse there at one place. It will walk about as the stars do. It is startled, as if a man were driving it. It is really startled; it gets up and walks. It is startled as if something has called it. It gets up, it walks because the star has aroused its heart, so that its heart will want to walk.[1]

That is why our mothers did not tell us only a little. They told us about it, about walking. When we have shot game, we must not hurry, at the time when we have shot game. For they (other people) look at our walk as we leave the hunting-ground. They watch us because they want to see how we will behave. They will do what they see our behaviour is like. They can tell by our actions that we have shot game, even though we do not tell them that we have shot game. They suspect us because of our walk. It is by that that they know we have shot game.

They do this when we come to sit down where they are warming food which they have put away for us: they give it to us, because they want to see whether we shall handle the food. If they see that we do not touch the food, then they know that we have shot game.[2] That is when we do not handle food.

[*10 December*] /Xam-ka !ei suspect a person because of what he does, when he does not behave as he ordinarily does. For he behaves differently. He feels that he makes water; therefore he behaves like this. He does not behave as he usually behaves.

We who are /Xam-ka !ei are accustomed to do this when we have killed something on the hunting-ground: we knock it down (cover it)

235

on the hunting-ground. We return home while the game lies knocked down (covered) on the hunting-ground. We go up to the people at home. This is what we do when we want to let them know that we have killed game: we do not want to say to them, 'I have struck game dead at such a place!' Instead, we do this: when we tell them about the game that we have killed, we say that we have merely come upon the spoor of game; we have found the spoor of game that behaves like this.

The others then understand that we are really telling them that we have killed game. They believe us because they feel that they are making us [*untranslated line*] when we have told them that we have shot a gemsbok. They do not ask us any more questions, but they just tell their friends that they should tell the children to go and dip up water for them so that they can take it to the place from which the man has come, to see what is there.

NOTES

1. Bella compares this sound to that made by a Muscovy duck.
2. When a man has hit (a buck), he does not take hold of food and eat, for he wants others to give him food to eat, which they know will not cool off the poison with which he shot the game. That food is what they let the man eat.

The ≠Nuturu

/Han≠kass'o
From his mother, /Xabbi-an

L. VIII. 9. 6786–6857
MAY 1878

[*4 May*] Her name was ≠Nuturu[1] when she was a woman. Therefore she is altogether used to dance for the children. She sang to herself. She sang,

> Yes, yes, yes, O ≠Nuturu.
> Yes, yes, yes, O ≠Nuturu.
> Yes, yes, yes, O ≠Nuturu.

Then she stood erect. She did this: she stood up, stood erect, for she wanted to ask the children. She asked the children whether the people who had gone hunting had returned. The children told her that the people had not come.

Then she danced again and asked the children again about the women who had gone to dip up water. She said, 'Have the old people not come?'

A child answered, 'They have not come.'

Then she believed the children. She said, 'Yes, yes!' For she believed the children. Then she danced again. Then she asked the children again about the people who had gone to get *!haken*,[2] who were gathering ants' chrysalides.

She said, 'Have the ants' chrysalides people not come?'

A child answered, 'They have not come.' To which she said, 'Yes, yes!'

Then she danced again. She asked the children about the people who were hunting. She said, 'Have the people not come?'

The children answered, 'They have not done so.'

She said, 'Yes, yes!' And she again danced. And she asked the children again about the old people, whether they had not come.

A child said, 'They have not come.'

And she danced again. And she asked the children and said, 'Have the old people not come?'

A child answered, 'The old people are coming.'

And she again danced. And she said, 'Are they near?'

And the children answered, 'The old people are not yet near.'

And she danced again. And she asked the children again whether the hunting people were not coming.

And the children said, 'The hunting people are coming.'

And she said, 'Are they near?'

And the children said, 'They are not yet near.'

And she danced again. She asked the children again whether the ant-gathering people were not coming.

And the children said, 'The ant-gathering people are coming.'

And she danced again. And she asked the children whether the hunters, who were deceiving the people, were near.

And the children said, 'The people are coming nearby.'

And she asked the children whether the old people were near. And a child said, 'The old people are coming nearby.'

Then she did this: she snatched off the horns of her face, and she went and hid. She walked along, she went. She did this: she lifted up her face, that part of her face on which the horns of her face had stood. It was beautifully white.

[5 *May*] The people thought, 'Our friend is the one whose face is beautifully white.'

As she sat, she lifted her face, for she wanted her face to be beautifully white as she sat. That is why she lifted up her face; she felt that that part of her face was really beautifully white. That was why she turned up her face.

Therefore the people who were returning merely walked, looking at her face. They just gave her the springbok breasts. She was the one who got the springbok breasts, which are fat. Therefore she was the one who ate them, while the wives of those men went without because their men had given the ≠Nuturu the springbok breasts. And she was the one who gnawed them. The wives of these men ate meat, but she was the one to eat fat.[3] That is why these women suffered want. They felt that it was she who ate springbok breasts, for the men felt that they had married her. They neglected their wives for her.

Therefore they withheld the fat from their wives because they married the ≠Nuturu because her face was pretty.

Then the children told their mothers. They said, 'O our mother, when you see the person to whom your sons are giving the springbok breasts, you seem to think that the horns of her face are not like this. They stand there. She does not nod her head nicely, as she does when she has taken off the thing which she keeps hiding. She takes it out; she sticks it on when you have gone. Then she dances for us. She does not nod her head nicely like this, O our mother.'

Then the mothers said, 'You must not tell her when we come; you must let us come so that we may also see. This thing must be what you are wont to put in the ground, while she is flaunting there. Therefore you must let us come. All the people must come home. They will catch sight of her. They will see what it is that she does.'

Then the people came home from all sides, gathering while she danced there. The people caught sight of her while she danced there. The people came home from all directions. The people thus saw the horns of her face.

The people said, 'You are like this. You don't act like this. We thought you were beautiful.'

And a child said, 'Allow me to go and get the springbok heart with my brother.'

When she found that she was caught, the ≠Nuturu darted away, while the child went to fetch the springbok heart with her brother. She did this when she thought that she would take off her face's horn. It stuck fast. She went to hide her face's horn. She hid her face's horn in a bush because she was angry with the children because they had not told her before the people had seen her face's horns.

The people gave her meat scraps. They said, 'How is it that we withheld the fat from the little mother? We thought that she was a beautiful person. We gave her only fat.'

Another said, 'Give grandmother that bone (the bone at the back of the neck), so that she may go to chew it. They felt that they blamed and scolded the ≠Nuturu because they had thought her beautiful. That is why they had withheld the fat from the women; they had thought the ≠Nuturu was beautiful.

And another said, 'I am telling you about that thing. I withheld meat from this mother, while the ≠Nuturu lay cooling off.'

She felt she was angry. She was angry with the children who had not told her. Therefore she lay cooling off, for she felt that she had done as follows: when she ate the springbok breasts, she had kept holding up her face. She kept on lying, cooling off. She was angry with the people, because she was eating the springbok backbone. She used to do this when she was eating the springbok breasts, she kept holding up her face, for she thought that her face would seem lean. That is why she kept holding up her face: she thought that the people did not know that her face's horn had been there.

Then the children told their people that her face's horn had been there. And the people told them not to speak to the ≠Nuturu. They would come to see how the ≠Nuturu behaved. The children must not tell the ≠Nuturu that they were coming, so that they might see how the ≠Nuturu nodded her head this way. They felt that the children thought that the ≠Nuturu did not nod her head nicely like that. Therefore they wanted the children not to tell the ≠Nuturu when they were coming. They would come to see how the ≠Nuturu nodded her head.

Then the children hid it and kept it secret from the ≠Nuturu; they did not speak to the ≠Nuturu. They did not do as they had been accustomed, to tell the ≠Nuturu when their mothers were coming.

Then the ≠Nuturu danced there because she still thought the people were not coming, but they were in fact coming. They surprised her.

The people said, 'You are really doing this, nodding your head nicely. That is what the children put in the ground when they stared at you when you behaved like this. We said that the children had been playing, but your soft ground (the ring she made in dancing) must have been like this because you did this there while you did not fetch water. Your soft ground looks as if it fell in with a dip where you stood dancing. Our children are those who did this: they played, while you were the one who behaved as you did there; you did not get wood. We dipped up water to give you to drink. We also brought wood to warm you. You are the one who ate fat when you were behaving like this.'

Then her face's horn stuck fast while she was dancing there. She stood erect. She asked the children. The children told her the people had not come even though the people had caught sight of her face's horn. She was dancing there.

Then one child said, 'Please let me go to get the springbok heart with my brother.'

Then the ≠Nuturu was startled. She wrenched off her face's horn, wrenched it off. She hid it. She went away. She lay down and did not stand upright. She lay in anger and did not look after the food. She lay down, lay in anger. Then she was silent.

When the children said, 'My grandmother, please play for us, as you used to do,' she was silent, for she was cross with the children because they had not warned her in time. The people had come and caught sight of her face's horn. The children had not told her when the people were returning. And all the people were at home. They had caught sight of her when she had thought that they had not come. She was dancing there because she still thought that the people had not come, when the people must have come already. That was why she was dancing there. The people caught sight of her while she was still thinking that the people had not come. That was why she was dancing there. She still thought that the people had not come because she thought that the children had said that they had not come.

The children felt that their people had spoken to them about it. They were not to tell the ≠Nuturu; they were to keep quiet so that all the people might see what the ≠Nuturu was like.

She nodded her head. The men did not give their wives the fat. They should see the ≠Nuturu; they gave the ≠Nuturu only fat, while they were eating meat. Their wives went without while the ≠Nuturu was supping on fat. Their wives were eating meat because the men had married the ≠Nuturu on account of her face. They gave her fat and that is why the wives went without while the ≠Nuturu was the one who kept eating fat. Their wives were eating meat; they felt that they had scolded their wives. They must only give the ≠Nuturu fat.

Then the women were afraid. The women gave the ≠Nuturu only fat because they had said, 'Take it to that person for me so that she can eat the thing and do not cut off any part.'

The women were afraid of them. They took the thing to the ≠Nuturu for they thought that the woman had wanted them to cut the thing, that they should cut off a little bit of fat.

They had said, 'You must leave the thing alone while it is whole and not cut it; you must give it to the ≠Nuturu while it is whole. You must not cut off a bit; you must take it whole to the ≠Nuturu.'

Then the woman was afraid of the man. She took the thing whole to the ≠Nuturu. They came to sit down, but they did not eat. The ≠Nuturu was the one who was eating there.

They were afraid of the men because they felt the men had married the ≠Nuturu because of her face which seemed lean. That is why they did not want their women to eat. The ≠Nuturu was the one who ate. The women ate old things.

Therefore the old women said, 'Oh children, see, the brothers do not want the sisters to eat fat, but that person is the one to eat fat, she at whom they keep looking while she sits over there. They do not want the sisters to eat fat. You must not tell her when the brothers will return, while she is playing there. The brothers will see what she is like while she is still playing there. Then the young men who have married the ≠Nuturu will stare at her when she is like this. [*7 May*] They will stare at her because they love her. They will see, getting her. They thought they loved her for her face, but they did not see what she was really like. The people who loved her will stare at her face's horn because the children told their mothers about it.'

Whereupon the mothers said, 'You must not stop her when the other people return from all directions if you wish the brothers to come and see the person at whose face they are accustomed to stare. That is why they do not let the sisters cut off [meat]. They keep looking at the ≠Nuturu because of her face. The sisters are afraid of them because they are not patient if the sisters eat and cut off meat. That is why the sisters are afraid of dropping the thing that they give to the ≠Nuturu and why they do not cut off even a little bit. They think that if they cut it, their menfolk will scold them. So they give the thing to the ≠Nuturu. Therefore you must let them come while the ≠Nuturu is still dancing.'

Then they came while the ≠Nuturu was dancing there. They came and saw the ≠Nuturu. They unloosed and set down the springbok, while they looked at the ≠Nuturu. They said, 'You are like that! How is it that we thought we would stint the mothers for a person like this? She is not at all nice. She is like this, though she used to sit making her face thin.

'But she must really be like this. She must have behaved like this.

She is not nice. I do not want the mothers to share the pieces of meat with this person who is behaving like this. Therefore I want her to give this piece, so that she may eat it. I used to think that she was a beautiful person. But she is a person who is like this; she is not nice. I have been depriving this person. She is a proper person, but an old person. She is not nice. She is really ugly. I have been depriving a beautiful person.'

Then their mothers said, 'I want you to look because you did not seem to unburden. You do not seem as if I had taught you. I taught you. You did foolish things, whereas a little child has sense when we have taught it.'

NOTES

1. Editor: The *Bushman Dictionary* gives ≠Nuturu as follows: a weevil. *Cleonis glacialis* (?).
2. *!haken* resembles 'rice' (i.e. 'Bushman rice'); the maggots' fat is like (that of) rice. *!haken* are food's things; there is not anything as nice as it when it is fresh.
3. Editor: Amongst the Kalahari !Kung, 'to eat fat' is a euphemism for sexual intercourse. This was probably also so among the /Xam.

The moon

The moon features prominently in /Xam folklore. Some versions of the creation of the eland end with the creation of the moon (Bleek, 1924: 2–9).

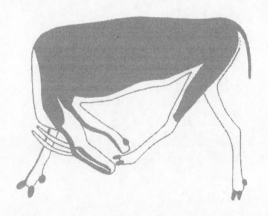

The moon not to be laughed at

/Han≠kass'o
From his mother, /Xabbi-an

L. VIII. 28. 8441–8443
MAY–JUNE 1879

The moon (*!kau-kauru*)[1] is that of which people say, 'The moon was angry, because people laughed at it because it was large; and it went into the sky.'

Therefore the people are accustomed to call it '//Kuan-ttu'. The moon's other name is //Kuan-ttu because they show respect to it, so that it will not go into the sky.

NOTE

1. Jantje thinks that this must have been the moon's name when he was a man. //Koon is the name of the moon's wife, when it is large.

Hunting with a dog and asking the moon for luck

//Kabbo

L. II. 1. 217–220
13 JUNE 1871

The Gipp[1] springs out of the hole. The dog runs after him. The dog catches him and bites him with his teeth. The man runs up and beats him. He beats him dead with a stick.

The '≠kaitchi'[2] springs out of the bush. The dog runs to him and catches him as the man comes running. The man beats his head, he beats him down.

The jackal comes out of his house, as the man comes. The man sets the dog on him. The dog runs and catches him. The dog bites him, while he lies and screams. The man beats him down dead. He falls on the ground; he dies.

They cannot ask the sun for anything, but they do ask the moon. They raise the right hand and say, 'I speak with the hand here, so that I may kill a springbok with my hand, with my bow.'

I lie down. I ask that I may kill a springbok early tomorrow. [*Two untranslated pages follow.*]

The moon lies there in the sky. I take a stick to poke out rice today so that I can eat it. After the moon has died and come out again small, the /Xam-ka !ei speak to it.

NOTES

1. Editor: The *Bushman Dictionary* gives '/kuken', the word translated 'gipp', as *Proteles* or aardwolf.

2. Editor: The /Xam informant /A!kunta identified a jackal species, *Canis variegata* as '≠kaitchi' (L. I. 2. 185). The word is probably a corruption of the Dutch *katjie*, diminutive of *kat*, cat.

The moon, moths and game

Diä!kwain

L.V. 16. 5206–5257

12, 13 & 16 AUGUST 1875

When our mothers saw the moon, when they saw that the moon did not lie hollow, they spoke, they said, 'This moon is a good moon; it does not carry people, for it carries as a man does when he carries food, when he has put food into the net. It seems as if it knew that our men will carry; therefore it carries with the net. It seems as if it knew that our folk will go out and find food, that their going will be fortunate.'

Our mothers spoke, they said 'Wait, we must watch because this moon it is like this: we must see if our men will not get a tortoise. For it is a thing that knows the time at which we shall get food. For the moon and stars are things which know matters which we do not know.'

When our mothers had thus spoken, when we were there for a short time, we looked there so that we should truly see the thing which the moon had been carrying. For the moon was the one who told us about it, that our fathers would carry food. Therefore when our mothers saw the moon, when the moon returned, they exclaimed, they said, 'That person has really been the one on account of whom my husband went out unsuccessfully because he feels that he has been lying down. Therefore, my husband's going was thus.'

When our mothers espied the moon, they exclaimed, they said: 'I have desired the moon to do this, to return for he really has been the one on account of whom the thing is like this; while he feels that he has been lying down.' They exclaim, they say: 'Wait for us, that we may look, when we perceive the moon, for, [*untranslated phrase*] we have not yet seen him. Therefore, the thing has not proved fortunate. For you are those who know, that the moon is a thing which knows things; for it sees things which will come to pass; it is the one who knows them, things which we do not know.'

That is why it was that the hare formerly spoke about the moon's doings. It is not a little thing. For he is a great sun. He is the one who knows the time at which a thing will come to pass.

Therefore, our mothers, when they perceived the moon, they exclaimed, they said, 'Behold! The moon is bloody, a man will shoot game; its blood will flow. That herd of game, its blood is that which is there (on the moon). That is why it is red.'

Therefore our mothers used to teach us who were children that we should, when we shot game, we should not look at the moon. For we appeared to think that if we looked towards him, he would swallow down the fat of the game which we had shot. The game's flesh would become black. The flesh felt that the moon was the one who had swallowed down the game's fat, even if the game had been fat. The moon was the one who had swallowed down the game's fat. We might think that the game had always been lean, but the game felt that the man who shot the game had looked towards the moon. Therefore the game was like this.

Therefore our mothers used to tell us that we must not look at the moon when we had shot game. If he did not swallow down the game's fat, he would not allow the game to die. He would cool the mouth of the game's wound, that the game might recover, the game would not die, even if the poison with which the man had shot the game had been strong.

[*13 August*] The moon would allow the poison to become as water. Our mothers used to tell us about it: Did we not behold the earth when the moon has made water upon the ground? These are the things with which he (the moon) cools the mouth of the game's wound.

Our mothers also did so with regard to the other little thing that resembles the moon.[1] Its name is also Moon. It is alive. It lives on the ground. Our mothers took it up when they saw it. Our mothers grasped it and placed it on their hands. They questioned it as to the time at which our fathers would get food.

When our mothers opened their hand, they did thus: their hands fell, they did thus. When they had not yet questioned it, they said, 'Rrrrrru! O Moon!' While they opened their hand, they exclaimed: 'O Moon! When shall I get food?'

This is what they did when they opened their hands, when they intended to talk with it. If the moon ran down their hand, they did thus. If they said that the moon ran down their hand, they exclaimed, they said: 'We shall get food; for the moon ran down over my hand.'

They do this when they see that it appears to die on their hand: they exclaim, they say: 'Behold! The moon has told one that we shall not yet get food, for it was the one which died upon my hand.'

This is what they do when they see that the moon acts in this manner; they exclaim, they say: 'Wait! I will question it again.' Then they shut their hand and exclaim: 'Rrrrr! O Moon! Shall I not really get food?' If, when they open their hand, the moon dies on their hand, they exclaim: 'Do you not see that the moon has told me that we shall not get food? You yourselves see that it does thus. When I questioned it about the time when I should get food, it continued to sleep upon my hand, and it told me that I should not get food.'

This is what they do when they see that the moon behaves in this way; they put it down and tell their companions about it. They exclaim, they say, 'You know that it is not a thing which deceives. We agree entirely with it when it tells [*16 August*] us about it. For it is not a thing which is wont to deceive us. For, it is wont to tell us the truth when we question it.' For a thing which possesses[2] game, it is. It knew the time when we would kill different kinds of game. It intends to show the game to us, when we have not yet killed the game.

That is why our mothers were accustomed to do thus when we sat, warming ourselves at our hut's fire at night: if a moth[3] came to our hut's fire, our mothers exclaimed, they told us about it. They said, they exclaimed: 'Behold! Why is it that the moths not a little come to our fire tonight? Father will shoot game, for the moths come to our fire tonight.'

The other moth resembles what the game looks like. Mother told us about it: 'Behold! A gemsbok will be wounded, for you see it is a gemsbok's moth. Things which live with the game, they are those which are accustomed to come to our fire at the time when we think we will kill a gemsbok. They come to us and burn themselves in our fire. They feel that the game with which they live, its flesh will burn at our fire. Therefore they come to tell us that we shall put the flesh of the game to roast at the fire which we possess. That is why they come to tell us about it.'

If we are a person who knows, we know that the game will die if the moths come to our fire. The moths do thus when our father will kill a quagga: black moths were coming to our fire.'

When our fathers saw that black moths were coming to our fires, they said: 'Look! Why is it that black moths are coming to our fire tonight? A quagga will be wounded, for a quagga's moths are those which come to the fire tonight.'

Our mothers did as follows at another time. About black moths which resemble the ostrich, our mothers exclaimed, they said, 'An ostrich is the one which will be wounded, for, you are those who see that these ostrich's moths come to the fire.'

NOTES

1. A small insect, called *!kao !kasso*, and said to resemble the moon, by means of which the women try to ascertain if the men will bring food home.
2. Editor: The /Xam word '/*ki*' has several meanings. In this context, it is best translated as meaning possessing the power to control the behaviour of game (see Lewis-Williams, 1988).
3. Editor: The *Bushman Dictionary* (p. 282) gives *g/oro* as 'moth, *Celeuna renisiga*, Walker'.

The moon and the hare

≠Kasin
From his mother

L. IV. 1. 3441–3447
4 NOVEMBER 1873

The moon was the one who ordered the hare to go to tell the people that a man who is ill will rise up, like himself. For he who is the moon, when he dies, he comes again, living.

The hare went, but he turned the story round. He said that a man who dies will not arise; he decreed that a man who dies shall die completely and be finished. That is why people do not rise up. People who die do not arise. Dying, they are finished. Therefore people who die do not come back living; they die and are completely finished. They do not arise, for they are truly finished.

This is the argument about which the moon hit the other one's mouth. Therefore we who are ill are finished; we do not arise again. We who are ill, we are finished. Our thoughts, ascending, leave us. Our bodies, our bodies are those which lie in the earth. That is why our thoughts leave us.[1]

NOTE

1. The moon was angry with the hare because it had given the message wrongly, and heated a stone in the fire, held down the hare, and burnt its mouth, which is why it has a wound or scar there. The hare gave the message intentionally wrong; and this is why we who are people, when we are ill, die and are finished, and this is why the moon fought the hare. He [≠Kasin] says he heard this from his father and mother; his father had heard it from *his* father.

Shamans

The /Xam-ka !ei believed in a supernatural potency that was, in some ways, like electricity. It could be in a number of powerful things, such as eland. In intense concentrations it was considered to be dangerous. This power was harnessed by shamans, who could number as many as half the men and a third of the women in a camp. Shamans performed their tasks by entering an altered state of consciousness (the spirit realm).

The /Xam word translated as 'shaman' is *!gi:xa*. It means full of (*xa*) potency (*!gi:*). The work of San shamans may still be observed among modern Kalahari groups. The San word *!gi:xa* was taken into the Xhosa language.

Kum 48

Shamans and swallows

Diä!kwain

L. V. 21. 5698–5707
15 DECEMBER 1875

Our mothers tell us that we should not throw stones at the swallow because it is the rain's thing. We can see that it is not like other little birds that eat earth. For they eat clay. It eats insects which are in the water.[1] That is why our mothers scold us severely if they see us children throwing stones at the swallow. They ask us whether we do not see that, when the rainclouds are in the sky, then the swallow flies about. But when there are no rainclouds in the sky, we do not see it flying about.

Our mothers[2] used to tell us that the swallow is with the things which the sorcerers take out and which they send about. Those are the things which the swallow resembles. That is why our mothers told us to leave off throwing stones at the swallow. They asked us, did we not see what had happened to Kki-a-//ken?[3] He had been carrying on in that way, throwing stones at the swallow, and he had nearly died because of the swallow. As he stood throwing stones at it, he fainted, while he was throwing them. He fell insensible. People went and carried him from the place where they[4] had been throwing stones. It did not seem as if he would live. He was so ill that his mother's people did not think that he would recover. They thought that he was really dying because the swallow had entered into him. A sorcerer had come out of the swallow into him. It had seemed as if he would grow up to manhood, but he would die another evening.

NOTES

1. Little things which are in water that has become small in quantity.
2. It means here all the children's mothers.

3. Kki-a-//ken was the name of a child who was the son of Nan-oro and !Kappem-
    an. Nan-oro was the younger brother of Xa:ä-tin (the latter being the father of
    Diä!kwain, my informant.) Kki-a-//ken was killed (when grown-up and the father
    of a family) by the half-white half-kkuobboo [*Dictionary*: *kwobbo*, Coloured per-
    son], a little before Diä!kwain came to the breakwater. Four Bushmen were killed
    at the same time. They bound them and drove them, making them go to the cliff;
    they went to lay them dead at the cliff, when they had driven Kki-a-//ken and the
    other with horses. The names of the men were as follows: 'Gert Rounabout',
    'Prince Sautkop' (a brother of 'Jan Rounabout's' father) or //Kum-!k'au; 'Swart
    Klaas'; Kki-a-//ken or 'Stuurman'.

4. 'They', referring to a whole party of little boys, D.H. says.

Karosses must not be beaten upon the ground

Diä!kwain
From his mother, ≠Kammi-an

L. V. 20. 5537–5556
NOVEMBER 1875

[*17 November*] When a Grass Bushman is angry with other people, he unloosens the things he is carrying, and he beats them on the ground. As he beats them, he says that he wishes that the heat will devour the people. He does this to make dust fly up to the sky. He says that the dust which he is raising will cause illness. It causes thirst, and the thirst will make us feel hot (feverish). That is why he is raising the dust.

Our mothers always say that it is not good for a person if we beat a kaross on the ground. For illness is caused by our shaking of a kaross. So whenever our mothers saw us children beating karosses, they used to scold us and ask us why we were beating the karosses. They asked us why we did so. Did we not know that dust is not a good thing? This is what the earth will do if we shake a kaross, striking it on the ground: a great deal of illness will come because of our beating it.

Our mothers said that the illness's departed people[1] would see us if we beat the karosses. For a sorcerer[2] is watching us at the moment when we are beating karosses. If it sees us do so, it races to us and carries us off, as if we had no sense and did not respect magic things.[3] It lets one of us die because we seem to have no sense. So our mothers used to say that we cause illness by beating karosses.

Our mothers told us that people bring illness; they do so because other people have killed one of their people. They cry because it is their friend whom the people have killed. They do not want to be like those who kill others with their hands, (for these) merely kill by magic (sorcery).[4] When they have cried for their friend, they say that they wish that the midday heat will surely cause a fever (heat) so that they may see the heat kill the man of the other people, surely kill him.

[*18 November*] They do not seem to realise that we are also people. They seem to think that we do not think of our own person. But they do as they say. They send little things which resemble flies, which are small and fly, they make them go to the place where people have killed their man and stay there.

A person who is a man-of-illness[5] goes to the place where he intends to cause illness. He goes to open the place in which the illness is. He speaks to the illness when he has opened the place in which the illness dwells. He says, 'Come out! You shall see whether we do not also send [sickness] and make those people cry, as we do.'

For they do not seem to know that we have people. Then the things like flies fly away to where the man has let them loose. They are like a cloud of dust.[6] They go out, and they go to the place where the people who have killed their man live. That dust goes to kill the people.

NOTES

1. Editor: *//xi-ta /nu*: the spirits of dead shamans who send sickness.
2. Editor: Lloyd translated *!gi:xa* as 'sorcerer'. Today the /Xam word is commonly translated 'shaman'. Most of the /Xam texts dealing with shamanism were published in *Bantu Studies* (1933a, 1933b, 1935, 1936a) by Dorothea Bleek.
3. Editor: The phrase used here, '*!gi: ka tiken-tiken*', may be literally translated as 'the actions of supernatural potency'.
4. Editor: *//ken*, a synonym or near synonym for *!gi:*, means the supernatural potency that was harnessed by /Xam shamans.
5. Editor: *//xi-ta !kui*: a living shaman who has the power to send sickness.
6. *!kho*: something like a blue mist which resembles fire smoke.

A rock painting[1]

/Han≠kass'o

VIII. 1. 6063–6068
13 JANUARY 1878

I think that it is the rain's navel that goes along here. I think that these people are addressing the rain so that the rain's navel will not kill them, so that it will be favourable towards them, so that the rain's navel will not kill them, so that the rain's navel will keep favourable towards them.

This man holds a thing that resembles a stick. I think that these are rain's people.[2] I do not know them, but I see that they are people, because they have arms; they resemble people. They feel that they are sorcerers. They are rain's sorcerers.[3] This man is holding a thing which resembles a */khoë*,[4] the sort of curved stick used in making a house. I do not know whether it is a */khoë*, but I see that it looks like a */khoë*.

These people (i.e. those on the lower side of the line, in the picture), I do not know whether the rain's navel divides them from the other people. They are people, sorcerers, rain's sorcerers. They make rain fall, and the rain's clouds come out because of them. That is why the rain falls and the place becomes green. This thing (i.e. what we should have called the right arm of the rain-figure) resembles a caterpillar,[5] the rain's caterpillar.

NOTES

1. Editor: The rock painting is shown on page 262 in a copy made by Thomas Dowson. For a discussion of the various interpretations that have been advanced for this now-famous rock painting, see Lewis-Williams et al. (1993).
2. Editor: *!khwa-ka !ke*. Literally 'people of the rain'.
3. Editor: *!gi:ten*, sorcerers, medicine people or shamans. *!Khwa-ka !gi:ten*, shamans

of the rain.

4. A curved stick ('*paale*') used in making a /Xam house.

5. Editor: The *Bushman Dictionary* gives *//kerri-si !kau* as *Scolopendra* and says that the species was identified in the South African Museum, Cape Town. A note by Lloyd on page 6067 rev.: 'There is another *!khwa-ka //kerrissi !kau*, Jantje says, which is found in the ground when digging out *!kuisi* [an edible bulb]. This is a very little one. The rain's one is the true one. The *!khwa-ka //kerrissi !kau* was seen by Jantje in a painting brought down by Mr Sanderson, executed by a [Bantu-speaking] artist.'

//Kabbo causes rain to fall[1]

//Kabbo

L. II. 5. 625–633
12 OCTOBER 1871

I dreamt that I told the rain to fall for me because my arm ached and my chest ached. Therefore I dreamt that I spoke. The rain consented. Because my chest ached, the rain would fall for me so that I could sit comfortably. The rain would wet the garden for me so that I could sit in peace while the rain was wetting the earth of the garden.

And I sat. The rain wet the bushes in the garden, as I sat quietly.

I used to dream when I was at my home. I dreamt, and the rain assented to me when I was at my own place. The rain fell for me. The rain fell when I was thirsty. That was why I dreamt of the rain, that rain should fall for me, so that I could drink; for I was dying of thirst. Then the rain fell, and I drank because the rain used to consent.

I told my wife that rain would fall for us so that we could drink.

I spoke to my wife about it: 'O Wife, I have been dreaming of rain so that it will fall for us, so that we can drink.' That is what I said. My wife agreed with me.

I also spoke to my son: 'My son, I have been dreaming that rain will fall for us, so that we may drink, for we are thirsty.' I said to him: 'We shall drink tomorrow; I see clouds.' I said to him: 'Do you not see the clouds? We shall drink tomorrow.'

My daughter spoke to her husband. She said to her husband: 'Father has told me that rain will fall for us, so that we may drink.'

I told my daughter's little child that rain would soon fall, and that we would drink.

The rain soon fell while the sun was at this place. The sun was warm. I spoke. My daughter's child was silent. 'The rain will come to us, and we shall drink.' But the child was silent.

The rain fell. The rain moistened the ground, and the waters ran off, the water's child. We drank it. We filled springbok skins. We filled

263

the springbok skin. We put away water. We filled ostrich eggshells with water. We put them away.

I have shot three springbok, and my son-in-law has shot two porcupines. Then we put the water away.[2] Our wives cook the springbok meat in a pot. We eat it; we lie down. We go out hunting in the dark. We go to look at another water which is level with the ground.

We have told our wives: 'We must move away. We will move to the water lying there.'

We move to it. We go to settle at it, at midday. The sun is warm, and we feel that the child cried for the water. We put down the water.

We climb the Brinkkop in the dark. We make a fire. We are two, I and my daughter's husband. My daughter's husband sees springbok coming, and they are many. We creep up to the springbok as they walk along.

I again get a male springbok; my daughter's husband also gets another springbok. We both get springbok while the sun is warm.

We carry the springbok home. We go and cut up springbok with our knives. We hang up the springbok meat.[3] We cook the springbok meat and eat it, while the sun is warm.

We go hunting again. We again climb to the top of the mountain. We again light a fire. [*14 October*] We again see other springbok. The other springbok walk along. We head them into the Little Swartkop. We steal up to them in the Little Swartkop. We again get two springbok. We again carry them home. Then we empty the pot.

My daughter's husband goes out at night. My daughter's husband goes to get two young porcupines at night. He comes and sees an anteater in the holes. They are the anteater's home. They are also the anteater's burrows; they are holes. The anteater is in them.

He went and told my daughter that we must go and dig out the anteater. My daughter told my wife what her husband said to her, 'O Mother! /Han≠kass'o has told me that they have gone to dig out the anteater, he and father. We will carry water while our men are with us.'[4]

NOTES

1. [*12 October*] Jantje Toorn told me on the 11th that he had asked for rain on the previous night, when lying down (in his bed), to make the garden wet, as his arms and chest were painful; and that it had come in the night. He told this with an appearance of satisfaction, so I today, [*12 October*], I asked more about it, and got the history, which appears to be that of a dream. He says he saw the rain coming, and also saw and spoke to his wife, his son, and his daughter in his dream. [*14 October*] The whole is, I believe, not a dream. I think he has branched off into ordinary life in the course of it.

2. 'Bera' the water, put it in the house's shadow, inside the house. Editor: '*Bera*' is a Dutch word meaning 'to put safely away'.

3. hang flesh (on bushes).

4. The women bring the water to the men, who are digging out the aardvark; with a stick. The sun being very warm they want to drink. They dig out the earth then shoot him in his hole. They throw out the ground with their hands.

New maidens

The /Xam-ka !ei practised numerous rituals concerning girls at puberty – the so-called 'new maidens'. They were considered to have 'the rain's magic power'. The Kalahari !Kung perform the well-known Eland Bull Dance at the time of a girl's first menstruation (Lewis-Williams, 1981: 41–54).

A ceremony performed by /Xam girls
at puberty

Diä!kwain
From his father and his mother

L. V. 20. 5592–5604
DECEMBER 1875

[*13 December*] A woman who is still a maiden¹ does this to the dog which her father takes out (hunting). She is still a very young girl, not a big girl. She does this before she eats. She protects² the dog that is with them because she wants him, when he smells an animal's scent, to seek out its heart. She cuts off meat and holds it in her mouth and chews it. Then she sucks off the dirt from her knee. When the dirt from her knee is with the meat, she tells the people to catch hold of the dog for her.

[*14 December*] A girl who is a maiden³ does this to a thing which a dog has killed, if her mothers wish her to eat it. She cuts off its flesh and puts it in her mouth. She then sucks the dirt from her knee. When the dirt of her knee is together with the meat, she pulls open the dog's mouth. She spits the meat into his mouth with her saliva on it. When the meat is in the dog's mouth, she shuts it. She pats his back; she pats his shoulder.⁴ She says, 'Sa sa, sa, sa, sa!', while she is patting him. She wishes that the dog will never look away from game that he has seen.

The /Xam-ka !ei say that a dog does as follows if a girl does not give him the dirt from her knee. The dog does this if she simply eats something that he has killed for her. The old people say that her saliva will lie on the dog's heart; the dog will become bad. When he is chasing something, he will sound as if he is playing with it, even though he used to be a dog that killed. He goes along playing with the game; he leaves it because the girl has eaten, bewitching and turning his heart from the things.⁵ That is why he does not feel inclined to kill anything. He turns back and leaves the game. He merely comes up to us, as if he did not know that he ought to chase and catch something.

He appears to do foolish things because the girl has, by eating, taken his heart away from the game. His heart does not think of the game he has killed [*15 December*] unless the girl's saliva (with the dirt from her knee) is on his heart. That is why his heart is not inclined to kill things.

Our mothers also told us these things about dogs and also about the bone of the upper foreleg. They said that we must not break that bone in any game that the dog had killed; otherwise the dog's foreleg would break when it was chasing something.

NOTES

1. Editor: A girl who is menstruating for the first time.
2. Editor: Here Lloyd has transcribed the /Xam word for ritual avoidance and protection, '*!nanna sse*' as '*!ko a sse*'.
3. Editor: On the second day of narration, Diä!kwain started again from the beginning.
4. The back between the shoulders.
5. Editor: Lloyd first translated this passage 'the girl has eaten the strength from his heart'. Then she changed it to 'the girl has bewitching turning his heart from the things.' This gloss adds the word 'bewitching', which is not in the /Xam text, as an explanation.

Men turned into trees by the glance of a new maiden

//Kabbo

L. II. 2. 295–305
JULY 1871

The man here climbs the mountain. He plays the *goura*.[1] The girls look at him, as he comes. He stands fast, as he comes. He holds the *goura* in his hand. He holds the *goura* in his mouth as he stands playing it. As he stands, the sun has set. He stands still, as he holds it; he holds the *goura* in his mouth.

The girl listens to the *goura* with her ears. The man stands. He stands[2] because the maiden looks at him with the maiden's eye. The maiden looks, fastening him to the ground.

[*21 July*] And it is so. His legs are those of a man, but he is a tree. His arms are those of a man. He holds the *goura* with his mouth. He is a tree. He has his eyes, because he was a man. He has his head. He has his head-hair. He is a tree which is a man. He is a man. He is a tree. He has his feet. He is shod. He has his nails. He has his mouth. He has his nose. He has his ears. He is a tree. He is a man. He is a tree, and it is so that he plays the *goura*. He is a tree. He plays the *goura*, while he is a tree. He is a man. He plays the *goura*. It is so that he is a tree that stands playing the *goura*. He looks with his eyes. And it is so that he plays the *goura*, because she looked.

Another man stands fast. He carried arrows. He held a bow. He was returning, holding a jackal tail's hair. The maiden looked at him, and it is so that he stands fast. It is so that he stands still, as he held the jackal tail's hair. He held it, standing fast. As he stood, he also held the bow. He stood. So it was that he became a tree as he stood there. He held the hair, for he was a man. It was so: he held the hair. He is a tree. He stands. He has his legs, because he (formerly) had feet. It is so that he does indeed stand. He was shod in gemsbok skin sandals. He has his legs. He has his feet. He has his arms. He has his nails. He has his eyes. He has his nose. His head remains. He has his head-hair.

He has his ears. He has his knife. He has his tinderbox.

Another man climbs the mountain for he seeks [*untranslated word*]. He comes over the mountain. As he comes, he carries a quiver. And it is so that the maiden looks at him, as he comes. He too stands, as he carries the quiver on his shoulder. He stands. He holds the bow. He stands. He holds the stick. He stands. He still has his legs, and he still stands. He carries the quiver. He is a tree. He is a man. He carries the quiver. He has his arms, and it is so that he indeed still carries the bow. He still holds the stick because he still has his hands. He still has his nails. He still has his eyes. He still has his nose. His eyes remain. He is a tree. He has his head. He has his head-hair. He talks. He is a tree. He was a man who talked, and it is so that he talks while he is a tree. He waits standing on the mountain. He carries the [*22 July*] quiver. He is a talking tree, one that talked standing there, for he was a man. The maiden looked at him, and that is why he became a tree. It is true that he talks, for he was a man. And it is true that he became a tree which talked, for he was a tree. He looked and he talked. His mouth remained; his tongue remained to talk with. He is a tree that has his head-hair. He also has his eyes. He looks. He is a tree that looks. He is a tree. He looks. He has his flesh, because he was a man. It is true that he stands there, because the maiden looked at him.

NOTES

1. Editor: A stringed musical instrument (Bleek and Lloyd, 1911: 321–325; Kirby, 1968: 171–192).
2. He has his legs. He has his feet. He is a man. He was a man. He becomes a tree. He has his arms.

New maidens and the rain

Diä!kwain
From his mother, ≠Kammi-an

L. V. 13. 4981–5022
JULY 1875

[*15 July*] The time when the porcupine was a man, that was the time when mother told me about the quillroots on the porcupine's back and on the back of the porcupine's neck. My mother used to say to me that the porcupine's younger sister had once been a girl. This is what she did when her brother told her that she should make something that he wanted, that she should make it for him. She would not do what her brother said. Instead, she did this: when her brother spoke, she scolded him.

Her mother said, 'Oh my daughter! Why do you not realise that you are now a new maiden? Why did you speak like that to your brother? Did you not remember that your brother is now going to the hunting-ground? You did not seem to know that this is what the rain does when a new maiden curses people and wishes that her rain will be angry with them: the rain is not a little angry with the people. The rain lightens, killing a man, because it feels that the maiden does not protect the people from the rain.'

[*16 July*] The rain resembles what the maiden said to the people. The rain does this when it falls upon their place. The rain smells the scent of the person whom the girl cursed. The rain is angry when it is at that place; it lightens out from the place where it has fallen. The rain lightens, killing the man on the spot where he is. These are things about which a maiden thinks. For, when she is a maiden, she has the rain's magic power.[1] These are the things of which she must think when she is a maiden.

The maiden's mother spoke. She told the maiden about it: did she not know that the rain is a thing which hears? For the rain's sorcerers are with the rain. By magic they lead out the rain[2] so that it may hear her brother when he sees that it does not a little fall and so that it may listen to him when he speaks to it. When he sees that the rain seems to be growing angry, he must address the rain. For the rain is not pleased when its sorcerers take it away; the rain is very angry.

He (the sorcerer) does thus: he speaks to the rain so that it will hear him and turn back, so that it will fall at another place. For when the /Xam-ka !ei see that the rain seems as if it will become angry, they arise and go out in front of the house. They stand opposite to the place from which the rain comes. And they strike their navels[3] with their fists, and they press their hands on their navels and they snap their fingers at the rain.

And they speak to the rain, they speak, they say, 'Falling, you must turn back, so that, falling, you may pass along to the place over there and not pass to this place. For you do not a little lighten; it seems as if you are very angry.'

The rain consents to the man if he does this. It turns back; falling, it goes along to the place to which he made it pass by snapping his fingers. His rain goes there.

When a maiden takes care of her people, the rain is not very angry with the people. The rain agrees with the man when he speaks to it; the rain does not spit at him. When a maiden takes care of her people, the rain will not become angry with them, if she takes care of them. This is what she does when her father talks to her: she speaks gently with her father when he speaks to her. When her mother talks with her, she also talks gently with her mother. She wishes that the rain will do this: even if the rain has become angry, it may become cool when her father has spoken to it. It will gently and not make a noise of rattling thunder.

If a maiden scolds her people, the rain (will not listen) if one of her people speaks to it, when they think that they will speak to the rain so that it will sound gently as it falls, so that it will not make a rattling noise of thunder. A place is not nice if the rain makes a rattling noise of thunder; for the rain is fighting if it makes a rattling noise of thunder. When the rain comes down gently, then it is not very angry. The rain feels that it is not displeased. For the rain resembles what the maiden did. The rain is also afraid of our scolding; the rain falls gently on us when it is not displeased with us. The rain does this when we speak to it: it consents to us.

These are the things that old people tell the maidens, about the

doings of the rain and of a storm which once did as follows. When
the maiden was on the hunting-ground, the storm came in the sky.
She saw the storm, but she did not think that the rain intended to
fall. She thought that it was a little waft of mist. She reflected, she
thought that there were no rain clouds there. It seemed to be only a
little waft of mist that seemed to have come with the wind. That was
what had come into the sky. She looked at the little waft of mist. She
reflected, she thought that she would still dig out *!koa*⁴ for a little
while longer because the house was not far off. And she reflected, she
thought, 'Allow me to look again towards the waft of mist so that I
may see what it can be.'

And she looked up at it; and she saw that it was a cloud. The
cloud became large. The cloud came over the whole of the sky. The
cloud came up [*19 July*] as she was looking. And she reflected, she
thought, 'How is it that it is a rain cloud that floats along there? At
first it seemed to be a little waft of mist. But the cloud has become
like a beast of prey. I shall first put down the bag of *!koa* roots so that
I can return home. I shall go and tell my younger brothers about it so
that they can come to fetch the bag of *!koa* roots. I shall not be able to
go quickly if I am carrying the bag of *!koa* and seeking food. I shall
hide it. I shall go quickly so that I can return home. For the rain
cloud does not allow me time; it seems as if the rain will fall on me
before I have reached the house. For the rain comes rolling up. I shall
go; I shall see why the rain is doing this.'

And a storm came. [*Untranslated line*] The storm seemed like
wind; it sounded as a little whirlwind does. And the rain fell before
she had reached the house.

Her mother thought, 'The child seems to be yonder; for there is a
storm yonder.' Her mother had spoken before and told the child that
she should not go out to look for food because she was a new maid-
en. She had recently lain down.⁵ 'That is why I told her that she
should not go, because she is not yet cleansed with rain liquid. When
she washes, then she will be able to do so because she will have been
cleansed with rain liquid. For her scent still has the "buchu"⁶ with
which she had lain down.'

And the wind blew. As her mother came to look at the place
where she saw the rain strike, cleaving the clay, this wind whisked up
the maiden. And the maiden ascended with the wind, while the rain

lightened at the place where the girl was. And the wind took the girl. The rain, lightening, split open the earth. The earth ascended with the maiden; it became a whirlwind.

Then the maiden's mother spoke. She said, 'You are those who now see the earth ascending over there. It rises from the place where the rain struck. [*Untranslated line*] It ascends yonder; it is the earth. The maiden truly became dust, while she felt that she was a snake.[7] Whirling, she ascended.

The people who possessed their noses (the sorcerers)[8] sang. They said, 'You are now those who see that maiden ascends over there into the sky. The rain is now the one who takes her away. She becomes a snake.[9] You are now those who behold that she is ascending yonder, whirling up because the children do not behave as if we had spoken to them. They now behave like this because of what they have done: they do not behave as if we had educated them.'

Notes

1.   Editor: /koöde. One of three /Xam words that Bleek and Lloyd translated as 'magic' or 'magic power'. The other two words are !gi: and //ken. A person who is full of power, a shaman, was called a !gi:xa (pl. !gi:ten).

2.   Editor: The /Xam spoke of the rain as if it were an animal. Shamans of the rain were said to lead the rain-animal across the parched land and then to kill it so that its blood and milk would fall as precipitation. They could also withhold rain.

3.   Editor: At this time Lloyd was unsure how to translate !^hai:n. Elsewhere and in the *Dictionary* the word is given as 'navel'.

4.   A root something like a potato, but hairy and rather bitter, eaten by the /Xam-ka !ei. The !koa is in clay; and when we dig out the !koa, we strike it on the ground, so that the clay, which it has been in, may break off, that we may clean it of the clay, for it has been in the clay. They do this when its roots that are in the ground sprout; the sprouts are together with the clay. [*Two untranslated lines*]

5.   Editor: At the time of their first menstruation, girls were secluded in a hut; they lay down as if sick.

6.   Editor: Aromatic herbs.

7.   A large snake, whose name is feared. It is, D.H. says, to be seen in one of the rock paintings sent down by Mr Stow.

8.   Editor: /Xam shamans sniffed sickness out of their patients. During a curing ritual, they frequently suffered a nasal haemorrhage.

9.   !nuin is another name by which the snake //kheten (//xeiten) is spoken of.

Kum 55

The girl who made locusts

/Han≠kass'o

L. VIII. 7. 6622–6624
8 APRIL 1878

A girl once scooped up *!kuisse.*[1] She threw it up. It did this: it went and it became locusts. It became young locusts. And they jumped away. She takes out *serru,*[2] she makes dust.

NOTES

1. Editor: The *Bushman Dictionary* (p. 450) gives this word as 'an alternative spelling of *!kuisi, kuise,* an edible bulb much eaten'.
2. Editor: The *Bushman Dictionary* (p. 167) gives this word as meaning 'some part of a locust'.

New maidens and frogs

Diä!kwain

L. V. II. 3864–3881

7 JANUARY 1875

She became a frog and went into the waterhole[1] on account of it, and
the mud made a noise like the report of a cannon on account of it.
And her elders[2] wondered what it could be that sounded like that.
And they looked towards it, towards the place where the thing made a
noise. They saw that the thing looked like a mist of mud[3] when the
water was angry. They asked what had caused the water to do that.

And the maiden's grandmother said to the girl's mother, 'Go and
look because it seems to be your daughter with whom the water is
angry, for she has not behaved as if you had spoken to her.'[4]

And the maid's mother looked in the house and said, 'She must
have gone to the water. She seems to be the one with whom the water
is angry.'

And the children said, 'That maiden is in the water spring.'

The maiden's mother said that she had really told her about it,
that she should not go to the spring. For she (the mother) knew that
it was a great pit that did not want young girls, for it became angry
with young girls, that is to say new maidens. This is why the water
became angry with her on account of her odour. She became a frog.

This is why the people say that a frog was formerly a person who
became a frog. The people say 'frog', when they remember that a
maiden once became a frog when she went to wash herself at the
spring. She altogether became a frog. This is why people are accustomed to be afraid when their maiden does not walk about. They
remember that a maiden had once fallen into the spring. This is why
/Xam women take care of their maidens, on account of it. They fear
that she will do what the maiden once did. She had not been willing
to listen to her mother when her mother spoke to her about it, that
she should not go to the spring because she was a new maiden. She

deceived her mother. She went to the spring. She went and washed herself. And she became a frog, on account of it.

This is why the old /Xam women are afraid lest their maiden should also become a frog when she is a maiden if she were to walk about. This is why they are accustomed to make a house for her. They want her to lie in the house so that she will not walk about. They also give her water and food so that she may eat as she lies inside her house. They do not allow her to drink herself. They give her to drink. They remember that the people would [*untranslated word*] if she ate a lot.[5] The people also would eat just as she ate, on account of it. The people wish that she might eat moderately, so that the people might also eat moderately. This is why the people themselves give her food moderately. The people do not want her to eat by herself. The people take her food to her.[6]

The people also wish that she should not drink much water. They want her to drink moderately, so that the people might also drink just as she did. She drank, on account of it, so that the people might drink moderately. For the people would [*untranslated word*] if she did not drink moderately. The people also drink like her, as she did. She drank [*untranslated word*]. This is why the people gave her small pieces of meat which were very little. They want her to eat moderately so that they might also eat like her.

This is why the people make a reed for her with which she might drink.[7] She must not drink from large things. For if she drank from large things, she would not drink moderately. This is why the people make a reed for her so that she will drink by means of a reed, so that she will drink from an ostrich eggshell with a little mouth, one which was very small and had a reed entering into its mouth.

NOTES

1.   A deep hole or pit.
2.   Her mother, grandmother, grandfather and father, D.H. says.
3.   The 'blaaws mudder' sprang up into the air like a black mist, when the girl fell down into the spring.
4.   Because the water does not like a new maiden.

5. Cut off little pieces of food, and give them to her. D.H. says, 'We do not put them into her mouth for her.'
6. She must drink out of a reed, placed in the mouth of the ostrich eggshell; an eggshell with a *small* hole, so that only a little water may come through.
7. If the eggshell's mouth were large, she would have got a great deal of water.

References &
suggested reading

Anthing, L. 1863. Report in 'Message from His Excellency the
Governor with enclosures, relative to affairs in the north-western
districts of the colony'. Cape of Good Hope Parliamentary Papers
A-39 '63.

Biesele, M. 1993. *Women Like Meat: The Folklore and Foraging
Ideology of the Kalahari Ju/'hoan.* Johannesburg: Witwatersrand
University Press.

—— 1996. 'He stealthily lightened at his brother-in-law (and thunder
echoes in Bushman oral tradition a century later)'. In Deacon and
Dowson (eds.) 1996. *Voices from the Past: /Xam Bushmen and the
Bleek and Lloyd Collection.* Johannesburg: Witwatersrand
University Press.

Bleek, D. F. 1924. *The Mantis and his Friends.* Cape Town: Maskew
Miller.

—— 1928. *The Naron, a Bushman Tribe of the Central Kalahari.*
Cambridge: Cambridge University Press.

—— 1928–1929. 'Bushman grammar'. *Zeitschrift für Eingeborenen-
Sprachen,* 19: 81–98 and 20: 161–174.

—— 1929a. *Comparative Vocabularies of Bushman Languages.*
Cambridge: Cambridge University Press.

—— 1929b. 'Bushman folklore'. *Africa,* 2: 302–313.

—— 1931. 'Customs and beliefs of the /Xam Bushmen. Part I:
Baboons'. *Bantu Studies,* 5: 161–174.

—— 1932a. 'Customs and beliefs of the /Xam Bushmen. Part II: The
lion'. *Bantu Studies,* 6: 47–63.

—— 1932b. 'Customs and beliefs of the /Xam Bushmen. Part III:
Game animals'. *Bantu Studies,* 6: 233–249.

—— 1932c. 'Customs and beliefs of the /Xam Bushmen. Part IV:
Omens, wind-making, clouds'. *Bantu Studies,* 6: 323–342.

—— 1933a. 'Beliefs and customs of the /Xam Bushmen. Part V: The rain'. *Bantu Studies*, 7: 297–312.

—— 1933b. 'Beliefs and customs of the /Xam Bushmen. Part VI: Rain-making'. *Bantu Studies*, 7: 375–392.

—— 1935a. 'Beliefs and customs of the /Xam Bushmen. Part VII: Sorcerers'. *Bantu Studies*, 9: 1–47.

—— 1935b. '!Kung mythology'. *Zeitschrift für Eingeborenen-Sprachen*, 25(4): 261–283.

—— 1936a. 'Beliefs and customs of the /Xam Bushmen. Part VIII: More about sorcerers and charms'. *Bantu Studies*, 10: 131–162.

—— 1936b. 'Special speech of animals and moon used by the /Xam Bushmen'. *Bantu Studies*, 10: 163–199.

—— 1956. *A Bushman Dictionary*. American Oriental Series Vol. 41. New Haven: American Oriental Society.

Bleek, E. & Bleek, D. 1909. 'Notes on the Bushmen'. In Tongue, M. H. *Bushman Paintings*. London: Clarendon Press.

Bleek, W. H. I. 1873. 'Report of Dr Bleek concerning his researches into the Bushman language and customs'. Presented to the Honourable the House of Assembly by command of His Excellency the Governor. Cape Town: House of Assembly.

—— 1874. 'Remarks on J. M. Orpen's "A glimpse into the mythology of the Maluti Bushmen"'. *Cape Monthly Magazine*, 9(49): 10–13.

—— 1875. 'Brief account of Bushman folklore and other texts'. Second Report concerning Bushman researches, presented to both Houses of Parliament of the Cape of Good Hope by command of His Excellency the Governor. Cape Town: Government Printer.

—— & Lloyd, L. C. 1911. *Specimens of Bushman Folklore*. London: George Allen.

Deacon, J. 1986. '"My place is the Bitterpits": The home territory of Bleek and Lloyd's /Xam San informants'. *African Studies*, 45: 135–155.

—— 1988. 'The power of a place in understanding southern San rock engravings'. *World Archaeology*, 20: 129–140.

—— 1996a. 'The /Xam informants'. In Deacon, J. & Dowson, T. A. (eds.) *Voices from the Past: /Xam Bushmen and the Bleek and Lloyd Collection*. Johannesburg: Witwatersrand University Press.

—— 1996b. 'A tale of two families: Wilhelm Bleek, Lucy Lloyd and the /Xam San of the northern Cape'. In Skotnes, P. (ed.) *Miscast:*

Negotiating the Presence of the Bushmen. Cape Town: University of Cape Town Press.

—— & Dowson, T. A. (eds.) 1996. *Voices from the Past: /Xam Bushmen and the Bleek and Lloyd Collection.* Johannesburg: Witwatersrand University Press.

Guenther, M. 1989. *Bushman Folktales: Oral Traditions of the Nharo of Botswana and the /Xam of the Cape.* Stuttgart: Franz Steiner Verlag.

Hewitt, R. L. 1986a. 'Structure, meaning and ritual in the narratives of the southern San'. Hamburg: *Quellen zur Khoisan-Forschung*, 2. Helmut Buske Verlag.

—— 1986b. 'The anteater's laws: animal classification and the social order'. In Vossen, R. and Keuthmann, K. (eds.) *Contemporary Studies on Khoisan 2. In honour of Oswin Köhler on the occasion of his 75th birthday.* 2 vols. *Quellen zur Khoisan-Forschung*, 5(1)–5(2): 37–49. Hamburg: Helmut Buske Verlag.

Katz, R. 1982. *Boiling Energy: Community Healing among the Kalahari !Kung.* Cambridge, Massachusetts: Harvard University Press.

Kirby, P. R. 1968. *The Musical Instruments of the Native Races of South Africa.* Johannesburg: Witwatersrand University Press.

Lewis-Williams, J. D. 1981. *Believing and Seeing: Symbolic Meanings in Southern San Rock Paintings.* London: Academic Press.

—— 1983. *The Rock Art of Southern Africa.* Cambridge: Cambridge University Press.

—— 1988. '"People of the eland": an archaeolinguistic crux'. In Ingold, T., Riches, D. & Woodburn, J. (eds.) *Hunter Gatherers 2: Property, Power and Ideology.* New York: Berg.

—— 1990. *Discovering Southern African Rock Art.* Cape Town: David Philip.

—— 1996. '"A visit to the lion's house": the structure, metaphors and socio-political significance of a nineteenth-century Bushman myth'. In Deacon, H. J. & Dowson, T. A. (eds.) *Voices from the Past: /Xam Bushmen and the Bleek and Lloyd Collection.* Johannesburg: Witwatersrand University Press.

—— 1998. 'The mantis, the eland and the meerkats: conflict and mediation in a nineteenth-century San myth'. *African Studies*, 26: 195–216.

—— & Biesele, M. 1978. 'Eland hunting rituals among northern and southern San groups: striking similarities'. *Africa*, 48(2): 117–134.

—— & Dowson, T. A. 1989. *Images of Power: Understanding Bushman Rock Art*. Johannesburg: Southern Books.

Lloyd, L. C. 1889. 'A short account of further Bushman material collected'. Third Report concerning Bushman researches, presented to both Houses of Parliament of the Cape of Good Hope by command of His Excellency the Governor. London: David Nutt.

Markowitz, A. 1956. *With Uplifted Tongue: Stories, Myths and Fables of the South African Bushmen Told in their Manner*. Cape Town: CNA.

—— 1971. *The Rebirth of the Ostrich and Other Stories of the Kalahari Bushmen Told in their Manner*. Gaborone: National Museum and Art Gallery.

Marshall, L. 1976. *The !Kung of Nyae Nyae*. Cambridge, Massachusetts: Harvard University Press.

Orpen, J. M. 1874. 'A glimpse into the mythology of the Maluti Bushmen'. *Cape Monthly Magazine*, 9(49): 1–13. Repr. 1919. *Folklore*, 30: 139–156.

Rosenthal, E. & Goodwin, A. J. H. 1953. *Cave Artists of South Africa*. Cape Town: A. A. Balkema.

Schmidt, S. 1989. 'Katalog der Khoisan Volkserzählungen des sudlichen Afrikas'/ 'Catalogue of the Khoisan folktales of southern Africa'. 2 vols. *Quellen zur Khoisan-Forschung*, 6(1)–6(2). Hamburg: Helmut Buske Verlag.

Schoeman, K. 1997. *A Debt of Gratitude: Lucy Lloyd and the 'Bushman work' of G.W. Stow*. Cape Town: South African Library.

Skotnes, P. 1991. *Sound from the Thinking Strings*. Cape Town: Axeage Private Press.

—— (ed.) 1996. *Miscast: Negotiating the Presence of the Bushmen*. Cape Town: University of Cape Town Press.

—— 1999. *Heaven's Things: A Story of the /Xam*. LLAREC Series in Visual History. Cape Town: University of Cape Town Press.

Spohr, O. H. 1962. *Wilhelm Emmanuel Bleek. A Biobibliographical Sketch*. Varia Series 6. Cape Town: University of Cape Town Libraries.

Stow, G.W. & Bleek, D.F. 1930. *Rock Paintings in South Africa: From Parts of the Eastern Province and Orange Free State; copied by George William Stow; with an introduction and descriptive notes by*

D.F. Bleek. London: Methuen.

Vinnicombe, P. 1976. *People of the Eland: Rock Paintings of the Drakensberg Bushmen as a Reflection of their Life and Thought.* Pietermaritzburg: University of Natal Press.

Watson, S. 1991. *Return of the Moon: Versions from the /Xam.* Cape Town: Carrefour Press.

Woldmann, K. 1938. *Das wahre Gesicht des Buschmannes in seinen Mythen und Märchen nach Original-Bushmannerzählungen von Dr. W.H.I. Bleek und Lucy C. Lloyd.* Basel: Kommissionsverlag Zbinden & Hügin.

Young, R.B. 1908. *The Life and Work of George William Stow.* London: Longmans, Green.